Call M

By
PHINEAS F. ELLIS

DEDICATION

This book is dedicated to my wife,

Mildred M. Ellis

Phineas Franklin Ellis

Table of Contents

FORWARD

Call Me Phin is an account of the life and times of Phineas F. Ellis from Castle Hill, Maine. He retired just five days before his 77th birthday and was immediately encouraged by his family to write a book. This is a wonderful story that chronicles the life of an amazing man.

Mr. Ellis was first and foremost a true public servant. From the bold stand he took that resulted in a new mail line out of Ashland, Maine, to the financial sacrifices he made to serve in the Maine State Legislature, to the many acts of service and kindness he rendered during the years he served as the Town Manager of Mapleton and Castle Hill, Phin gave a great deal to all around him.

As we join Phin on his journey we are able to watch over his shoulder and catch a glimpse into the lives and observe the culture of the people in rural Aroostook County during the early to mid 20th century. We learn of the infamous lynching of Jim Cullen, hear the story of a U.S. Senator's grandfather nearly losing his life at a remote lumber camp, and are told of premonitions received as he relates stories of being inspired to help others.

Even though this book was originally published in 1977, it remains an intriguing account of the life of a fascinating man, a work that will hold great value to all who take an interest in the past. Phin's story was not professionally edited nor published, but its simple folksy style will help immerse you into his unsophisticated yet admirable life.

Phineas Franklin Ellis was a pioneer who understood the value of hard work. He was full of humility and determined to help those around him by taking an active role in bringing positive changes to their lives.

This book will inspire and delight. It will remind you of where you came from and will help you see what is most important in life. As I have read and reflected on this story, through my involvement in preparing it to be republished, it has certainly changed me for the better.

Thank you Grampy Ellis for the legacy that you left us. You truly are one of the noble and great ones who did what ever you could do to help and serve others. You are a great example who truly made a difference and left the world a better place.

Timothy Ellis Hotham
2010

Chapter 1

The Beginning of My Life's Journey

My journey on the road of life began August 15, 1896, in a small modest farmhouse located on the State Road in the town of Castle Hill, Maine. I, Phineas Franklin Ellis, first born child, oldest of ten, of Jasper O. and Lucy E. Wilcox Ellis was ushered into the world by the good and kindly Dr. Lindley Dobson.

Mrs. Rose Archer, who was fourteen year old Rose Richardson at the time, was working as a hired girl for my mother. She always delighted in reminding me that it was she who had the honor of putting me in pants for the very first time.

The house in which I was born was entirely made of wood. The outside was covered with cedar shingles. It measured fourteen by eighteen feet, with a shed on the east side, fourteen by twelve feet. The lower floor was one room, lathed and plastered; steep narrow stairs led to the chamber that was divided into two rooms that were never finished.

My memory takes me back to those very cold and windy winters which were much more severe than they are now, more than three quarters of a century later. Wood burning stoves were used with tin stove pipes leading up through the roof. A great deal of care and caution had to be taken with this type of heating system to prevent fires. The stove pipes were stayed with hay wire on the roof. Green wood was used mostly and this caused a lot of creosote to collect in the stove pipes. Quite often, and just before a thaw, the creosote would burn causing the stove pipes to become very hot and sometimes quite red. A ladder was always kept leaning on the house and another on the roof itself, ready to be used in case sparks would light on the roof causing a fire.

During severe storms, when the wind was of great force, the house creaked and groaned until my parents were fearful we were going to be blown over. The house did not have a cellar but was built on sills that were not in any way anchored down. In winter when the house was banked with dirt, which became frozen, the danger of toppling over was not as great.

Often in the winter, water would freeze in the pails and care had to be taken not to leave liquid in kettles for the frost would cause the kettle to bulge. Iron kettles would crack. Slop buckets were kept indoors when snow drifts blocked the path to the outhouse. Sometimes these also froze. Mother always kept a few small sticks of wood, clean and handy, to stand in the water pails at night. This made a vent for the air in the water to escape, keeping the pail from bulging at the bottom.

As the family increased, our little home became very crowded. By 1909 there were five children. During the summers of 1907, 1908 and 1909, I slept up in the hay mow in the barn with John DeMerchant, the hired man who worked summers for my father. In his later years, he made our house his permanent home for he was a bachelor. We were quite comfortable sleeping on the hay, with the heavy blankets used winters in the lumber camp. About the time school started in the fall, with approaching cold weather, I moved back into the house.

During the summer of 1909, our spacious new home was built with rooms for all.

Sanitary conditions were very poor around our home during the years we lived in the old house. The windows and doors were without screens and the slops and wash water were thrown out the door in all directions, often not very far. After the snow had melted in the spring, the yard was raked and cleaned as much as possible. Due to the lack of lime or some disinfectant, the area became a breeding place for flies, as did the little outhouse standing in back. Hard wood was used for fuel and my parents knew the ashes were good for spreading over the places where flies hatched; however, Mother saved the ashes for another purpose.

In the spring especially, when a lot of ashes had accumulated, leaching barrels were filled. A leaching barrel was just a plain hard wood pork barrel. Near the bottom a small hole was made in which a wooden plug or stopper was placed. The barrel was then filled with ashes, water was poured over them, and the mixture was left to set for several days. A pail or kettle was then placed under the bung hole, the bung was removed and the lye seeped into the container. Sometimes when the lye didn't seem strong enough, Mother would return it to the barrel and let it seep through again. Throughout the year waste fat was always saved. Every scrap of fatty meat was boiled in a kettle. The fat would rise to the top; this was skimmed off and placed in an empty lard tub. After the lye had leached long enough, Mother would mix the lye and fat together then boil the mixture. This mixture was soft soap. It was stored in bottles or earthen jars and used for washing clothes, scrubbing floors, washing dishes and most of the time had to serve as hand soap as well. Soap making continued until about the time we moved into the new home in 1909.

Butter was also a product made at home in those days. We had a milk house, built of common soft wood boards, that measured about six foot square, a little higher than one's head, with a small door about two by four feet. Alder bushes grew all around this little building, preventing the sun from shining through after the leaves came out in the spring.

The milk house was built over the brook, about one hundred fifty feet from the house. It had a plank floor with an opening so that the milk cans could be set in the cool running water. Milk always kept nice and sweet by this method. The only exception was that when there were heavy thunder showers, the milk soured. No one ever explained to me why this occurred; however, it seemed to always happen.

Meat also could be kept fresh for several days if put in an earthen jar and placed in the cool running water.

The milk cans held about four gallons each and had a glass window in the front. At the bottom there was a faucet from which the skim milk could be drawn. After each milking, the milk was strained into the cans and placed in the milk house for the day or night. When the next milking time came, the cream had risen to the top and was skimmed off. The skim milk was drawn off through the faucet and fed to the calves. The cream was churned into butter in an "up and down" churn. This was an earthen vessel with a stick called a dasher, which was hoisted up and down until the butter fat separated. The milky liquid remaining was called buttermilk. The butter was washed, salted and prepared for use. It was stored in earthen jars in the milk house.

About 1907, Father purchased a second-hand cream separator. This was an improvement over the old method of skimming off the cream by hand and the cream could be separated from the milk while it was still warm from the cows.

The little milk house was still in use even when I began high school in 1911.

Life, even to exist, was a continuous struggle as farming and lumbering were the only means of livelihood in the area. My father farmed in summer and worked in the woods during the winter months.

Tough and rugged was the life back in those days and one almost had to provide the greater part of the living off the farm. We always kept a small flock of sheep. A small garden provided vegetables for the family and a cow or two kept us in milk, cream, and butter. Hogs were raised for their meat and were butchered when the weather became quite cold. Hens were also a source of meat and provided us with eggs. Father always planned to get at least one deer in the fall. There was a time when each family was allowed to have two.

Father grew potatoes and grain. Most years, only what potatoes that could be stored would be grown. The new house, built in 1909, had a cellar which provided storage for about eight hundred barrels. Up until that time an outdoor cellar was used. This cellar had sides of logs banked up with dirt. The top was poled over and covered with dirt and straw. As I remember, this would not hold more than three or four hundred barrels of potatoes. This "dug-out" also provided storage for our apples and vegetables.

Before 1912, it was rather hard to market potatoes in any amount. The only market for potatoes was at Ashland or Presque Isle. Ashland was eight miles away and Presque Isle, twice the distance.

A few potatoes were sold in the fall. Hauling was a slow process as only twelve or fourteen barrels could be taken at one time. A few were also hauled in the winter. For winter hauling, tote-sleds, boxed up on the sides, were used. Straw was placed on the sled's bottom and blankets covered the barrels. On very cold days, a lantern or two would be placed between the barrels of potatoes to prevent freezing. Mostly potatoes were hauled in the spring after "breaking camp" in the woods. The better price was usually at Presque Isle due to more competition among the buyers. The horses used in the woods hauled the potatoes.

When the Bangor & Aroostook Railroad built a branch from Mapleton to the State Road Siding and Washburn, we hauled to the siding, a distance of only seven miles.

My father, born in Ashland in 1869, began working the lumber mills when he was fourteen years old. He later was considered qualified to be Woods Boss. This was good for the family because he and Mother could save some of his earnings with which to build a new house. A good Woods Boss had to have a lot of experience with where to locate the best places for cutting lumber, where to land the logs, how and where to build a set of camps without wasting time, and how to cruise out the roads for hauling the logs to a woods yard or the landing at a river. He must hire a good filer to file the saws, for very sharp saws were needed to get the most lumber at the least expense.

Father never allowed card playing or gambling in any of his crews and everyone was used alike; there were no favorites. The wood and lumbering business was his life for fifty eight consecutive winters. Many of those, he took charge for others and some years cut on his own, cutting by the thousand. The last twenty-four years that he was working for others, he was in charge of the woods operations of the H.D. Collins Lumber Co. located in Caribou, Maine.

The house I was born in.

Chapter 2

"Uncle Bill" Coffin Comes To My Rescue

During those early years when sanitary conditions were very poor, with numerous flies roaming at large, cholera was very common during the summer months. Cholera, once started, usually spread throughout the entire family and often the entire neighborhood.

Although the supply of food was plenty, we weren't getting much of a variety. I was one of the children who hankered for something that was lacking in our diet. The walls were papered with newspapers which mother put on with flour paste. Tearing off this paper and chewing it seemed to satisfy my hunger for something different. After a time, the acid content in the paper poisoned my blood to the extent that the Doctor had "given me up."

In 1901 the cholera was with us. My younger brother, Byron, became very ill and Doctor Dobson was called. He left medicine for Byron and told my father, "I cannot think of anything that we can do for Phin." I was white as chalk, very frail, without an appetite, and awfully skinny.

Uncle Bill was present when the Doctor made the remark that he did not know of a medicine that would cure me. After the Doctor had taken his leave, Uncle Bill made this statement, "That old pill peddler doesn't know what he is talking about. I'll prove to him that what he does not know will make a larger book than what he does know, and I'll prove to you all that there is help for Phin."

He asked Mother for a five pound lard pail. After it was washed and cleaned he said, "Phin, you carry the pail and we will go hunting. (There was a piece of woods not far from the house) We will go hunting up in those woods for medicine." After roaming about for awhile he shouted, "Ah, here is what we are looking for." With his jack-knife, he whittled a pointed stick saying, "Phin, you take this stick and dig up this plant, roots and all." On the bottom of the plant there were yellow roots. He said, "Here Phin, you chew one of these and tell me how it tastes." I did as I was told and found the roots to be very bitter and told him so. He replied, "Good, good, good, and I see a large number of these plants, they are called Gold Thread. Let's dig a whole lot of them."

Uncle Bill located the plants and kept me digging for a long time. After awhile, he looked into the pail and said, "Probably that will be enough Gold Thread, now we'll hunt for something else." As we moved about the woods, he cut off different kinds of bark from trees until our pail was full.

"Uncle Bill" Coffin

We arrived back at the house, both very tired. Uncle Bill said, "Now, if I had some nice fresh water I'd wash this stuff that we have in the pail and steep it." There was a small brook nearby from which we got our wash water, etc. but the drinking water was carried from a spring down across the road. Mother took a couple of pails and went to the spring for the water.

I fell asleep on the floor. When I awakened, the Gold Thread and bark, thoroughly cleaned, was on the stove steeping. This steeping process continued until the next day when Uncle Bill allowed that the mixture had steeped long enough. He asked Mother for a milk strainer (the milk strainers were made of several layers of cheese cloth). Through this, the liquid was strained a couple of times, sugar added, and then boiled down to about a quart. After this process was completed and the liquid cooled, Uncle Bill tasted it saying, "My, oh my, this will sure cure Phin and in a hurry, too." My parents were very happy about his prediction and hoped he was correct. I was given a spoonful. "How does that taste?" Uncle Bill asked. "It is awfully bitter but I like it," I replied. The medicine was put in a fruit jar. Mother was instructed to give me a spoonful several times each day until it was gone.

The day we tried the medicine, my father was going to town for groceries. Uncle Bill gave him fifty cents with which to buy bananas. Uncle Bill was with us for the next several days. He fed me bananas and saw to it that Mother did not forget to give me the medicine which he had prepared. I did not hanker for any more wallpaper. Color came back to my face, my appetite for food returned and I rested and slept much better. This was no less than a "miracle" for just a few days before the Doctor had said there wasn't a thing he knew of that would help me.

Now "Uncle" Bill was Bill Coffin, a native of Ashland, well over seventy at the time, fondly called "Uncle" by us all. His birthplace was on the Sheridan Road, on the farm now occupied by Paul Ayer (1974). As a young man, he staked a Squatter's claim on the north side of the State Road, just west of what was then known as Sheridan Plantation, which bordered on the town of Ashland. The piece of ground that he staked out was one-half mile along the road and extended north to the Aroostook River.

During his early years, he farmed in summer and worked in lumber camps during the winter. When still a young man, he became very ill with rheumatic fever, which left him crippled. One leg became so badly twisted that he could not get around without the aid of crutches.

When Uncle Bill became crippled, he gave his property to his sister, Mrs. Nancy Gardner, but continued to make the farm his home. Not wanting to be a burden, he learned to knit and would go from place to place each year, among relatives and friends and do their knitting. He'd live with the family he was knitting for at the time, receiving his board and what money they could afford. This explains his presence in our home at the time of my illness.

My father always kept a few sheep. After the spring shearing, Mr. Crocket, a partner in the Caribou Woolen Mill, would come along with his horse and peddle cart. Mother would exchange the wool for yarn. By weight it probably was two pounds of wool for a pound of yarn. If Mr. Crocket was unable to take all the wool at one time, he returned several times during the summer and fall.

Uncle Bill would then come and stay at our home for several days until all the yarn had been used. He could knit anything and everything: mittens, stockings, caps, sweaters and drawers for the men.

People for whom he knit tried to have wool dye in various colors on hand. His knitting was truly an art. He created many beautiful patterns and designs with this colored yarn.

Chapter 3

Off To School

It was the fall of 1902, at the age of six, that my mother dressed me up for school. Up to this time, my hair was hanging down in the back and Mother kept it curled. I wore buttoned shoes in summer and shoe packs in winter. This fall, Mother or Father cut my hair and the curls were saved. The buttoned shoes became a thing of the past. Gum rubbers, low with a buckle, were bought for me to wear to school. I still had to wear knee pants.

Late in September, after potato digging, I was sent off to school. The first day, a dozen or so of us children waited at the Little Red School House for the teacher. About noon, when a teacher still hadn't arrived, we all went home. That evening, my father inquired as to what happened. I never knew but was sent back the next morning. Again we waited until noon, but still no teacher came. The third day, I refused to go to school. I was only six years old and rather small for my age, so the folks gave in and let me stay home.

The next year, at the age of seven, I was dressed for school and sent again. This time there was a teacher, Mr. Archie Watt, who farmed in the neighborhood. I knew and liked him and became interested in school right from the beginning. I attended the Little Red School House until I passed the State Examination for High School in the early summer of 1911. The attendance varied from sixteen to eighteen to perhaps twenty some. There were seats made of boards and two of us sat in each seat.

Grades were not known to us in the Little Red School House. The beginners were in the Primer class, and then came the First Reader, Second Reader, and so on until the Fifth Reader. When we had passed the tests through the Fifth Reader, we were ready to take the State Examination for High School. There were three terms of school each year and, if I remember correctly, they totaled up to thirty-two weeks. Sometimes a teacher would serve but a single term. Mr. Watt taught two terms. Lizzie Nason taught a single term. Kitty

The Little Red Schoolhouse

McLellan, Josephine Bernard, Constance Cross and Alanda Smith were my other teachers.

The distance I traveled to school was three-fourths of a mile. The roads were very muddy in wet weather and bad in the winter time. It was very cold and windy much of the time and the roads often drifted so we had to wade through snow drifts most of the way. I vividly remember the landmarks along the way to and from the school house. After a few days, I had them all named and could describe each place to my mother.

As I left the driveway at home, there was a cedar stump, then, going east, was George Alley's first turn. Next, was Alley's second turn, then came Big Rock. This was a very large boulder, flat on the top, with the words G.M. Liniment painted on it. Uncle Jim's driveway was next on the right. There was a "spring road" opposite on the left from which he carried his drinking water. A short distance beyond was the flat which was really a bog. Quite often teams of horses with loads would get mired here in wet weather and another team of horses would have to be hitched on to pull out the load. Next, of the named landmarks, was The Hill. Beyond that, a short distance on the left was the Apple Tree. Rob Wood's first driveway came shortly after on the left. His second driveway, a few feet further on. Then there was a log culvert over a stream of running water, called Rob Wood's Brook. The Little Knoll wasn't much further on, and then came Perry Prosser's home. His barn was on the opposite side of the road. As we reached the school, there was the School House Hill, where we used to play at noon and recess time. These places that I've mentioned were talked about to my mother all of the years that I attended this school. Almost every night, she would inquire about school and I'd tell her about the condition of the road, or something that happened or about someone I'd met at one of these locations.

At the beginning of school, some person in the town was appointed School Supervisor. One incident that I vividly remember was when Mr. Waddell, the Supervisor, came to visit the school. It was the general practice, when he came to visit, for the teacher to retire to the back of the room and he would do the teaching for an hour or so. He would call us down front, one at a time, and review some of our lessons with us. When my turn came, Mr. Waddell asked me to read for him. He named the page on which I was to read. It was all review work so I got along well. When I finished he called me over to his side, placed his hand on my shoulder and said, "My boy, my boy that was wonderful. I'm going to predict that some day you will be president." This was like a booster shot. I would try and do a little better each day and as time went on I never forgot the statement "Some day you will be President."

Many years later, I was chosen President of the Aroostook Town and City Manager's Association at a monthly meeting which was held at Van Buren. At that time, I told the members of the Association this story and although Mr. Waddell had passed away many years before, his prediction had come true.

The last two years that I attended the Little Red School House, I was appointed janitor. The salary was twenty-five cents per week. One of the janitor's duties was to arrive early and build a fire in the box stove, which was located approximately in the middle of the school room. This building was awfully cold in winter. The teacher would have us place our dinner pails around the stove. Quite often our food would still be frozen at lunch time.

The little building, paraphrased by James Whitcomb Riley, stood out back. There was a single board partition between the boys

Schoolmates inside the Little Red Schoolhouse (circa 1909).

FRONT ROW: LEFT: Eva Alley, Abbie Hanson; CENTER: Georgia "Nellie" Alley, Hazel Turner; RIGHT: George Anderson, Jesse Watt
BACK ROW: LEFT: Braighton Alley, Harold McLellan; CENTER: Beatrice Anderson, Inza Alley, Leona Ellis; RIGHT: Phineas Ellis, Byron Ellis

and girls sections. On the first school day, each term, the teacher would have the older girls help put wall paper on either side of the partition and she'd give a lecture that there weren't to be any holes made in this paper. As I remember, all were loyal to the teacher and the paper remained whole.

Usually, the teacher would come out in the school yard at recess and noon time and teach us to play games. This was great fun. When recess was over, the teacher would ring the bell and we'd line up and march in. Just inside the door, on the right, was an iron bracket on which the water pail was hung. Under the large bracket was a smaller one, to hold the dipper. Each morning, a couple of the older boys would go and get a fresh pail of water. In good weather, the water was brought from a spring down by the woods in back of the Prosser place. In bad weather, the water was carried from McLellan's, a much shorter distance.

As we marched in, each one could stop for a drink of water. The portion not drank was thrown into a bucket placed under the water pail. The water pail was a tin or galvanized pail and the dipper was made of tin. Sometimes the dipper became very rusty. The teacher always took it home week-ends to be washed, but when many of us had colds or runny noses, it was washed every night.

In the spring of 1910, I was given the State Examination for High School and did not pass. I told my parents that I was glad I didn't pass so I wouldn't have to go to school anymore. Sometime during the summer, Mr. Libby, Superintendent of Schools, and Mrs. Parker (Alanda) Smith, came and talked with my mother and they coaxed me to go back another year and try again. At first I refused, but after a few days I gave in and told my mother, "Yes, I'll try another year." This last year at the Red School House was the best thing that could have been done for me. All of the studies were a review. I received higher rank all along and every study seemed to have a meaning that I had not understood the year before. In the spring of 1911, in my fourteenth year, I passed the State Examination with flying colors and from then on had a great desire to go on to high school.

Sunday School was held every summer, for three or four months, at the Red School House. Mrs. Louise Wood was my Sunday School teacher several of the years that I attended. The latter part of each summer, a minister would come and hold meetings. This was very interesting. I especially enjoyed listening to the gathering sing hymns. One of my favorites was "Bringing in the Sheaves," and another, "When the Roll is Called up Yonder." There were many more but those two were sung nearly every evening that the series of meetings lasted.

One fall, there was a minister, who after a short while would get real excited, start sweating, unbutton his coat and preach until he was thirsty. He would then go to the water pail for a drink of water. He made several trips to the water pail during the evening. If there was any water left in the dipper, he would turn it back in the pail instead of in the bucket below. We scholars noticed this and wondered why someone hadn't mentioned to him "Cleanliness is next to Godliness," as that is what he preached and what the teachers had taught us.

During the winter of the school year 1907 and 1908, my father was away in the woods. I was eleven years old and my brother Byron was two years younger. We were doing the barn chores before and after school. Byron would hold the lantern and I would feed the stock and pitch down the hay. At night I turned the cows out of the tie-up and they would go to the brook for water. While the cows were out for water, we would clean out the tie-up and bed the stalls down with fresh straw. My mother raised a few geese that were penned up in the rear of the barn. Sometimes they would break out of their pen. One night after school, it was getting quite dusky as the sun had gone down. For some reason Byron wasn't with me and I was going to do the chores alone. Our father had always instructed us to not set the lantern down in the barn, so this night it was left outside. As I opened the barn door the gander, which had broken out of the pen, began pounding me with his wings. I'd kick him and he would charge again and again. After a time, I managed to reach a pitch fork and tried to drive the gander away. While punching at it, I stuck the fork in my right leg. Finally I subdued the gander, drove him back in the pen and continued on with the chores. After supper, Byron came out with me and we finished the chores.

I did not realize the seriousness so didn't tell anyone about hurting my leg. During the night, I became very restless and feverish. When morning came my leg had swollen to at least twice its normal size. There were red streaks all the way up my side and swelling had begun under my arms. When my mother got up, I called her to look at my leg. "My, isn't that awful!" she exclaimed. She allowed that we would have to wait until Byron went to school and she could send a note by him to Mrs. McLellan asking her to hurry right up.

Mother went with Byron to feed the livestock, then hustled him with his breakfast and off to school with the note. Mrs. McLellan came right up on the run. She lived three-quarters of a mile away.

Mrs. McLellan was the neighborhood "nurse" and in many ways could do as well as the Doctors. She was known as Anna or sometimes Grammy McLellan. She attended when babies were born and seemed to have a remedy for everything. In the summer, she gathered many kinds of herbs and prepared medicine that was good for "most everything."

When she took a look at my leg, she became quite depressed and looked awfully sad. She told my mother that gangrene had set in. She said, "My, oh, my, it may be too late. I wish that I could have been here sooner. However, we will do our best." She asked my mother to bring in a round of salt pork and cut off the rind. She said, "While you are doing that I'll get some hot water and salt and be bathing the leg." By the time Mother returned with the pork rind, the swollen area had been bathed, this gave me some relief from the pain. She placed the pork rind over the wound and bandaged it on tight with strips of an old sheet. She then told Mother to feed me a little breakfast of broth and soft toast. Mrs. McLellan went back to her home, but stated she would be back before night.

Towards night, she returned to look me over. She said, "Oh Lucy (my mother's name) come look. I guess that we did get started in time. The swelling is not so bad and just look at the pus that the pork has drawn out. Get a new pork rind and we will dress this up for the night." I was given broth again for supper. The fever began to go away and I slept better that night.

Mrs. McLellan came twice a day for several days and then once each day for awhile. In a week or so the swelling was gone but a pocket of pus formed a few inches below the injury. She would squeeze up on this and cause the pus to come out of the wound. The odor was terrible. Mrs. McLellan said, "The Doctor would probably lance this place and the wound would heal quicker, however, we'll keep applying the pork rind and perhaps it will break by itself." After a couple of days, this treatment worked and the wound healed very fast

I lost about two weeks of school but survived with both legs.

Chapter 4

Preparing For High School

After passing the State Examination in June of 1911, I began to wonder how I'd ever earn the money to buy clothes and be ready to enter high school in September.

During the summer, my father helped Uncle Jim complete filling a pulp wood contract with a Mr. Wessenger. As I remember, only some thirty or thirty-five cords were involved for which Uncle Jim had been overpaid. Therefore, no money was involved in this deal. Father was to furnish the horse to yard the wood and I was to come along to lead the horse. Uncle Jim was to furnish a man. An expert pulp cutter and woods worker, Eli Oakes, was hired for one dollar per day. A few extra cords were to be cut to get money to pay Eli with.

It took several weeks to complete this deal. Time had to be taken off to care for the potatoes and do the necessary work on the farm. Things worked out fine. The pulp wood contract was settled and Eli was happy that he had earned a few dollars. I felt sort of down-at-the-heels to think that I did not receive a cent during all this time, neither did my father.

For clothing, I wore a single shirt, a pair of overalls and a pair of canvas sneakers. Many of the days in the woods were very hot and the flies were terrible. My clothes collected pitch from the fir wood and were so rough my body became chafed. The sneakers became full of holes by the middle of August. I began wondering more and more just how I was going to get to high school, with no money in sight and my clothes were unsuitable to wear away from home.

My father and Calvin Ellis used to exchange work many times due to the lack of machinery. About August fifteenth, my fifteenth birthday, we were up to Calvin's helping thresh. We were there a couple of days, and then Calvin, who owned the thresher, and his brother Eben, came down to our place to thresh. Their stay was short for all Father wanted, at this time, was some oats for the horses and the straw for bedding. After a few hours, Calvin and Eben loaded up and headed back to their own neighborhood to do custom threshing. We got busy and hauled the balance of the grain that was harvested and stored it in the barn to thresh later in the fall or winter.

Time was running out. It was now late in August and I still did not have any money with which to purchase clothes. School was to start the second week in September. While threshing, my father had talked with Calvin about me wanting to go to high school. He stated many times that he'd like me to get an education so that I "wouldn't have to work for a living." During the discussion he had with Calvin, he said, "I haven't any money and he will have to hoof it alone." Calvin advised us to go see Mr. Towne, who was Principal of Ashland High School or still better go see Penn Craig, who was Chairman of the Ashland School Board. Father was well acquainted with Mr. Craig as he was a potato buyer in Ashland and we had hauled potatoes there to sell.

Father got me up early one morning and said, "Phin, get ready and come along. We will go see Mr. Craig." It took a couple of hours to reach Ashland. We found Mr. Craig at home and he and father talked the matter over. Penn told us there would be a charge for tuition which the Town of Castle Hill would probably pay and quite often someone was looking for a boy who liked to work, to do chores in exchange for room and board. Father told Penn, "We are anxious for Phin to get a high school education so that he 'won't have to work for a living'." Penn's reply was "We all have to work pretty hard for a living, yet Phin can go on to high school and college and become a doctor or a lawyer. Perhaps it will be better than the rugged work that we have to do." Mr. Craig asked me if I really wanted to go to high school. I informed him that I'd passed the State Examination but I'd have to work my way through school and for clothes I was stuck. "Well, well," he said, "School begins in about three weeks, have your father bring you up and in the meantime I'll do my best to find a place for you to work. As for money with which to buy clothes, perhaps your father will sell me a few potatoes and that will start you off."

On our way back, Father and I talked about how he would manage at home when I went away to school. "Ah, don't worry," he said, "We will find a way. Byron is old enough to help and we will get along." We finished cutting the grain and after it was dry, stored it in the barn. Next was the annual job of hauling the manure, from around the barn, out into the fields and spreading it. This was a tedious job.

The odor from the manure was RANK. We would pitch it on the wagon with forks, drive into the fields and pitch it off the wagon, spreading it around.

The days passed quickly and the end of the month came. Now there were only a few days left before I was to enter high school. Not a word had been said for several days as to how I was going to get some clothes suitable to wear. The manure was about all hauled out. It was very hot one day and after we had loaded, I stood the fork against the barn and said, "I'm all through farming, but how am I going to get started to high school?" Father said, "I'll go spread this load and you see if you can 'figger' out some way for yourself." When he came back, he asked, "Did you think of some way?" "Yes," I replied, "Why don't you dig and sell a load of potatoes as Mr. Craig suggested. That will give me a start."

"Well," he answered, "Let's figure on that idea. A load of potatoes hauled to Ashland would bring about $1.10 per barrel and the most we could haul at one time would be twelve or fourteen barrels if the roads are dry and good. The potatoes are green yet, so we can't dig them until about the time school starts. The most we would have would be $15. Some of this would have to be spent for groceries and the money left would buy only a small part of the clothes that you will need." Then he came up with an idea I hadn't thought of. "Why don't you sell your sheep?" he asked.

It was back in March of 1907, when my brother Luther was born, that my Grandmother Wilcox came from Bangor to help Mother for awhile. My father was carrying on a lumber operation up at Beaver Brook and his camp was some three miles away. He came home nights for awhile to look after the barn chores and see that we had plenty of wood and water. He would get up very early in the morning and call me to come to the barn with him. I'd hold the lantern while he harnessed the horse and got ready to drive back to the camp. He said he had to be back in time to have breakfast with the crew and get them out in the woods as soon as "we can see to work."

The weather was very cold and one of those cold mornings about March 12th, Father said, "Listen! What is that noise?" He was ready to leave, but he hitched the horse to a wheel of a wagon that was left in the yard and we went into the basement part of the barn where the sheep were kept in winter. Here was a newborn lamb with the wool on its hind parts frozen in the ice. Father said, "This lamb is ahead of time. I'll just have to bump it off because it won't live anyway." He pulled the lamb from the ice and some wool was left there. He said, "Now we'll find a stick to kill it with." "Oh, wait!" I exclaimed, "Perhaps it will live, let me have it and I'll try to make it live." "See, Phin," he answered, "His hind parts are all iced over. You haven't a chance. Oh well, I'm in a hurry so you can do what you like but when it dies bury it out back of the barn in the manure pile."

Although it was well below zero, I held the lantern for Father to get the horse untied from the wheel of the wagon. As he hurried off to his lumber camp, I took off my jacket and wrapped it around the little lamb that was shaking with the cold. The house was some four hundred feet from the barn. I hurried over and put the lamb on the floor behind the cookstove. It didn't show much sign of life, but I found some rags that I kept warming and putting on the lamb. After awhile, the ice thawed off the hind parts and it began to show some signs of life. It would raise its head up and then down again. After a half hour or so it began to bleat. My grandmother heard the strange noise and tiptoed down the stairs to see what this was all about. I explained about finding the lamb, about it being stuck in the ice, that my father had wanted to kill it and I stopped him with the idea that perhaps I could make it live. Grandmother said, "Phin, you did just the right thing. That lamb will live. We will make it live." She made an examination and stated that it was a ewe lamb. "We can make it live," she said, "and someday you will have a flock of sheep all your own. You find a can and get a little kerosene and I'll find some more rags and we'll make that lamb live." Its hind legs seemed to be paralyzed. Gram said, "I think the lamb has been chilled so that his hind legs will be affected. I'll have to make some bread for breakfast, get the kids up and ready for school, and then we'll doctor up the lamb."

When she caught up to the point where she could come and help me, we both got down on the floor. Gram told me she would have liked to have helped the lamb sooner but "your mother would have a fit if I got kerosene on the food." We went to work. I soaked the rags in kerosene and Grandmother bandaged the hind parts, tying the rags on. Mother wanted Gram to have me take the lamb back to the barn but Gram insisted, "No, no, we can't do that because it can't stand up, its hind legs are too weak from being chilled." Mother asked Gram if she thought the lamb would live. Her answer was, "I know it will if we can find some way to feed it. If we can find a nipple, we'll be in business." "We don't have a nipple here," Mother said, "but perhaps Phin can run down to the McLellan's. They raise sheep and perhaps they'll have a spare one." I started on the run. It would take fifteen or twenty minutes to reach McLellan's. About half way there, I stopped at Mrs. Woods and asked her if she might have an old nipple saved. "What's up?" she inquired. After I gasped out the story of the lamb, she said, "Well, well, just get your breath and I'll look." In no time, Mrs. Wood came back with a box of various things that she had saved. Sure enough there was and old nipple. "May I have it?" I asked. "Sure you can have it." Mrs. Wood, who was our Sunday School teacher when it was held in summer, replied, "And I know God will help you and your Grammy make that little lamb live."

In not much more than twenty minutes, I was back at home with the nipple. Byron and Leona were all ready to leave for school. Gram said, "It is school time now, you kids hustle off. Hurry, don't be late. I'll warm up some canned milk and take good care of the lamb until you get home this afternoon."

The lamb was on my mind all day. When I got home that afternoon, I found Gram had fed the lamb and rebandaged the hind legs with clean rags. It was very much alive and kept trying to stand on its feet. However, its legs were so weak that it couldn't stand alone. It was decided that I take the lamb to the barn to see if the mother sheep would let it nurse. Sure enough, after a few minutes, the mother was nursing her lamb. Soon its little belly was full, so I took it back to the house and placed it behind the cookstove, making a fence around it with sticks of stove wood. Before bedtime, I made another trip to the barn with the lamb for another feeding. The old mother sheep became very cooperative and we got along just fine. My father was some surprised when he came home that night and boy, didn't my grandmother give him a lecture. She told him, "Where there is life there is hope; also, never, never discourage a boy, for you know boys make men."

The lamb improved every day. Due to the hind parts being paralyzed, a small syringe was used to help it have bowel movements. This procedure became less frequent and when the mother sheep got on grass, the syringe wasn't needed at all. It made so much noise in the house that, after a few days, I made a pen in the barn for the lamb and the mother sheep. The mother sheep was kind to her lamb throughout the many weeks before it could stand on its feet. The hind legs were stiff. The lamb learned to get up and nurse and by the time they were turned out to pasture was playing with the other lambs. It hopped along, peg-leg like, for many months before its legs functioned in a normal way. By the summer of 1911, I had six sheep from this one.

There was a Mr. Wilmont Crouse who bought cattle, sheep, hogs etc. He drove a team to pick up the livestock that he bought. As I remember, it was the same day Father and I talked about selling the sheep that Mr. Crouse was driving by. We could hear the rattle of the wagon a half mile up the road before he drove in sight. The wagon was full of sheep and calves. The wagon was hauled by a team of four very small horses. I ran to the road, stopped Mr. Crouse and asked him if he would like to buy my sheep. "Sure," he said, "How many do you have?" When I told him there were six, he looked over the load he already had and replied, "Yes, I guess there is room for a few more." He drove the team to our barnyard. The six sheep that belonged to me were all pets. It was easy to call them into a yard that we brought the cows to at milking time. Mr. Crouse came into the yard, looked them over one by one and stated, "I can pay you \$36 and maybe a little more." Father was telling him that the sheep were being sold so I could obtain the money I needed to begin high school. "Well, well," said Mr. Crouse, "I see where I can pay you \$38.50 for the six." The sheep were such pets that I dreaded to part with them, yet I said, "Sold."

Father helped Mr. Crouse crowd them into the wagon body along with the load he already had. Mr. Crouse paid me the \$38.50 and I was very sad as he drove away with my pet sheep. Father and I sat down and he said, "Don't feel so bad. You have the money to start you off for high school. Perhaps someday you can become a doctor or do some kind of work that is not as hard as the work we do now. You look after things and do the chores here tomorrow and I'll drive to Presque Isle and buy you some clothes."

Presque Isle was sixteen miles away. It would take nearly four hours to drive there with one of the work horses. However, bright and early the next morning, Mother prepared an early breakfast and Father was off toward town. I was left to do the chores and split some wood ahead for “diggin’ time”. The day was a long one. I hustled and did all the work I could and waited patiently for my clothes.

Father returned late in the afternoon and had spent $23 of the money. He’d bought me a shift of underclothes, a suit with two pairs of pants, a couple of shirts, some stockings, a pair of shoes, a cap and an overcoat. He had $15.50 left over. After supper, Mother checked over the slips for the clothing. Of the $15.50 left, it was agreed that I’d have $.50 for some school supplies that might be needed. I was to take the $5.00 bill and pin it in my shirt pocket and Mother would put away the $10 until a later time when I needed it.

Chapter 5

Getting Through My Freshman Year

The second Monday in September came. About four o'clock in the morning Mother had breakfast ready and Father had the horse and buggy at the door. As soon as we had eaten, we were off toward Ashland. As we drove away, Father said to Mother, "I'll try and be back about half past eight. It will be about a two hour drive each way and we'll be stopping at Mr. Craig's for a few minutes."

We arrived at Mr. Craig's before he was up and he came out in his nightgown saying, "Well well, what is all this about, you folks getting me out of bed at this time of day." Father reminded him of the time we were there a few weeks before. "Well," he said, "By golly I had forgotten all about the boy coming up to school." There was a long pause before he said, "All right, now that you are here, I'll keep my word. Hop out and we'll work you here for your board until I find a place for you to stay."

For the next hour and a half, I had to work very hard cleaning out a room in which I was to sleep. About 7:45, Mrs. Craig came and reminded me that it would be school time in a little while. She told me what street would be the shortest way to the school building, which sat up on a hill toward the northeast. I was feeling hungry about this time but was too bashful to tell her so. When I arrived at the school, three of my cousins were there: Climena Mosher and Avis and Hazen Walker who were also beginning their freshman year. Everyone else were strangers to me.

We were seated, books were distributed and lessons were assigned. School opened with Mr. Towne, the principal, reading a verse from the Bible. We all said the Lord's Prayer, just as we'd done at the Little Red School House. Mr. Towne then sang a solo and gave us instructions as to how he would expect us to behave. He explained about the four grades in high school. Recess came and I got acquainted with some of the others. For after recess, the principal and the two teachers had prepared a get-acquainted program. Noon soon came and I was so hungry that I felt sort of faint. I didn't know if I could make it back to Craig's for dinner, but I took my time and arrived okay. Mrs. Craig had a nice dinner prepared and I have often wondered what she thought about my appetite. I just couldn't get filled up and ate everything that was passed to me. Soon it was time to hurry back to school.

I hesitate to write about how I looked. Although I had on new clean clothes, my hair badly needed cutting and my face was covered with "fuzz" as I had never shaved. Mr. Craig and I talked about this at suppertime. I told him that I had the money to pay the barber but would like to wait until Saturday. He agreed to this, for there was much work to be done around his place. There was a cow to milk, chickens to feed and his driving horse to care for. The supper was wonderful, with more of a variety of food than I was used to having at home.

After a good night's rest, I was called at 5:30 in the morning, had a good breakfast, got along fine with the chores and was off to school at 7:45. This day, school did not go so well. Several of the boys in the upper classes began teasing. I learned later, the way freshmen were treated when they first entered school was called 'hazing.' All day I heard, "Where did 'this' come from? I'll bet 'this' came from Buffalo." "Where is Buffalo?" I asked, "About four or five miles above Portage," they replied. "I'm sorry boys," I answered, "I have never been up to Buffalo. My home is in Castle Hill." They retorted, "Well probably Castle Hill doesn't have a barber either."

This teasing continued on all day Tuesday, Wednesday, and Thursday. Quite often one of them would reach out and pull the fuzz on my face. By Friday, I began to feel that perhaps I'd made a mistake in coming to high school. At recess time on Friday, I was being used rather rough when a big stocky girl came along and asked, "Why do you put up with that? Wade right into them and fight back, kick hell right out of some of those boys." My reply was, "Oh, I do not believe in quarreling. I suppose they call this fun." Just then one of the boys reached out and pulled the fuzz on my face. The stout girl said, "Mother told me at noontime today that she and your father are cousins and she said if I was that boy I'd fight back." She went on to say, "My name is Helen Allen and I'm ready to take sides with you any time you want to pile up some of these fellows." About that time someone stepped back and thumbed his nose at Miss Allen. Quick as a flash, she grabbed him by the shirt collar and the seat of his pants and gave him an awful mauling. After she let him go, I said, "Boy, it is too bad to be so rough." She replied, "Too bad nothing. No one in this school is going to thumb their nose at me and get away with it."

Saturday came and I spent the morning choring around at the Craig's. As I was cleaning up about the barn and yard, an elderly lady surprised me. I later learned her name was Mrs. Medkiff and she did the washing and scrubbing for Mrs. Craig. She said, "Good morning, young man. I want you to catch a chicken and bring it in so I can make it ready for Mrs. Craig to cook on Sunday." I chased the chickens about the yard until I caught a good heavy one and took it to her. She exclaimed, "My God, that is still alive. Why didn't you cut its head off?" That was a chore I'd never done before and I inquired as to where I'd find the axe. "Oh, look out around, there is one somewhere," she answered. Holding fast to the chicken, I looked and looked for an axe. After awhile I found a block with a couple of nails in it and an old dull axe out behind the barn. After looking over the dull and rusty axe, I didn't have the heart to cut off the chicken's head so returned to the house still holding the chicken. I told the lady about the dull axe saying, "It is so dull I didn't have the courage to even try to kill the chicken." "Well, of all things," she remarked. "Don't you live on a farm? Just wait and I'll come along. Perhaps the two of us can kill the chicken." She showed me how to put the chicken's head between the nails, pull back hard on the feet and then use the axe. I did as she instructed until I raised the axe. "This axe looks like the one Abe Lincoln used splitting rails, it won't cut anything." I said. "Here, here," she muttered, "let's stop fooling around. You're chicken. Give me that axe." As she made several whacks to cut off the chicken's head, she kept repeating, "You're chicken, you're chicken!" After she finished, she said, "Bring it down to the house after it stops kicking and I'll dress it."

In the afternoon, after all the chores were done, I went to visit the barber shop. This was a new experience for me. I had to wait for a few customers to get barbered before the barber said, "Next, next" and beckoned for me to get in the chair. The barber, Fred Michaud, kept asking me questions and talking steady while he was shaving me and cutting my hair. He inquired as to who I was, where I lived, how it was that I was in town for the day, where I was staying etc. He said, "Boy, you've never shaved before have you?" After nearly half an hour, he finished, held up a hand mirror and said, "Who do you see? By golly I've made a new boy out of you. Now that I've learned who you are and about what you intend to do, I'm sure you will make good." As I climbed out of the barber chair, he said, "That will be thirty cents, ten cents for the shave and twenty cents for the haircut." I handed him the fifty cent piece. He said, "Boy, this is a lot more than you owe me," and gave me back twenty cents.

After returning from the barber shop, Mrs. Craig had me take the wash tub up to my room, carry up some water and take a bath. Gee, when the day was ended, I felt like a new person. Sunday morning came and Mr. Craig asked me if I was going to church. "I'm a stranger," I replied, "and guess I'll go some other time after getting better acquainted with the people."

Monday I sort of dreaded going back to school, fearing the rough boys might continue to torment me as they had the first week. When I arrived at the school house, the principal said, "Good morning," and remarked how clean and nice I looked. As I met the boys who had teased me so much the week before, they each said, "Good morning, Phin" and shook hands. One of them said, "Now that you have got barbered, you look like a different person. We are sure that you will like us and we feel that you may become the most popular boy in school." After that things went along just fine at school, day after day and week after week.

In the Craig family there was a little boy about two years old named Benton. We became acquainted and whenever I could spare a few minutes, I had great fun playing with him. One Saturday afternoon, I was left to care for this little fellow. Mrs. Craig went for a ride with her husband up to Squa Pan Siding where he also bought potatoes. Leon Stone had purchased a Tin Lizzie (new Ford). Leon was a barber and sometimes he would close the shop and take people for a ride. He offered to take both Mr. and Mrs. Craig up there for a dollar. It was a ten mile trip, five miles each way. They were late coming back so I was late getting the milking done.

I heard a noise out in the shed and tiptoed out very quietly to see what was going on. Opening the door very quickly, I saw a boy about eight years old drinking milk out of a pan. He did not seem to get excited and drop the pan but sat it back on the shelf. As he stopped drinking the milk, a slab of thick cream hung from his upper lip. I have wished many times down through the years that I could have taken a picture of the scene. I inquired, "What are you doing?" He replied, "I was just tasting to see if it was ours." This little fellow had been coming every night about this time to get a couple of quarts of milk, which I suppose Mrs. Craig sold to the family. About this time, the Craig's returned so I hustled out, milked the cow and measured out the boy's milk.

I found plenty to do about Mr. Craig's and began to wish that I might stay with them all along, but as I came from school on Friday, the end of the sixth week, there was a man with a horse and buggy waiting there. Mrs. Craig had my clothes all tied up in a box and broke the news to me that Penn had found a place for me to stay and work my board, just as he had promised my father. I was introduced to Mr. Abe Sloat. Mrs. Craig complimented me for the good work that I had done for them and she assured Mr. Sloat that he was getting a good and efficient chore boy. It was about a one mile drive to the Sloat's farm. When we arrived, I helped unharness the horse and he then took me in and introduced me to Mrs. Sloat, saying, "Here is our new chore boy." He then said, "We will go out and look around and I'll instruct you as to what we will expect you to do. It must be understood at the beginning that the work will take care of your board and you'll pay Olive (Mrs. Sloat) for your washing." I inquired as to how much she would charge me. She answered, "Well, twenty-five cents a week will be okay."

We then went out and he showed me about. I learned that they were milking five cows, had a pen of pigs, a colt and a team of horses. Mr. Sloat showed me a pile of wood that had been split up and seasoned out-of-doors. "In your spare time," he said, "I want you to carry this in and pile it in the woodshed." There was a large orchard and apples had fallen all over the ground. "I'd like to have you pick these up and put them in the barn," he said. "I'll show you where. Perhaps it would be well if you picked these apples up this weekend so that they won't freeze and spoil. We will feed them to the hogs. The apples are fattening and we will feed them a few each day." The cows were still out roaming around in the field out back. "Now you drive in the cows," he ordered, "and we'll bed them down. By that time Olive will have supper ready for us." I inquired as to how much of the chores

I would be expected to do. "Why, this will be your job to do all the chores except taking care of the work horses," he answered. "I have hired to go in the woods and will be taking the team and going away in a few days."

Mrs. Sloat had prepared a good hearty supper. After we finished eating, I began doing the chores. There were so many things to do, it seemed I would have to make a schedule and arrange things so that the chores would be well done and in a certain time. That night Mr. Sloat got in the wood and water and took care of the work horses, leaving all the other chores for me. That first night, it took about an hour to milk the five cows. After a few days, I found they could all be milked in less time. After a while, I could complete the milking in about thirty-five or forty minutes as all the cows were kind and permitted me to milk fast. After the milking was done, the milk had to be separated from the cream. A hand cranked separator was used and it took quite some time to do this job. Sometimes Mrs. Sloat would help with the separating.

Saturday arrived and I began to gather the apples. Some time before noon, Mr. Sloat came and told me that my little sister, Leona, had passed away and that her funeral was to be held that afternoon. I was to be dressed and ready to ride to the cemetery with my folks when they came along. Burial was to be in the Ellis Cemetery out on the Masardis Road that afternoon.

My sister, Leona, was born March 27, 1900. She always seemed well and rugged, even more so than the rest of us children. She had reached the age when she was beginning to be a great help to Mother. The last time that I remember seeing her was the day before I left to go to high school. At that time Mother was teaching her to cook. The morning I left, Leona, Dorcas and Luther were not up yet. Opal was awake and playing in her cradle. Byron was up and helped with the chores. Leona attended the Little Red School House and was in the Third Reader. I learned that her illness was of very short duration. She was up around in the morning but rather feverish. The folks did not think it was serious enough to call the Doctor. During the day she gradually became worse. When Father came home from hauling a load of potatoes to Ashland, he called the Doctor. The Doctor came but he was too late. Leona passed away that very night. The date was October 29, 1911, and her illness was scarlet fever.

The news of her death was such a shock that I just couldn't work and I was so sad that I felt like quitting school and going back home that very day. The hearse came along, prearranged perhaps; it stopped, giving me time to get in the wagon with my parents. This was a very sad day. Mother and Father were all broken up. After leaving the cemetery, I asked them if they wanted me to come back home and help. "Oh, no," Father answered, "We understand through your Aunt Abbie Walker (my mother's sister who lived in Ashland, mother of Hazen and Avis who were in my class in high school) that you are doing well in school and everyone thinks a lot of you. Although you have quite a long walk to school, you have a good home in which to stay and work your way. Hang to it, study hard and someday you may become a doctor and won't have to work as hard as we do to earn a living."

Although this was a very sad day, I went back to doing the chores. Mr. Sloat said, "I understand how you feel and I'll help you tonight." We finished the chores early and I went right to bed. My room was up over the wood shed. There were two beds there. It was a good place to sleep at the time but became awfully cold during the winter months.

Sunday morning when I awoke, there was a man in the other bed. I inquired, "Who are you?" He said, "I'm Charles Sloat. This is my home." He told me where he was working, etc. This was a surprise as nothing had been said about there being children in the family. For dinner on Sunday, a young woman came and was introduced to me as "Our daughter Matilda." This was another surprise and I wondered if they had any more children in the family. I learned that it was customary for Mr. Sloat to work in the woods some each winter and up to this time Charles had been home to do the chores when his father was gone. Now that Charles was away working they needed a chore boy.

Everything went along fine all winter. I got the wood in before snow came, cleaned up about the yard and put banking around the barn where it was needed to keep out the snow and cold. They were good to me. Mrs. Sloat kept my clothes mended and washed for the twenty-five cents each week except for one time. Whit Martin (Mrs. Sloat's brother) came early one Saturday morning and wanted to hire me to help thresh grain as he was short of help. I told him that I would be awfully busy all day cleaning up around but it would be up to Mr. and Mrs. Sloat. He said that he would pay me a dollar to come and help him for the day. "Well, okay Phin," Mr. Sloat said, "You can go and help and catch up with the chores tomorrow."

It was a fine spring day, late in March. The machine was ready to go when we got back. It was a hand fed separator and the power was furnished by two horses walking in the "horse-power" or "tread mill" as it was sometimes called. My job was to take away the straw from behind the separator and pitch it up over the beam (a girder that was called "girt"). Mr. Martin had a man there to spread the straw and a horse walking around to keep the straw from piling up to much. Things went fine and I enjoyed the day until about the last couple of hours. Mr. Martin had some barley to thresh. The thresher stopped until the horse could be taken out of the mow. The straw was packed down enough so there was plenty of room for the barley straw. I had never helped thresh barley before and soon found out that the little barbs stuck fast to my clothes and worked in, much the same way as porcupine quills. By the time we had finished threshing, I began to feel that I had contacted the old fashioned itch. Mr. Martin got out his wallet and paid me the dollar he had promised. I hustled back to the Sloat's, happy to have earned some money, but I was very tired and awfully hungry.

When I arrived, Mr. Sloat inquired, "What in the world are you plastered with?" I told him that Mr. Martin said the last grain we threshed was barley and that this was barbs from the barley. Well, I cleaned off the stuff the best I could, had supper, did the barn chores, took a bath in the wash tub and got into some clean clothes. That night, I went to bed happy to think that I'd earned a dollar. Nothing more was said about threshing until the next Saturday morning. I took my dollar, which I had pinned in my shirt pocket and handed it to Mrs. Sloat to pay for my washing which I supposed would be the usual twenty-five cents. She thanked me for it saying "Phin, I'll have to keep all of this because I couldn't wash out the barley barbs so I kept picking them from the clothes. I hope that I got them all out." Boy, I could have dropped through the floor. Was I ever disappointed not to get back any change. However, I felt Mrs. Sloat had earned every cent of the dollar getting my clothes fixed up. As I worked about doing the chores that day, I felt angry with myself for going up to help thresh.

We have to live and learn, so decided I'd better not find fault about that deal.

Vacation came the early part of April. There had been so much hard work to do just for my board for the past five months. I was told I wouldn't be needed anymore as Mr. Sloat wasn't working out now and that he could do the chores. He said that he would try hard to find another place for me to stay and work my board. My folks called for me and I went down to Castle Hill for a week's vacation, hoping I'd be able to go back for the spring term.

A few days later, Mr. Sloat phoned and said he understood that Mr. Colbun, the Station Agent, had purchased the Burnham Holm's Farm and that perhaps he would need a chore boy. I thanked him for the information, and then called Mr. Colbun. He allowed that he had made a few statements about getting a chore boy. He asked all sorts of questions, as to who my people were, my age, about my qualifications as a chore boy and if I might care to give some references. I told him I was fifteen years old last August that my father was a farmer and lumberman and that I'd always lived on the farm and done chores as soon as I was old enough. I also told him that I had stayed with Penn Craig for six weeks during the fall term and spent the balance of the fall term and winter term at Abe Sloat's home doing his chores. I informed Mr. Colbun that this was my freshman year in high school and that I didn't have any money to continue on with and that the only way for me to go on would be to find a place to work my board. He seemed quite interested but said he wanted to talk things over with Mrs. Colbun and he'd call back in a day or two. I think it was the very next day that Mr. Colbun called back and said, "We have decided to have a chore boy and you are just the boy that we are looking for, a boy who likes to work and one who has the 'know how'. You come up Sunday and we will meet you over in Ashland after church and bring you over to the farm."

My folks took me to Ashland with a sleigh and from there Mr. Colbun took me to his farm with a horse and wagon. When we arrived at the farm, which was more than a mile from town, Mrs. Colbun prepared dinner and I helped take care of the horse. The Colbun's told me they had recently purchased the farm, had just completed moving from their old home, and that neither of them knew anything about farming. Mr. Colbun showed me around the place. There was a pile of wood he wanted me to saw up and prepare for stove wood. He had a couple of cows, a flock of hens, a double team and a few hogs. He allowed that all of this stock came along with the purchase of the farm. After the dinner was over, Mr. Colbun and I went out again and walked around the place. We talked more about the chores. He told me that he would be hiring a farm manager and this fellow would be taking care of the double team. He then asked, "Do you think that you can take care of all the rest of the things I have shown you?" I replied, "It's a long walk to school, must be nearly a mile and a half; however, I'll do my best to try and satisfy you." I inquired about how much feed he wanted me to give the stock. I said, "There is some pig feed here and some grain for the horses but I do not see any meal for the cows." "Now, Phin," he answered, "I do not have the least idea how much feed to buy or how much to buy at a time, we are going to leave that up to you. Just tell Mrs. Colbun and she can take the driving horse and bring back whatever you need." That afternoon, I made a study of the chores and planned out how, what time, and in what order each one was to be done so I'd have thirty-five minutes left in which to get to school on time.

In checking around, I couldn't find any salt for the stock. We would also need some meal for the cows. The cows looked so rough that I included a can of lice powder on the first list of things for Mrs. Colbun to buy.

Mr. Colbun was still holding his job as station agent and as he left for work Monday morning, he wished me good luck. He said, "Do the best you can. Oh, yes, did you ever cut potato seed?" I told him that I was an expert at cutting potato seed. "Well, then," he replied, "we may want you to cut some seed when the time comes." I told him not to worry about any of the things he wanted me to do, that I knew how to do the work and hoped that I could please him in appreciation for having a chance to finish out my school year. The first few days, I hurried to clean up around the place and learn just what I should do to please Mr. Colbun. He always had a compliment when he came home.

One night when I came home from school, about a week after I'd arrived, a man was working there. Mrs. Colbun introduced him as Mr. Ray Page, our farm foreman and manager. Ray and I became friends. We worked along doing the best we could. He arranged for a man to come with a circular saw and engine on his first Saturday there and we sawed all of the wood that day. This pleased Mr. Colbun. I managed to split and prepare the wood for the stoves before the end of April.

As I've mentioned earlier, the Colbun's had just recently purchased and moved to the farm. Every little noise and the different sounds seemed to bother Mrs. Colbun. Quite often she would remark, "Well, do you think this place might be haunted?" Some mornings she would ask Ray Page or me if we had heard a strange noise during the night. "Perhaps this place is haunted," she'd say. Sometimes when I was awake, I'd listen but never heard anything except the wind blowing through a large tree which stood nearby or sometimes a loose board would rattle in the wind or the wind would rattle a door or the shutters outside of the windows. Sometimes one could hear the horses stomping out in the barn. One time, I assured Mrs. Colbun that there wasn't such a thing as a ghost. "Well," she said, "I can't help it, but I'm nervous in this strange house." She allowed that perhaps we were right, that there weren't any ghosts and that she would overcome the idea.

Ray used to go over town on Saturday nights. He and I shared the same bed. He would often come home late and I would not even hear him come in the room. Probably because of Mrs. Colbun talking about ghosts, Ray was prompted to try a stunt all his own. It was one Saturday, about the first of May. The weather was warm and the frogs were singing. I had raised the window about a foot so I could hear them sing. I had dropped off into a deep sleep, listening to the frogs. Ray came home and I didn't hear a sound. He got ready for bed. He then took off all the bed-clothes, put a sheet, over his head and squatted down at the foot of the bed. Soon I became chilly and reached for the quilts to cover up with but there weren't any. I was about to light the lamp when there came a sound like a cat's meow. The first thing that came to my mind was that a cat had climbed into the room through the window. The "meows" became louder and louder. Then a white object began to rise slowly at the foot of the bed. There was a loud "MEOW" just as I was lighting the lamp. Then it dawned on me that Mrs. Colbun could be right and perhaps the house was haunted. In a second, I reached the window and was climbing out when I heard "Phin, don't jump, Phin, don't jump. This is Ray. For God's sake don't jump out that window." When I realized what was going on, I was shaking like a leaf. Ray put the bedclothes back on the bed and sat there quite awhile watching me shake. He allowed that he never would try a trick like that again on anyone. After a time he came to bed but I just couldn't sleep anymore that night.

Mrs. Colbun had heard the noise from their room downstairs and in the morning inquired as to what all the noise was about. "Was it you boys or was it a ghost?" I told her what happened, that I had my doubts about ghosts; however, I had seen one and never wanted to see another. Ray and Mr. Colbun had a hearty laugh about the affair but Mrs. Colbun cried and said, "What if it had been a real ghost?"

Now that it was the first of May, the question came up again about cutting potato seed. Some seed potatoes had been purchased and stored in the barn where they wouldn't freeze. I told them although I could cut seed I felt I had plenty to keep me busy. About the third Saturday that I was there, Ray said, "Let's see just how good Phin can cut potato seed." A knife was brought to me which I placed in a board. Mrs. Colbun stated, "Potato seed can't be cut on a contraption like that, can it, Ray?" "Oh, yes," he answered, "Phin seems to know what he is doing. Let's leave everything to him regarding cutting potato seed."

They agreed to stay away and let me cut a barrel of seed. In about an hour, I had filled a barrel right to the brim. I hunted up Ray. He examined the seed and picked out about a bushel to show Mr. and Mrs. Colbun. He told them he had examined every seed that he had picked out and found an eye in every one. He said, "If you want to arrange for Phin to cut some seed it will be okay with me. I'll guarantee that every seed he cuts will grow."

After some deliberation, Mr. Page allowed that it would be okay for him to pay me ten cents per barrel for what I could cut. That was in addition to doing the chores for my board and washing. I agreed to the arrangement and would try and cut about four barrels each day. For a time I managed to cut approximately the number of barrels I had promised but it was a hustle from the time I awoke in the morning until bed time. After the first four days with the seed, Mrs. Colbun came and said. "I'd like to make a bargain with you." "What's up?" I asked. She said, "Will is very pleased with your work and Ray especially is happy with the way you cut potato seed and I'll tell you just what I'd like to do. We have a house maid coming and if you'll work right up to just a few minutes before school time, I'll have the horse harnessed and here by the door. Your dinner pail will be ready. We'll allow you time to wash up and then come and jump in the wagon with me and I'll drive you to school and meet you there just as school is dismissed." I said, "Well, okay, but always have me there on time so that I will never be tardy." She answered, "Okay, it's a bargain."

Mrs. Colbun was a good driver and she knew just how fast to drive the horse to get me to school on time. Sometimes she used the whip but after a few trips, the horse seemed to know just what was expected. Some days I'd get six or seven barrels by this arrangement and on Saturday, I'd do a lot better. I would be up at dawn and cut after school until dark. This became very tiresome by the time Mr. Page finished planting early in June. I kept account of the number of barrels that I cut. At ten cents per barrel, I earned more than ten dollars.

The Colbun's were quite religious and always attended church on Sunday. There wasn't any work done on Sundays, except the regular chores. There was a light plant or power house at Big Machias River. This was just a short distance from the Colbun farm. I went up there quite often on Sundays to observe how the thing worked. The plant was owned by George Moores. His brother Wilmer was usually in attendance when I visited. Inside the building was a large electric generator. Power to operate the generator was furnished by a water wheel. This power house was built almost over the dam and the water coming over the dam kept the wheel going, this in turn kept the generator working. Mr. Moores had constructed a power line over to Ashland village and furnished electricity for the town. This gave good service most of the year. Sometimes in summer, the lights would dim due to low water at the dam.

One time when I was up there, logs were being driven down the Machias River. It was interesting to see the river drivers poling the logs along down the stream. I remember that these logs were to be boomed at the Sheridan Mill. There were a few times that I was lucky enough to see the main drive of logs on the Aroostook River passing by under the covered bridge at Ashland.

When school finished, the Colbun's paid me for cutting the seed with a ten dollar bill. Boy, wasn't I rich. I said goodbye to them.

Mrs. Colbun drove me to the village where my father was waiting. On the ride home, I told him about the deal and about how hard I had worked. He said, "Well, that was okay if your ranks didn't suffer on account of it."

In those days, we had to drive three miles to Morin Corner for our mail. This was on R.F.D. No.1 from Mapleton. The rank card came in the mail a few days later and in all of my subjects I had scored well above 90.

Chapter 6

Life with Dr. Hagerthy

After coming home from Will Colbun's farm, the summer of 1912, I pitched right in helping with the farm work. I drove the team to hoe potatoes, to cut the hay with the mowing machine and to haul it in. I did most any kind of work that a man could do and found it very interesting. Before going to high school, my work, for the most part, was doing chores and milking.

After a few weeks had passed, I began to wonder about going back to high school in the fall and mentioned it to my parents. Mother assured me that I needn't worry for she had heard many compliments about my work and that someone would be wanting a chore boy.

One day, about the first of July, word came to us that Dr. Hagerthy was looking for a new chore boy. I phoned the Doctor to see if what I had heard was true. "Yes, it is true," he said, "Gene (his former chore boy) graduated this spring from high school and I have to find a boy to take his place." He also said, "Do not promise anyone else until I have had a talk with you and your parents." He came along soon after for an interview with us. He allowed that there was an awful lot of work to do but he was willing to give me a try. He wanted me to go to his place right away on account of milking the cow. I begged off, telling him that I was driving team and helping with the farming as much as I could but would like to come when school began in September. "Okay," he said, "That will be fine. Be ready a couple of days before school begins and I'll come for you."

When September rolled around, I had passed my 16th birthday and had been doing much of the heavy work and liked it. Dr. Hagerthy phoned at the appointed time and said to Mother, "Have Phin get his duds on and pack his clothes. I'll be down for him today."

At the beginning, I inquired of Mrs. Hagerthy as to how much I would have to pay per week for my washing. She replied, "Don't worry about that. We have a hired girl all of the time and while you are one of the family your washing will be done." I was very bashful at first, since their ways were somewhat different than ours were on the farm. However, I became acquainted in a short time and my work always seemed to please them. I became very busy arranging things my way about doing the chores.

I learned at the beginning that Dr. Hagerthy was a graduate of Bowdoin Medical School in 1903 and that he interned at the Maine Medical Center in Bangor in 1903 and 1904. While at the Maine Medical Center, once in a while a patient would come from the Ashland area for treatment. One day someone mentioned that Dr. Chapman of Ashland was thinking of leaving. Dr. Hagerthy inquired about this with Dr. Chapman and then decided Ashland would be a good place for him to begin his practice.

He came to Ashland in the fall of 1904, driving up with a horse and wagon he had purchased. He made arrangements with Dr. Chapman for the use of some of his equipment. In the beginning, Dr. Hagerthy had his office located up over Whit Hallet's store. Mr. Hallet was Postmaster and operated a grocery store at the same place. Dr. Mansur, a dentist, also had an office nearby. The Telephone Company later located their office in the same room Dr. Hagerthy had occupied, after he had purchased a home with ample space for his office. The Hallet building was later taken over by the Ashland Trust Company and remodeled, making it suitable for a bank. In recent years, the Washburn Trust Company of Washburn purchased the building and acquired the bank. It is now a branch of the Washburn Trust Co. Dr. Hagerthy purchased the Vinal home about 1906 and continued to live there until it burned on December 30, 1934. He then purchased the Frank Webster house and moved in.

Before going to Ashland to attend school, I heard a great deal about Alf Trafton. Mr. Trafton was a lumberman and a farmer. He always took part in the annual fairs at Presque Isle. He owned a team of horses which he entered in the horse pulling contests each year. He owned several trotting horses. Some of them were Queen Inez, Silk Patchen and Revena Wilkes. They were very good and won many races at the fairs. I learned that Mrs. Hagerthy was one of Mr. Trafton's daughters. Mrs. Hagerthy (Belle), before her marriage, had taught school in Sheridan. It was four miles from her home to Sheridan. I was told she used a pung in winter, a single wagon in summer and rode horseback in the fall and spring when neither wagon nor pung could be used very well.

Mr. Trafton was one of the many people bidding to have another doctor come to town. Dr. Chapman was leaving. Dr. Dobson was located in Ashland but a young doctor, who could rough it and travel the many miles to the lumber camps, was badly needed. When Dr. Hagerthy first came to Ashland, Mr. Trafton made his driving horses available to him so he wouldn't have to buy several horses and pay barn and stable rent for them.

This perhaps, is how the Doctor and Belle became acquainted. Mrs. Hagerthy was always kind to me and saw to it that my clothes were washed and pressed.

Dr. Hagerthy and his wife, Belle.

The Hagerthy's had two small sons, Dana and Bert. Just about the day the Doctor came for me, the oldest son Dana who was six years old, got ptomaine poisoning and became very ill. Other doctors and a nurse came to help but all was in vain. The poor little fellow died a few days later. The Doctor managed, with the help of the other doctors, to care for his patients through this period. Sadness prevailed for many days and I was on my own with the chores.

A week or so after Dana's funeral the Doctor found some time to spend with me. Two horses were already being used and three more were over in a pasture on the Portage Lake Road. We went over and brought them home, one at a time, behind the car. He instructed me which harnesses to use on which horse, for a harness was adjusted to each individual horse. I was to exercise a pair each night after school so that they would be conditioned for fall and winter. The road conditions were so bad in those days that he used horses quite early in the fall until late in the spring. Most people used their horses for transportation all year, but Dr. Hagerthy owned one of the very few cars in the area which he drove during the summer months. Sometimes when the weather was rainy and wet, the roads became too muddy and slippery for the car and he had to use horses even in the summer.

I soon learned that life doing chores here would not be an easy one. I also learned that the Doctor was on the "go" around the clock. There were no regular rest periods for him. Duty bound, he worked day or night, rain or shine, day in and day out. Meals were always ready for him at regular times but he was not always there to eat them.

The Hagerthy home was a very large place. It was built by a Mr. Vinal who lumbered, cutting long lumber for the Ashland Mill Co. There were many rooms in it. Some thirty or forty cords of wood, in four foot lengths, were purchased each year. A man would be hired each spring to buck saw the wood into stove lengths and then split it, leaving it to season for the next year. The furnace was very large. It needed to be filled each morning, noon and night and there was always plenty of heat from it. There was a cookstove, a laundry stove, a stove in the front chamber and a fireplace in the living room. It was part of my job to keep these going.

The barn was very large. There were regular stalls for five horses and a cow or two on one side of the barn floor. On the other side there was room for more horses when it was needed. Above the barn floor was a hay loft that was filled with loose hay each summer. Loose oat straw was also stored for bedding the horses, etc. The arrangement for feeding was well planned. Hay was pitched from above to each individual stall. Also, traps were located in the floor through which the waste and manure was dropped to the basement. A cow was always kept and one or two hogs, but never hens.

I was instructed about keeping the horses groomed, about keeping the wagon axles greased and oiling the harnesses from time to time. After a few weeks, when I became acquainted with all of my work, the Doctor took me along with him many times. I was known over the entire area as Doctor Hagerthy's "portable hitching post." As time went on, he taught me a great deal about medicine and permitted me to assist with many cases where it was proper to do so.

On weekends, we would check the equipment for repairs. There was a first class harness shop in Ashland at that time. The shoes on the horses had to be calked often and sometimes even new shoes were needed. Walter McKay and his son Charles did most of this work for us. Keeping the driveway shoveled in winter and the lawn mowed in summer was another part of my work.

One job that took considerable time was pumping the water used in the home. There was a large reservoir made of wood in the attic. This held around three hundred gallons of water. Water was pumped each night. Sometimes about an hour was required to fill the tank. Each night after school, I would pump the water and then hitch up a pair of horses and hustle out to exercise them.

One night I hitched up Dan and Lady and drove off. They made a grand team and as I drove up through the village someone came running beside the wagon and hollered, "Here I am. I knew you would come and give me a ride and I've been right here watching for you. Just how do I get up in that rig where you are?" I answered, "Just come around the other side." I helped the lady in and to my surprise it was Miss Cronin our English Teacher at the high school. I tried to explain that this was a complete surprise and that I knew nothing of her waiting for a ride, but couldn't seem to get even a word in edgewise. It was a nice fall afternoon in early October and there were still some colorful leaves on the trees. For the next hour and a half, I answered many questions for this girl. "What do you call a rig like this?" she asked. "This is a double hitch," I replied. "Why is it called a double hitch?" she wanted to know. I answered, "It is called a double hitch because we use two horses at one time." "What are the horse's names?" she asked. "Dan and Lady," I replied. "If this is part of your chores, what do you call it?" she inquired. "This is jogging the horses, exercising them so that when the Doctor has to put his car away they will be muscled up to make long trips such as to Oxbow, Portage Lake, etc." I answered. "This rig that we are riding in is what is called a wagon isn't it?" she inquired. "Yes," I replied.

She told me that this was her first year up in the wilderness, that this was her first ride in a wagon and that her home was in the city. After we had driven a ways, I began to jog the horses and Miss Cronin became very nervous or perhaps frightened. She said, "Please don't drive so fast that I will fall out and get hurt. You won't let me fall will you?" I stopped the horses and asked her if she was frightened. "If you are," I said, "I'll take you back home." "Oh, no," she answered, "Don't take me back, I have on a good warm sweater and it is such a lovely afternoon. You are such a good driver and I want to have the experience of having a buggy ride. Just don't let me fall out." "Boy, oh boy, Miss Cronin," I said, "I've just got to drive along much faster." There was a blanket folded under the wagon seat and I got it out and gave it to her saying, "Here, you wrap this around yourself and get a hold of my arm for I must hurry along." I got hold of the horse whip and spirited the team along a little faster, thinking all the time there was something fishy about this deal.

I called her attention to the landscape, to the hills and the color that was still on some of the trees. We arrived on the Ridge to where the Snowman's lived, turned and headed for home. "My, oh my," she said, "This is a lovely ride and now I'm not afraid of falling out." Then the questions began again.

By the time we arrived back to the village, Miss Cronin had learned most everything about the wagon, the names of the parts of the harnesses, etc. She wanted to know why I was working for the Doctor instead of staying home. I explained we were a poor family and didn't have any money for education and the only way I could go to high school was to work my way.

She asked if I would please drive by Mrs. McQuarrie's where she boarded. "This will save me from walking back up town," she said. As we arrived at her boarding place, she allowed that she was not frightened any more and perhaps she might like to go along again when I was out jogging the horses. She also stated that it would be nice to ride down sometime and meet my people. She said, "They must be very nice people to have a son who likes to work as you do." As Miss Cronin climbed down from the wagon, she stated, "I have enjoyed the buggy ride and I will see you at school tomorrow."

The sun was sinking in the west when I returned back to the stable and it was the beginning of a lovely evening. As I was doing my chores, I was praying the Doctor wouldn't find out about my giving Miss Cronin a ride for he might not like it. I went in to supper a few minutes later than usual; however, it did not cause any inconvenience for the Doctor had not yet arrived for his supper. During the meal, Mrs. Hagerthy stated, "Phin was a little later than usual, but that's okay." Nothing else was said about my trip that night or the next morning, so I made up my mind nothing would be mentioned about it.

When I came home for dinner, the Doctor was there and he began kidding me about taking the English teacher for a buggy ride. I listened and tried to take the ribbing all in a good way. Before I went back to school, Mrs. Hagerthy told me about the deal. She said, "Don't take the Doctor's ribbing too seriously. He was behind all of it. He had someone up the street arrange for Miss Cronin to stop you and ask for a buggy ride." I later told the Doctor about all of the questions Miss Cronin asked and said to him, "What if she had fallen out and got hurt. What would have happened then?" He replied, "Oh, I would have had another patient, perhaps."

After winter came and the outside work was done, putting in the wood, etc., I went along with the Doctor many times, especially on weekends, on trips to Portage Lake and Oxbow. Portage Lake was ten miles away and it was twenty miles to Oxbow. Very often when we were returning from these long trips, he would let me drive the team and he would sleep. The Doctor was very good about not taking me from my studies on weekdays. That is why most of my longer trips with him were on weekends.

Several times I went with the Doctor when he received calls to go many miles up in the woods beyond the hotel at Oxbow. Arrangements were made in advance with Mr. Libby, owner of the hotel, to have a fresh team ready when we arrived there. Very often it was nine o'clock or even later. The Doctor would hop out of our pung and someone would drive him to a lumber camp or perhaps to several camps before returning. I would stable our team, go in and go to bed. Many times it would be in the wee hours of the morning when he returned. I was called and would get our team hitched up while the Doctor had a hot lunch. When the weather was very cold, we would have a hot "soapstone" to put in the bottom of the pung to keep our feet warm. As we were leaving Libby's, he would look at the clock and state, "The roads are pretty good so you take the reins. Try and make it home in two hours and I'll sleep."

In minutes he would be sound asleep and snoring away. Very often on a long trip like this he would sleep all the way home.

One night, I remember, it seemed we were ahead of schedule so I let the horses slow up on the hill coming out of Masardis. The Doctor was awake in an instant, wanting to know if there was trouble. I assured him that we were making extra good time so I'd just tightened the reins to let the team have a breather while going up the hill. "Well, okay," he said, "but when you reach the top push them along a little, there may be calls waiting for me when we get home."

The bells we used at night were quite heavy and could be heard for miles. Sometimes, when returning from a trip like this, a farmer would be standing beside the road waving a lantern and I would stop the team. Either the Doctor was wanted at that place or Mrs. Hagerthy had left a message for him to call at another place. It was not unusual to see the farmer's lights come on as we were driving by, between four and five o'clock in the morning. They would be getting up to start a new day.

While riding together, Dr. Hagerthy and I would talk about most everything. Just a few months after I went there to stay, he inquired as to my nationality. I told him I was Scotch. He stopped the team and said, "Gee, I wish I'd known that before." "Why?" I asked. "Well," he answered, "The Scotch and Irish never seemed to get along together very well." He told me that he had a friend one time that claimed to be Scotch and one day he was taken to jail and locked up. "Why did they lock him up?" I inquired. "Oh, he had too much scotch in him, I guess," he answered. I was puzzled for a minute or two as to what was up and wondered if he really minded that I was Scotch. He then said, "Well, I guess I can fix things up this time. By the powers invested in me as a surgeon, I now declare you a true son of Erin and the title Phinagin is bestowed on you for now and forever." As we drove on, the Doctor thought this was a great joke, having me guessing for a few minutes. Thereafter he always called me Phinagin.

Dr. Hagerthy inquired, "How in the world did the Scotch ever get over here in the first place?" I informed him, "I was always told my ancestors acted so bad over in Scotland that they were driven out of the country and some of them landed in America."

I asked the Doctor, "There seems to be an awful lot of Irish people living in America, how did they happen to be over here?" His reply was, "Oh, the Irish were imported and some became doctors but the most of them were made cops to look after the other people and keep order in this country."

On one occasion, he inquired about religion. He said, "You don't smoke, I've never heard you swear, you don't drink and you are always honest with us at home. Just what is your church background?"

I told him that we did not have a church close by at home but up until I came to Ashland, I attended Sunday school that was held in the Little Red School House. "That was a nice thing to do," he said, "Do you remember something that you've learned?" "Well," I answered, "We were taught that God helps those who help themselves." After a long pause, he said, "Maybe so Phinagin, maybe so, but I was just wondering why it is that when people are sick, they send for the Irish."

Life with the Hagerthy's continued like this the rest of my high school days. I would ride with him at every opportunity, listen to his stories and help him with minor cases whenever I could.

One thing that always impressed me was what the doctor knew about the weather. Riding in at night when the stars were out, we would talk about the weather. Different bells were used at different times on the harnesses while making calls. The Doctor claimed it was restful to listen to a different tone of bells. Sometimes he claimed that the tone of the bells seemed to change and in this way helped predict the weather. The way the horses looked or acted was an indication of what the weather would be. If they were garping, it was a sure sign of rain. If their hair stood up that was an indication of a cold snap. If the hair was lying down, it indicated that we would be having a warm spell or good weather. Fog going up the river against the current was an indication of rain or a storm. Fog on the hill indicated rain. Cows resting on higher ground indicated a foul day. Cows resting on the lower part of the pasture was a sign of a fine day. If the sunset was clear on Friday, watch for a storm before Monday night. A sweet Saturday night meant watch out for a storm Monday morning. Quite often his predictions were accurate.

The Doctor told me his father was a sea Captain, who would lie on his back on the deck of a ship and study the stars. By this method, he could forecast fairly accurately as to what the weather would be for several days ahead.

He often mentioned that it was possible that the change of the moon delayed or sometimes hastened the birth of a child. Years later when I was administrator of the A. R. Gould Memorial Hospital, when the census in the maternity ward was quite low, I'd tell the nurses, "Cheer up, the moon will change (and I'd name the time it would change) and you will be crowded with maternity cases." Sure enough things most always happened that way.

The Golden Calf

About March 10, 1913, as I began to do chores in the morning, a strange noise came to my attention. After feeding the horses and pitching down some hay for the cows, I found that one of the cows had given birth to a new bossie. The cow was taken to a box stall along with the calf. The newcomer was found to be a heifer and a very pretty one. The calf was already up and around and had sucked some milk from the mother cow. I finished milking what milk there was left in the udder.

The Doctor was notified about the new calf. He came and looked it over and instructed me to pass by Lawrence Coffin's home on my way to school and ask Mr. Coffin to come for the calf. "What will Lawrence do with the calf?" I inquired. "Oh, he will bump it off," he answered. "What do you mean, bump it off?" I asked. "That means to kill it," he replied. I did a lot of thinking before school time. This was such a pretty heifer. I had a feeling I'd like to have it.

Before school time, I looked at it several times and before leaving asked the Doctor if I might keep it. I explained that I would purchase some calf meal, make it grow and it would be a fine cow someday. "If you are interested in taking care of the calf, I will make you a present of it. You may feed it meal from what we have for the cow and you won't have to buy any yourself," he informed me. So I kept the calf. After separating the milk each time, some of the skim milk was used for the calf. It soon learned to eat dry meal and in short time it looked slick and grew like a weed. After a few weeks, the Doctor was taking folks out to the barn to see the calf. He seemed to enjoy watching the calf grow as much as I did.

Mrs. Will (Maria) Rafford brought butter and eggs to Hagerthy's place every Saturday morning. When the calf was about six weeks old, Mrs. Hagerthy told her about how nice it looked. "Really, Maria," she said, "You should have Phin show you that calf." Mrs. Rafford drove to the barn. We hitched her horse and she came to see the calf. She was surprised and allowed it was the most handsome calf that she had seen for a long time. "It is a heifer. Well, well, what do you plan to do with it?" she asked. I answered, "Oh, I may sell it sometime." Mrs. Rafford said, "Let's make a deal right now. I'll give you ten dollars for it if you will keep it until it is ten weeks old." I hesitated a minute or two then said, "Well, okay, I'll keep it for you."

When the ten weeks were up, I told Mrs. Rafford. She paid me the ten dollars and sent her husband with a wagon to bring the calf home. Here I had a ten dollar bill and wondered what to do with it. It was fastened in my shirt pocket. Some time during the next week, posters were posted around town telling of an excursion on the Bangor and Aroostook Railroad to a circus in Bangor, the second week in June. The excursion tickets were listed as $2.50 and the tickets to the circus were to be $1.00 for adults and $.50 for children. My grandmother Wilcox lived in Bangor and I thought this would be a grand time to visit her. The only hitch was to have someone do the chores while I was away. This came the last week of the school year when it was time to be taking tests. I talked the matter over with Mrs. Hagerthy, one night after school, and she made some suggestions. She said, "We will arrange to have someone do the chores for a few days. You tell Mr. Towne, the Principal, about your plans. I'm sure he will arrange to give you the final examinations in advance so that you can take that trip." I always felt the Doctor went and saw the Principal, for when I went to him he seemed to have already learned of the plans that I had, relative to going on the excursion. Mr. Towne said, "Don't worry; we will see that everything will be taken care of and you can take the trip."

I had never before been on the train and had never been to Bangor. I hadn't seen my grandmother since she helped me care for the lamb. After a day or so, I began to hesitate about going alone. One day at school, I told my cousin, Hazen Walker, about the plans and asked him to arrange to go with me. Hazen allowed it would be a wonderful trip but he told me he did not have the money to go. At this time, I showed him the ten dollar bill and said, "Let's see, perhaps this will be enough for both of us." Hazen became excited and interested. We took paper and pencil and figured things out this way. Two railroad tickets to Bangor would be $5.00. Two circus tickets @$1.00 each, $2.00. "This will be only seven dollars, we can stay with Gram for nothing and we still will have $3.00 to spend," I said. "Okay, if my mother is willing, I'll go with you," he answered. We both went to the principal to see if Hazen could take the exams in advance, too.

"Wonderful idea, boys," he remarked, "Hazen can take the exams in advance, too."

Hazen went home that night and told his mother. She was all excited and said, "Phin won't have to divide his money with you. Your father can give you the same amount and you boys will have a nice vacation, see your Gram, see the circus and have a ride on the train. It will be wonderful."

Wednesday came of the last week of school. We each took the exams and were ready to leave on the train on Thursday morning. Hazen came to the Doctor's home and the Doctor took us down to the train. If I remember correctly, the train left Ashland around eight o'clock. The Doctor introduced us to the conductor at the depot and we were off on a new adventure. It was a long and tiresome day. The train was crowded by the time it arrived at Oakfield. At Oakfield, another passenger car was connected on and this too became crowded before we reached Bangor. Seems, as I think back, it was nearly five o'clock when the train arrived at Bangor.

Hazen and I had enjoyed watching passengers crowd on from one station to another. It was interesting to watch the conductor as he went through the cars after each stop taking tickets. It was also interesting to see him hop off at every station, watch up and down and keep saying "All Aboard-All Aboard" and he would wave his hand, a signal to the engineer on the locomotive, meaning "we are ready, go ahead". During the afternoon it became so warm in the cars that the windows were opened. All during the day a man kept walking through the train shouting at the top of his voice, "Popcorn, peanuts and cracker jacks, Popcorn, peanuts and cracker jacks." Some trips through, he was selling sandwiches. We each had brought some sandwiches and did not spend money for anything that day except for our tickets.

When the train arrived in Bangor, our Aunt May Morrison was at the depot waiting with her car to drive us over to where Gram lived. Gram was happy to see us. She said, "Wait a minute," and brought a mirror so we could see how we looked. Each of us was quite a sight. During the trip down we had become sweaty and having leaned out of the window once in a while, had collected a lot of coal dust. What a sight we were. Aunt May said goodnight and allowed that she would be back early in the morning to give us a ride all over the city. Gram showed us the washroom and gave us some soap and water so that we could clean up. Neither of us had an extra shirt along so she took our shirts and washed them because the collars had collected so much coal dust. We had a wonderful supper like only Grandmothers used to make. We told her about our school, about things back home and about how we enjoyed our first train ride. I also told her about the lamb that she helped save. That it had lived, eventually had six lambs and in 1911 I'd sold them for $38.50 and this money helped me to begin high school.

My grandmother, Eucebia Gilman Wilcox, with her daughter, my aunt, May Wilcox Morrison.

The next morning, Gram had ironed our shirts before Aunt May came to take us on a tour of the city. The first place we visited was Jones' Fish Market where Uncle Guy Wilcox worked. Guy showed us all through the plant, how the fish were packed in ice, etc. He also told us the fish were brought in by boat loads and explained how they were prepared to sell. Some were salted and some smoked.

Later she parked her car somewhere near the street car line. Uncle Don Wilcox was conductor on the car. Aunt May bought a ticket for each of us. The tickets were, as I remember, ten cents each. We made several transfers which took us about all over the city on the same ticket. After coming back to where we had started, Aunt May took us for a tour with her car and we arrived at her home six miles out on Union Street. She hurried dinner and then we went to the circus grounds. Aunt May took a dollar from each of us and bought the tickets. We found some good seats inside the tent where we could have a good view of the performances. This was a three ring circus and boy, oh boy, what a happy afternoon. How we enjoyed the many acts. We saw the wild animals, the elephants, stunts by the acrobats and the clowns. This was to me the treat of a lifetime.

After the circus was over, Aunt May suggested we buy our mothers a present to take home. We landed at a store where most everything was sold. I asked Aunt May to make a suggestion. Her suggestion was that we each buy our mothers a shirtwaist. These were one dollar each. We each gave Aunt May a dollar to buy something for Gram. We were taken back to Gram's on Pine Street late in the afternoon. It had been the best day in our lives. We enjoyed another evening with Grandmother, had a good night's rest and were called early the next morning. After one of Gram's special breakfasts, Aunt May came and took us to the train. A lunch had been prepared for us to eat on the way home. As we each had spent only $5.50 each, we allowed we would buy some of the things being sold on the train on the return trip.

We arrived back in Ashland late in the afternoon after a wonderful experience and each of us had $4.00 left.

The Woodpile

Spring vacation came and at breakfast the first morning I inquired just what I might do to keep busy all week.

"Oh, yes," the Doctor said, "Come along." We went out back of the house where there was some 30 cords of 4 foot cordwood piled. He said, "I'd like to have you bucksaw this pile of wood this week. Some of it we will cut just once. This will be 2 foot wood for the furnace. The rest of it you can saw into 16 inch wood for the cookstove and fireplace."

"Do you think you can do the whole pile this week?" he asked. He allowed it was a big job. "Where is the bucksaw?" I asked. We went out to the barn and located an old bucksaw. It was very rusty. Later, when I began to saw wood, I found it to be very dull.

I tackled the job in dead earnest, peeled off a sweater and loosened up my other clothes. As the morning passed, I worked with every ounce of energy I had and sawed as much as I could. When the hired girl called DINNER, I looked the pile over and estimated that at the rate I was going it would take at least three months, working everyday, to do the job. At dinner, the Doctor inquired about how I was getting along. I allowed that everything was going well but the saw was rather dull. However, I'd continue with the job. "Perhaps," I added, "It would help me along if you would stop by often and shovel away the sawdust."

I was awfully sweaty and Mrs. Hagerthy cautioned me to be careful and not catch a cold. The Doctor came out and looked to see how much I had done. He told me to rest for a few minutes and that he'd be right back. He kept his word and in a few minutes returned with a laborer, one Nelson Fisher, who had a good sharp, saw. Mr. Fisher and the Doctor agreed on a fee for cutting the whole pile. The Doctor allowed that I'd better take the afternoon off and rest. He stated, "I didn't intend in the first place for you to bucksaw all of this wood but I wanted to try you out just to see what stuff you are made of."

The End of a Perfect Day

After school one night, about the first of May in 1913, the Doctor had a hurry call to Portage Lake. He hollered for me to hitch up a horse. Although it was the first of May, the roads were not suitable much of the time to use the car. The horse was about ready when the Doctor came along. "Boy, Phinagin," he said, "I'm sort of tired and dread the ride to Portage in a wagon tonight. Put that horse back in the stall and come along. We will go with the car. I think we can make it. This has been a drying day. Come on, hop in and let's go." He drove out in the yard and tooted the horn. Mrs. Hagerthy came to the door.

"We are going to Portage with the car," he informed her. Mrs. Hagerthy shouted, "Hey, wait. Supper is on the table." The Doctor replied, "Keep some warm for us; we will be back in about an hour."

He hurried the car along. As we came in sight of McCormack's, out beyond the woods, there was a mud hole in the road. We got out and looked the place over. The Doctor walked back and forth and then said, "By golly, the Irish never did get stuck, get in and let's go." We only got part way through the mud hole when the car bogged down. The Doctor took off his hat, scratched his head and said, "NO, the Irish never were stuck! Here you take off your jacket and run like Hell up to Jim McCormack's (which was about a mile away) and ask him to come with his team and give us a pull." I guess I made a record mile for I soon was at Mr. McCormack's and delivered the message.

Jim was eating his supper and said, "Sure I'll give the Doc a pull. I have been harrowing some this afternoon and the horses are all harnessed. Come and we will hitch them up." I helped put the bridles on and we took a crotch chain and the whiffletrees off the harrow. "Pick up a twitch chain out there by the barn and let's go," Mr. McCormack said. He hurried the team down the road and, as I was about out of breath after my long run, it was difficult to keep up.

The chain was fastened to the front axle and in jig time the car was pulled out of the mud hole. The Doctor said, "Now Jim, wait right here. I'll make the call, leave some medicine and we will be right back." In a very few minutes we arrived at Portage village. The Doctor made the house call and, as we were about to leave, the man who lived there came running saying, "Here, Doc, I want to pay you. How much is the bill?" "Oh," the Doctor said, "Five dollars will be okay." The man paid the five dollars and in a jiffy we were on our way home.

When we came back to the mud hole, Mr. McCormack was waiting. He had gathered boughs and filled some of the deepest ruts. "Doc," he said, "I think if you will go slow and keep on the boughs, I won't have to hook on." The doctor tried it and went across just fine. He hopped out of the car and went back saying, "Jim, how much do I owe you?" Mr. McCormack answered, "Forget it, Doc. I'm glad to do this for you." Dr. Hagerthy said, "That is not good business. You were harrowing, you haven't finished your supper and besides, you have waited here for an hour or more." He took the five dollars that he had received at Portage and tucked it in one of Jim's pockets. "Thanks a million, Jim," he said and we were off. It must have been about eight o'clock when we got home. The supper had been kept warm for us and I still had a lot of chores to do.

After supper, the Doctor was singing and Mrs. Hagerthy said, "Why, Doctor, you seem to be especially happy tonight." He answered, "Why shouldn't I be happy? We made the trip to Portage with the car; I made the call and got cash on the barrel head for it. Mr. McCormack saw that we got through the mud hole and I had money to pay him with. We are back home safe and sound and have had a good warm supper, so why shouldn't I be happy?"

A Trip to Presque Isle

(Spring of 1913)

After dinner on Saturday, the roads were dry and the Doctor had some business to do in Presque Isle. "Come along, Phinagin," he said, "We will take the car and go to Presque Isle."

It was quite warm. I put on a summer cap and a sweater that was not very heavy.

When we drove over the Emerson Hill leaving Mapleton, the Doctor stopped his car. "Look out there in the field and see what I see," he said. I looked and looked and looked some more and couldn't see anything but the stump of a tree. "Only a stump there, Doc," I said. "That is what I wanted you to see," he remarked, "I've been told that Jim Cullen was hanged on the tree that once stood there. Did you ever hear tell of Jim Cullen?" he asked. "Sure I have," I answered, "Many times." I told him that Edith Ellis had married Minot Bird, who, but for a chance of luck could have been killed at the same time Hayden and Hubbard were killed out in Swan Back. "I've heard much about the lynching since coming to Ashland nearly nine years ago," he said. As we drove along, he told me some of the stories that had been told of the affair.

When we came to the Presque Isle town dump, the Doctor stopped his car again. "Now, look the place over carefully and see if there might be something that could cause you to ask a question," he said. I looked for a minute or so, then got out of the car and walked up and down a few feet each way. There were bushes all around and a road leading into the dumping ground. "Keep looking, keep looking," he said. Suddenly a voice seemed to say, "Look down, look down." I looked down along the ditch of the road and spied a depression in the ground. "Perhaps I have discovered what you wanted me to see," I said. "That hole down there looks as if it might be a grave and has sunken in."

"Atta boy," the Doctor exclaimed, "You may make a good detective some day. I've had that hole pointed out to me many times. It is said to be the grave where Jim Cullen was buried."

We continued to Presque Isle and he told me more of the story, as he had heard it, of the lynching of Jim Cullen.

While in Presque Isle, the Doctor learned that Arthur Rand, who owned and operated a livery stable, had a horse to sell. We called at the stable and the Doctor bought the horse and a wagon. "Say Phinagin," he said, "Would you be willing to drive this horse back to Ashland?" I allowed that perhaps I could. The horse was strange to me; however, we hitched it up and I started for Ashland. I was still in my sixteenth year and having a strange horse I dreaded the trip. I did not enjoy the ride home very much. The spring air became chill and there wasn't any robe in the wagon. Before I reached Mapleton village, the horse seemed to have a sore foot. It seemed okay when walking so I let it walk. As I passed some of the bogs along the way, the frogs were singing. The chilly air began to get the best of me and I guess I shivered for more than an hour before reaching home.

The Doctor had passed me with the car, soon after leaving Presque Isle. I was taking longer than he expected so he began to worry about me. He inquired by phone and was told, "The boy just went by. He is coming along okay."

By the time I reached home, the sun had gone down. They all felt sorry about me being so cold. The Doctor did not think about the clothes I had on or he would have come back with the car and brought a heavy coat. I explained why I did not make better time. We looked the horse's feet over and discovered the trouble was with the shoeing. The horse's shoes were changed on Monday and everything proved to be okay from then on. The doctor and Mrs. Hagerthy both complimented me for observing the trouble and letting the horse walk.

The Boat Ride at Portage Lake

During the summer of 1913, Dr. Hagerthy had a call to go to Portage Lake and asked me to come along. After we arrived at the Lake and he made the call, he came and told me that this turned out to be a confinement case (childbirth) and that he would be there quite awhile. "Too bad," he said, "But you will just have to make the best of the situation." About the same time the Doctor was telling me that he did not know just when we would be going back home a whistle blew, "Here is a chance for you to have a ride on the steamboat, perhaps," he said. We drove down to the lake shore. Here was the steamboat taking on passengers for a boat ride. The Doctor introduced me to Mr. Oscar Iverson, owner and captain of the boat. The Doctor paid a fare and Mr. Iverson invited me to come aboard.

When all of those waiting for a ride were on the boat, Mr. Iverson looked at his watch, blew the whistle and we were off. Mr. Iverson had a regular schedule for the several trips he made daily. Coal was used to generate the steam. Mr. Iverson shoveled some coal into the boiler after the boat was in operation and headed up the lake. The trip was eight miles each way, he said, five miles across the lake and three miles up Fish River to the Hay Shed landing. At the landing a few other people came on the boat. These men, perhaps, were returning from some lumber camp to their homes.

I sat in the bow of the boat with Mr. Iverson and asked him many questions. He told me he had purchased this boat in Bangor, Maine and that it had been used there as a ferryboat between Bangor and Brewer. He said it was one of three such ferryboats that had been used there. The name of it was Bon Ton. At regular intervals or just at certain locations, Mr. Iverson blew the whistle. The trip was very interesting. When we arrived back at the landing, there were several loud blasts of the whistle. This trip was a wonderful treat for me and an incident I've always remembered.

In later years, I learned from my relatives living in Bangor, that this boat, once owned by the city of Brewer, was the Bon Ton 2. Bon Ton 1 went to Lake Erie and Bon Ton 3 burned. The boats were always tied up at the Brewer shore at night and housed there in the winter.

A Very Serious Burn

One time, Peter Morrow of Frenchville was clearing land and he had some of his children help gather the brush into piles so he could burn it. One day, one of the girls, Alfreda, got too near the flames and her little dress caught on fire.

Just how her father managed to extinguish the fire remains a mystery. He was so excited he just couldn't remember. "Probably did the most of it with my hands," he replied.

The girl was taken to the house and the Doctor was called. One side of her body was burned very badly. There weren't any ambulances available in those days and the Doctor had to act quickly, using his best judgment as to what would be the best thing to do. As he explained to me later, "Gee, Phinagin, this was a case much worse than I ever had but something had to be done. I got the sterilizer on the stove and some instruments to work with, peeled off my jacket and went to work. It was necessary to give the child an anesthetic. It was sure a task to remove the burned clothing. Boy that was one time I wished you had been along to help."

He explained he did more of a first aid job at that time and went home and studied some of his medical books. He later returned with gauze, ointment, and some special forceps and did a real job with dressing the burned area.

A trip was made everyday to dress the burn. He brought candy or a present of some kind to give the girl to quiet her down so he could put her to sleep.

It was an education in itself to see how carefully the Doctor worked, cleaning off the pus and burned flesh each day. One day I asked, "Do you think this girl has a chance?" His answer was, "Oh yes, Phinagin, remember where there is life, there is hope."

The girl got well, finished school, eventually married and raised a family. She and her husband have prospered, own a home in Connecticut and are financially able to spend their winters in Florida.

I never have forgotten this case and always had the idea a miracle had taken place.

While administrator of the hospital, I saw many burn cases. However, the doctors worked under circumstances much different from those Dr. Hagerthy was forced to work under in the old days in the individual homes.

Mitchell Bernard Accidently Shot

On Sunday, February 24, 1914, a phone call came from Castle Hill saying Mitchell Bernard had been accidently shot and the Doctor was to come as quickly as possible. One of the worst storms of the season had just occurred. The wind had blown Saturday and through the night and the roads had not been broken out when the Doctor received the call. The distance down to where the Bernard family lived was a little over eight miles, about a third of a mile beyond where my parents lived.

"This is going to be an awfully hard trip, do you want to come along?" the Doctor asked. "Sure, I'll go," I answered. He allowed that perhaps we could not get through; however, we must try. I was told which horses to get ready, to bring along two pairs of snow shoes, some rope, and extra mittens. It was about ten o'clock when we got started. As we were leaving town, Arthur Walker's milk delivery team was just coming in with the milk to be delivered. For three miles, at least, we had a track to follow but there was so much snow the horses could only walk.

After we left Walker Hill, for the next three miles there was not a sign of a track. The horses were pretty good following the road. For some two and a half miles, we got along fairly well. The snow was pushing up on the front of the pung all along. The horses stopped quite often to get their "wind." When we came to the foot of the Clark Hill trouble began. The drifts were so bad and so high the horses could not go. They would get down and we would have to pile out, unhitch and the Doctor would then urge the horses to get back on their feet. After some flouncing around they'd make it. The reins were buckled together and the Doctor would put the loop over his arm and reach for the pole on the pung. In some way I managed to work the pung ahead until he could reach the pole, then we would both pull it ahead. In this way we managed to get the horses hooked up and then we'd try to go again. I waded behind to make the load lighter. It would be but a short time before the horses were down again. It was about one half mile up the hill. The team was unhitched several times before we reached the top. It consumed about an hour of time, making this half mile. When we arrived at the top of the hill, the doctor and I were about all fagged out. Mr. Clark lived on this hill. He was Mrs. Bernard's father. He had his team out breaking the road down to the Bernard home. This distance was a little more than a mile and a half and the road was broken out pretty good. Several other teams were out helping break out the road. They were all anxious for the Doctor to come. The horses could walk along better and we made very good time.

It had taken about three hours to make the trip. My father was beside the road pacing back and forth. He told us that Mitchell had just passed away. The Doctor said, "Jasper, we did our level best. I'm awfully sorry we could not have arrived sooner. Perhaps I could have done something to save the man."

The road was broken out so good between my father's and Bernard's that the Doctor said, "Phinagin, you take the team in and feed them and give them a little water. I'll walk down and see Mitchell. When I return, we will be ready to go back home."

My father had a stall ready and we put the team in. We wiped the frozen snow off their legs, blanketed and fed them. I went in to see Mother and the others. Mother was busy getting the Doctor and me some dinner. The Doctor returned in about an hour and we ate a nice warm meal. While the doctor and my father were talking about the shooting accident, I hitched up the horses and cleaned the snow out of the pung as best I could.

The road was broken out much better going back, yet there wasn't a place the Doctor could jog the horses. We just had to let them walk and take their time.

It was five o'clock when we returned and chore time began. As I was doing the chores, I kept wondering how in the world the Doctor managed to live working like he had today.

The next morning, I was so tired and lame that I didn't care if I went to school or not. The Doctor allowed "the trip" yesterday was only one of the many he'd endured for nearly ten years and he'd probably have to tackle many more such trips in the future.

Helping with a Bad Fracture

In February or March of 1914, the Doctor received a call that there was a serious accident at Acil York's in Yorkville. I wasn't told what had happened, perhaps the Doctor had not been told, however he asked me to hitch up a pair of horses and "hurry like hell." In almost no time, a pair of horses was ready to go. Along came the Doctor giving orders. "Bring along two pairs of snowshoes and some rope, put on one of my old heavy coats and let's go," he said.

The going was fairly good and the horsewhip was used some. "Boy, Doc," I remarked, "Something serious must have happened to have to drive like this." "Well," he answered, "Word came that it was something serious and we will soon find out how much, if anything, we can do." It was about four miles out to Mr. York's. In about one half of an hour from the time the call was received, we were there. Mr. York was waiting and said, "There was an accident up in the woods. Lewis has a broken leg. My God, Doctor, hurry. He is in here. We managed to get him down out of the woods."

The Doctor hurried into the home, then came out and got a couple of satchels and said to me, "Blanket the horses, hitch them there somewhere and come in as quick as you can." In about five minutes, the horses were tied and blanketed and I was in with the Doctor. Here I found Lewis, a young fellow in his teens, lying on the bed. The bed was one of those old fashioned ones just like we used at my home when I was a youngster. There were ropes tied crosswise and lengthwise on a wooden frame, on which a straw tick was used to sleep on. The ropes had not been tightened, by the looks, for quite awhile and the arrangement looked more like a hammock.

The Doctor said, "Peel off, Phinagin and let's get busy." He handed me a pair of scissors saying, "Here, take these and get those clothes off of Lewis. Be as careful as possible. He has a bad fracture."

The clothes the boy had on were woolen and of the heavy kind as used in the winter. The boy's mother helped me get the jacket off and the stockings. All the while, the Doctor was arranging splints and preparing material for a leg cast. I told Mrs. York, "I'll have to take the scissors and cut off the clothes." As I started to cut the pant legs, Mr. York pulled my arm back and shouted, "No, you don't, those pants cost three dollars. To cut them will spoil them and Lewis will need them just as soon as he gets around." Getting the pants off was no less than being wicked. Each move brought a scream from Lewis, however, amongst us the pants came off. His drawers were knit from yarn. "Come, Doc," I said, "and help this time." He answered, "Oh, better use the scissors, it will be too much for him to remove them as you did the pants." I picked up the scissors again. This time the boy's father took them from my hand. "No you don't cut those drawers," he said, "There has been too much hard work mixed up in making them. Louise (Mrs. York) sheared the sheep, she washed the wool, she carded the wool, she spun the yarn and she knit those drawers. Now, don't spoil them."

"What will I do now, Doctor?" I asked. "Oh, you are doing alright," he answered, "Mrs. York will help you remove them just like you did the pants." I paused for a moment, wondering if I could continue helping. Something seemed to say, "Just grin and bear it." Mrs. York and I, with the help of the boy's father, removed the drawers; my, how that boy suffered while we were doing it.

The Doctor was watching, now I said to him, "It is your turn, where are you going to place this fellow to set the fracture?" "Oh, he will be okay right here," he answered. "Here take this can, here is a towel, just put him to sleep and I'm ready to take over." I placed the towel over Lewis's face and started to open the can of ether. Mr. York said, "What are you up to now?" I replied, "This will put Lewis to sleep and the Doctor can then set the fracture." Quick as a wink, Mr. York took the can away from me saying all the time, "NO, you don't, no you don't, no you don't."

"Now, Doctor, what shall I do?" I asked. He answered, "Just have Lewis lock his hands under his head and I'll go to work." The doctor and I worked a sheet under the boy's hips, then Mr. York and I lifted his body up. The Doctor told us, "That is good." Some pillows were placed under the boy's hips to hold the body fairly level. Then as "cool as a cucumber" the Doctor examined the fracture and applied the cast.

A few pain pills were left for Lewis. The doctor told the parents, "If the boy becomes uncomfortable just call and I'll come." Soon I had the horses ready and the Doctor and I were on our way home.

As we drove along, he asked me if I would work with him if he could arrange to build or have a hospital. "Sure, I will," I answered. "Yes," he said, "Someday we will have a hospital all our own, right here in Ashland and then we won't have to endure the hardships that we have to contend with in the homes."

I can't remember if the Doctor ever mentioned this case again to me, but twenty-five years later, in 1939, I was First Selectman in Castle Hill. During that winter, we had a W.P.A. road construction job going on, on the Demerchant Hill, from the Welts Brook over the hill to the Demerchant Brook. We worked as many unemployed as came along from Castle Hill and Mapleton. Each man was allowed to earn up to $14.40 per week. Things were going along fine. One morning, a man came along and said he had come over to work on the project. He gave me his slip. I looked it over and told Mr. MaGill, the road foreman, to put this fellow to work. After awhile it dawned on me that I'd heard the name before. When I came by where this man was working, I stopped and asked him if he knew me. "Well, no," he answered, "I don't believe that I do." I looked at the slip again that he had given me and asked him to walk across the road for a short distance. "Well, okay," he said, "But what's up?" He walked up the road a ways and came back. I thought to myself, what a miracle, this is the same boy, now a man, that had the bad fracture a quarter of a century ago up in Yorkville.

"Do you remember having a broken leg?" I asked. "Yes, I do," he answered. "Has it bothered you much down through the years?" I wanted to know. "No, not much," he said. "Do you remember the pain you endured while Dr. Hagerthy fixed you up?" I asked. He answered, "Damned right I do, never will forget about that. What do you know about all of that?" I replied, "I am the fellow that worked with the Doctor that day." As we shook hands, he said, "Well I'll be damned if it ain't you. Well, I can say that you fellows did a good job for me. I've been able to work. I have a family and live over at Mapleton."

Machias Lake

One spring morning, perhaps it was in April or late March, in 1914, the Doctor had a call to go to Machias Lake. The going was risky with a team or even with a single horse and pung. The call came very early in the morning. I had fed the horses and was doing other chores. The Doctor came out to the barn and told me about the call. "Phinagin," he said, "I've got to go but how shall I try? The snow is too soft to take a double hitch and the going is too risky to take a pung at all." He paced the barn floor for a few minutes and looked the horses over trying to figure out someway to make the trip. When I went in for breakfast, Mrs. Hagerthy had prepared a breakfast for the Doctor also.

I sat down and listened to them trying to find a way to see the people who had called him. After awhile, the Doctor decided to take Perdy, the older of his horses. "I'll put a riding saddle on him and make a try," he said to us, "Trying was never beat."

Mrs. Hagerthy gave me a clean soft blanket to put under the saddle. The saddle probably had been used many times, although, I had never seen the Doctor ride a saddle horse. The saddle was cleaned some and put on the horse with the blanket under it. The Doctor came with Mrs. Hagerthy and inspected it and some adjustments were made. He climbed on and off a couple of times. Mrs. Hagerthy was instructed to prepare a knapsack and include things that he might need when he arrived at Machias Lake, if he got there okay.

The distance to where he was going was about twenty miles. It was still very early in the morning and, as I remember, this took place on a Sunday. The trip was made to the camp where the Doctor's services were badly needed. After resting for a while and letting the horse feed and rest, he began the trip to return home.

There were a few places along the way where word was relayed by phone to Mrs. Hagerthy that things were going well.

Late in the afternoon or early evening, I kept watching down the road to see when he would come into sight. After awhile, he showed up. The horse was walking along very slowly and when they arrived at the house, I helped the Doctor climb down from the saddle and then cared for the horse. About forty miles had been made that day. The horse must have been at least fourteen or fifteen years old. As the saddle was removed, blood showed up. The saddle had caused a gall. I reported this to the Doctor. He was too tired to come to the barn. Mrs. Hagerthy prepared something with which to wash the sore and came out with me. After Perdy had rested for awhile and I had curried and brushed him, some straw was put in a box stall where he could stretch out and rest.

The sore did not heal. After a day or so a veterinarian was called from Presque Isle. The veterinarian did not give the Doctor much hope that the horse would live. The wound was dressed and treated several times each day for a few days. The swelling became enormous and the Veterinarian advised the Doctor to have the poor old horse "put away." The instructions were carried out.

The trip to Machias Lake proved to have been worth while and the patient became well, but the Doctor was the loser. When the people where the Doctor had called learned of the loss, they offered to contribute to the purchase of another horse. I never learned that the doctor or Mrs. Hagerthy ever accepted any money.

This incident was only one of the many hardships the Doctor endured while I lived at his home.

Dr. Hagerthy Makes a Deal

One morning, early in the spring of 1914, about 4:30, Dr. Hagerthy had a call to go to Portage Lake. He allowed that the roads were dried up quite a lot and said, "I feel that we can make the trip with the car if you have time to come along with me." "Okay, let's go," I said, "Just get me back in time for school." He answered, "That's a promise" and we were on our way. Things went well and in about twenty minutes, we drove into Isaac Crory's home at Portage Lake. We had covered ten miles. The doctor made his call, came out with his satchel and said, "Now to get you back to finish the chores."

Just as we were to drive out, Mr. Crory came from the barn with two pails of milk. "Hey, Ike, how many cows do you have?" the Doctor called out. "Only one," Mr. Crory answered. "Would you mind if I saw that cow?" the doctor asked. "Sure not." Mr. Crory answered, "Wait, 'til this milk is taken in. I'll be right back." Mr. Crory returned and he and the Doctor went to the barn. Shortly after, the Doctor waved for me to come in. "Well, Phinagin," he said, "What do you think of a cow that size giving two pails of milk at one time?" I inquired of Mr. Crory if the cow had been milked last night. "Oh, sure," he said, "she gives two pails of milk each night and morning." Then I answered the Doctor's question. "This is a wonderful cow, must be a cross between a jersey and a Guernsey." Mr. Crory said, "This boy is correct, the cow is part Jersey and part Guernsey."

The Doctor took the milking stool down from a hook, asking me to try and milk and see how I would like milking a cow that gives two pails of milk. I sat down, went through the motions of milking and allowed that I had never milked any cow in my life that was any more perfect than this one.

"Ike, how much money would you take for this cow?" The Doctor asked. "Oh," Mr. Crory answered, "I do not want to sell her at any price. Say, Doc, if you are looking for a cow you should be able to find one for around fifty dollars. This cow is so good that we wouldn't even consider anything less than seventy-five dollars." "Okay, Ike," the Doctor said, "If you ever decide to sell the cow promise to give me the first chance." We were about to leave when the Doctor climbed out of the car again, saying, "Ike, I'll make an offer for you and your good wife to consider. The offer is that I'll give you the seventy-five dollars and have Belle (Mrs. Hagerthy) send you a receipt in full for all that you owe me. Give us a ring after you have talked the offer over."

We had spent so much time that I was getting worried about getting some breakfast and finishing the chores and being at school on time. As we were about to leave, Mr. Crory asked the Doctor to wait just a minute. Perhaps we had waited nearly five minutes, when both Mr. and Mrs. Crory came out. "Okay, doctor," they said. "We agree right at this time to accept your offer." The Doctor paid the Crorys the seventy-five dollars and said, "Thank-you folks, I'll send for the cow today." Mrs. Crory said, "Perhaps it is our turn to say 'thank you'."

When I came home from school that night, the cow was in the barn and seemed to be very contented although in a strange place. When milking time came, I found two milking pails and went to the stable to milk. As I left the house for the stable, I said to the hired girl, "If the Doctor comes along in a few minutes, send him to watch me milk."

I patted the cow for a minute or so then took a brush and brushed her. This she seemed to appreciate. I then took a cloth that was hanging nearby and wiped off the udder and proceeded to milk. I filled one pail right to the brim then began milking in the other pail. About this time, the Doctor came, found an old chair and sat down to

watch. The second pail was soon filled and the froth was running over. "Well, Phinagin," he said, "this has been a wonderful day for us. I never thought I'd live to see the day we would own a cow like this." He asked, "What do you think of the deal?" I answered, "This is better than the story of Jack and The Beanstalk, because that story was a fable and this is true."

We took the milk to the laundry room and run it through the cream separator. By the time I'd finished separating, all of the others were watching. "My, what a lot of cream," Mrs. Hagerthy remarked. She turned to the Doctor and said, "You have very good judgment in making a deal."

It was not long before we could turn the cow out back of the barn in the pasture. Many times the Doctor took people to the stable to see the cow and after I began milking her out in the pasture, the doctor said one night, "I'm having company tonight. How about bringing this fellow out to watch you milk?" I answered, "It will be okay with me but bring along an extra pail when you come."

Probably it was about half an hour later than my usual milking time when the fellow came. I took two pails and hustled out to the pasture and began milking. I milked fast so there would be a lot of foam. The doctor and his company came and stood by the fence watching. I filled one pail, handed it over the gate, filled the second pail and handed it out too, reached for the pail that the Doctor had on his arm and began to milk in that one also. While finishing milking, I chanced a look to see what expressions the men might have on their faces. Tears were running down the Doctor's cheeks. The gentleman with him was saying, "MY God, doctor, seeing this done is almost unbelievable. I'll never question your word again if God lets me live to be a hundred."

Sarah

One morning, in 1914, the Doctor said, "Phinagin, I have received a call to go to your home in Castle Hill. I have been informed that your baby sister, Sarah, is very ill."

The Doctor hurried off to make his call. Upon arriving at my parent's home, he examined Sarah and found she had pneumonia. He sadly told my father, "Jasper, her lungs are full. I'm afraid you are going to lose her."

Upon his arrival back in Ashland, I inquired, "How is my little sister?" He answered, "Phinagin, I dread telling you this but she has pneumonia and I don't think she is going to make it."

He went immediately to his study and closed the door. He looked over the shelves containing his many medical books, selected one and sat down to study.

After a time, he came rushing out and prepared to make another trip to Castle Hill. He said, "Phinagin, there just might be a chance to save Sarah."

He arrived back at my parent's home. He said, "Jasper and Mrs. Ellis, we've got one chance to save the little one. I want to take that chance otherwise there is no chance at all. I want your permission to tap her lungs. I'm not sure that it will work, but by golly I have to try."

He made an incision in her chest and inserted a tube. The "green stuff" began to seep out. He stayed for some time then returned to Ashland after promising my parents that he would return the next day.

My parents sat with her throughout the night. They were hoping for her recovery but were so afraid that she might not live.

When the Doctor arrived the next day, he informed my parents, "Yesterday she had one chance in a thousand but today, she has a fifty-fifty chance."

In the weeks that followed, the doctor made many trips to Castle Hill checking on his little patient.

She was afraid of him and used to cry when she saw him approaching the bedside. One day, he gave her a stick of gum. She accepted the gum and began to like this nice man who gave it to her.

On his next visit, my mother informed him, "Sarah chewed that gum you gave her and she began spitting stuff up. The chewing seemed to loosen it up." The Doctor was happy to hear this. The very next day, he returned with lots of gum. He put it on Sarah's bed saying, "Chew all you want. If that helps, fine. Chew."

Sarah was a very sick little girl for a long time but she gradually became stronger. She had just learned to walk and after regaining her strength, had to learn to walk all over again.

The Doctor helped many people many times and I'll always remember and be grateful for the time he saved my sister, Sarah.

A Day That Everything Seemed to Operate in Reverse

In the winter of 1914-15, the Doctor received a telephone call from a lumber camp around thirty-five to forty miles from Ashland, up to and above Big Fish Lake. This was in the evening and I was told of the difficulties that were ahead of him in making the trip. Plans were made with a fellow at Portage Lake to have a team ready about six o'clock in the morning that the Doctor could use to go to the Fish Lake region with. I was to have our team ready so that he could make Portage Lake by six o'clock in the morning. I was up early, fed the horses and did up all of the chores, thinking he might want me to go along with him. Sometime, probably about 4:30, Mrs. Hagerthy came and told me, "Breakfast is ready and as this is Sunday the Doc wants you to go along."

Soon we had finished a good warm breakfast, the team was made ready and we were off. On the way to Portage, the Doctor drove a little faster than usual. I remarked, "Seems you are pushing a little this morning." "Well, that will be okay," he said, "We are to change horses at Portage and will have a fresh team from there." We arrived at

Portage at about the appointed time and went to the Mill Company stable. The Doctor said, "We will stable our team here I think, wait a minute and I will find out." Shortly, the Doctor returned with a fellow. They were having a heated argument. The trouble was that a team was not ready and if one could be made up, we would have to wait an hour or better. The Doctor walked around our horses a couple of times, then came and said to me, "I hate to do it but it 'must be'. We will just have to go along with our team. An hour will be wasted if we wait."

The Doctor told the man, "It is better that we push on. Call ahead and see if a team can be ready so we can exchange horses at the Hay Shed Camps." He turned to me and said, "Button up good and cover you face. It will be awfully cold going up across the lake but that is the only way." It was probably more than thirty degrees below zero but with the wind we faced it seemed much colder. The track across the lake was visible and fairly good and we found it better going after we had reached the river. We got up to the 'Hay Shed' early. We stopped at a camp there and gave the horses some water. There wasn't any team available here to exchange, so we continued on. We came to another camp above the falls and still no relief team; however, a man at this camp said, "A team is waiting at another camp about five miles up stream."

The forenoon was about gone when we arrived at that camp, but a fresh team was waiting. The proprietor there insisted that the Doctor come in and have a 'bite'. I was to unhitch our team, feed and water them and then have some dinner. The Doctor left by bobsled to go another four or five miles further on. The horses had a good long rest. Four hours passed before the Doctor returned. Word had been phoned ahead for me to have the hitch ready at a certain time and be ready to return to Portage. I asked the man who helped take care of the horses as to how far it was back to Portage. His answer, as I remember, was "It is about twenty-five miles."

Much better time was made coming back as the horses had rested and the wind was in our backs, which seemed to push us along. We arrived at Portage probably around seven o'clock. We stopped at the Mill Company Stable to let the horses eat some grain and rest for about half an hour. The Doctor was taken by another team, from the stable, to make a couple of calls. I warmed the soap stones, the robes and our mittens in the office of the Mill Company stable.

The Doctor returned and inquired if we were ready. Where we would be so late returning home, I asked him to call Mrs. Hagerthy and perhaps she could find someone to milk the cow and feed the other horses. The caretaker at the stable helped me hitch up and we were on our way again. Boy, what a cold night it was. As we swung out on the main road, the Doctor asked me how I was feeling. I answered, "Oh, I'm alright. We have some warm soap stones under our feet and some warm mittens ready in case we have to change mittens." "Well, here Phinagin," he said, "You take over. I'm awfully tired, you drive home." I asked, "Shall I give the horses plenty of time or push them along?" He answered, "Oh, use your own judgment. We will hope one of them does not play out before we reach Ashland. If things end well, you will have made about seventy miles today and I traveled by bobsled up another four or five miles." The Doctor was sound asleep in minutes.

The horses were getting pretty tired so I let them walk most of the way home. We must have been about two hours making the ten miles. My, what a day. The Doctor slept about all the way in from Portage. Mrs. Hagerthy had found someone to do most of the chores, for which I was very grateful. After the team was driven into the barn, and the doors closed, Mrs. Hagerthy came and wanted to help. "No, I'm alright," I said, "You get the Doctor in, feed him and put him to bed. I'll do what I can here in a hurry and come in for supper."

I unharnessed the team, brushed the frost off and wiped them over the best I could and went in for some supper. After eating supper, the Doctor wanted to come and help finish in the barn. They both apologized for keeping me out so late and away from studying my lessons. "Oh, you couldn't help that," I said, "Don't worry. I'll study when I come in from the barn."

When I returned to the barn to see if everything was in order, it appeared that one of the horses was trembling quite badly and was not eating. This horse had been driven to Mapleton the day before and driven again some seventy miles today. What should I do, I asked myself. There was an empty box stall across from the single stalls. Plenty of straw was pitched in and the tired horse was taken there for the night, where it would have a chance to stretch out and rest.

This team wasn't used again for several days. If my memory serves me correctly, one of those horses never recovered from the long jaunt. Instead of being sent to the pasture in the summer, it had to be "put away."

I took many long trips with the Doctor but this one to the Fish Lake region was the worst. As we talked about the trip later, the Doctor stated, "Oh, Phinagin, it was all in my line of duty. I've had to do about the same thing before and probably will have to many more times in the future. Such is the life of a Country Doctor."

Getting Poisoned

Sometime during my senior year at high school, four of us got ptomaine poisoning from eating shrimp salad. The victims of the poisoning were Mrs. Hagerthy, the hired girl, a Mrs. Jesse Howard who had been a guest for supper and me. At supper, Mrs. Hagerthy mentioned that perhaps the hired girl had not understood fully about fixing the salad and had put too much mustard into it. This hired girl was new at Hagerthy's. She was French and could not understand English very well and she was blamed for the salad being so strong. Bert, the Hagerthy's young son was not allowed to have any of the salad, which turned out to be a blessing.

Mrs. Howard was the first to become ill. She was attending a dance at the Opera House and flopped right on the floor. Those who witnessed this allowed they had never seen anyone having such terrible cramps. I was the next to feel the effects of the poisoning. I woke from a deep sleep with those awful cramps and began vomiting. My bowels let loose at the same time. After making several trips to the bathroom, I became dizzy and seemed to be getting awfully weak. I managed to get downstairs and call Mrs. Hagerthy. She said, "The Doctor is still at Portage. (He was not home for supper and escaped the salad). I'll check and see how long before he will be home."

Mrs. Hagerthy called the Doctor and learned he was still busy. He told her to call Dr. Knowland "and in a hurry." Dr Knowland was located at the Ashland Opera House doctoring Mrs. Howard, He was trying to arrange to have someone get a team and drive her home. As soon as he got word to come to the Hagerthy's "in a hurry", he came standing up in his pung and putting the whip to his horse. He rushed in, took a look at me lying on the couch in the kitchen and said, "Where is the mustard? Where is the mustard? Oh! Where is the mustard?" I told him to open the cupboard door and probably he would find some in there. Sure enough, he found the can of dry mustard. He then got a two quart dipper that was hanging above the sink and poured some mustard in it. He then filled the dipper with water and came to where I was lying and said, "Here, drink some of this." I took a mouthful. "Oh, here drink a cupful," he insisted, "It will wash out your stomach and you will feel better." "Now who else had supper here tonight?" he wanted to know. I told him that Mrs. Howard was here for supper, the hired girl and Mrs. Hagerthy. "Where are Mrs. Hagerthy and the hired girl now?" he asked. Just then we listened and the hired girl, up in her room over the kitchen, could be heard vomiting. Dr. Knowland hustled up the stairs with the dipper of mustard water. He gave her a drink of it and hurried back. "Now, where is Mrs. Hagerthy?" he wanted to know. She hollered, "I'm here." He found her sitting on the slop jar and awfully sick. He gave her a drink of mustard water and phoned Dr. Hagerthy at Portage, telling him about the condition we were in. "Come as quick as you can," he said, "Drive like Hell for I need some help."

Dr. Knowland then looked at the kitchen clock and asked me to watch it and "see how quickly Dr. Hagerthy can make the trip." He then went from one of us to another, always carrying the dipper of mustard water, checking our pulse, temperatures etc. He left once on a trip to Mrs. Howard's home to see how she was getting along but hurried back to watch us.

It was just fifty-five minutes later when Dr. Hagerthy came through the door. "How are they? How is Bert?" he wanted to know. He was very much concerned because his son Dana's death was due to ptomaine poisoning. "Golly, Doctor, I hadn't thought about the boy," Dr. Knowland said, "Where is he?" They raced to Mrs. Hagerthy's bedroom and learned that Bert had not been given any of the salad. Dr. Hagerthy said, "Boy what a blessing, now, let's get busy with the others." The doctors made the rounds together checking on each of us. Dr. Knowland said, "Everything seems to be under control now. Let's get our horses stabled out of the cold. I will first check at Howard's and then come back to help you the rest of the night."

Dr. Hagerthy got his horse stabled and blanketed. He hurried back in and phoned Portage. He told the nurse or attendant, where there was to be a confinement case (birth) that she would have to do the best she could alone, since he wouldn't be back until the danger was all over with his family at home. Dr. Hagerthy and Dr. Knowland paced the floor all the rest of the night and kept checking on each of us. While they were together in the night, they hunted around and found the shrimp can, looked it over, smelled it and decided it was rancid shrimp that had caused the trouble. Both of the Doctors agreed it was an awfully lucky thing that Bert had not been allowed to eat any of the salad.

When morning came, someone was called in to make breakfast and "clean up after the sick folks." A man was called in to look after the chores.

Seems as if it was a week or more before Mrs. Hagerthy got around again. The hired girl recovered in a couple of days, packed up her clothes and went back to her home. The Hagerthy's tried to explain to her that she was not to blame for what happened; however, she did not understand about the whole affair and did not care to work there any longer.

If I remember correctly, I lost about twelve pounds during this ordeal. The Doctor stated several times, "That was a close call for you folks. I'm thankful that Bert did not get poisoned. With Dr. Knowland's help things have worked out okay and you have all survived."

More Memories While at Hagerthy's

One summer Dr. Hagerthy purchased a new Stutz auto. My, how he was able to get around in the summer time. He attended to his calls much quicker and had a little more time at home.

One day, dinner was just about ready to be served, when the Doctor received a call to go to Squa Pan. The woman working there at that time was called Hannah. Hannah said, "Dinner will be ready in just a few minutes. Come and eat before you go." The Doctor replied, "Put it on the table. I want to take Phinagin for a ride and we will be right back in a few minutes. Come on let's go."

Up on the Masardis Road, on our way to Squa Pan, there was quite a long stretch of road that was fairly straight. The Doctor opened up the throttle and I became nervous. When he slowed down, he said,

"Did you notice the speedometer, Phinagin? We were up to eighty-six miles an hour at one time."

The Doctor made his call and we were soon back home eating dinner. The Doctor told Mrs. Hagerthy about reaching the eighty-six mile mark on the speedometer. "Well, Phin," she asked, "How did it seem to be riding at that rate?" "Oh," I answered, "I couldn't see very far for the telephone poles looked as close as teeth in a fine-toothed comb." The Doctor had a great laugh at this remark and added, "Say, Belle, you know that when I had to slow up, I looked around and there was Phinagin down on his knees counting his beads."

Shortly before graduation, the Doctor said, "Boy, oh boy, Phinagin, we will soon have to get along without you." One day he made the remark, "Belle and I have decided to have a girl graduate with you." This remark seemed rather amusing to him. One night, not long before graduation, as I came home from school, I was introduced to a nurse, Miss Gertrude Mutty. Someone added, "Perhaps she has come to graduate with you." Now wasn't I puzzled. When I had a chance I asked Lottie, the present hired girl, "What is all this joking about? This woman has not attended our school. How is she going to graduate with our class?" Lottie then told me, "The Doctor has been kidding like he has always done. The truth is, Mrs. Hagerthy is 'expecting' soon and she and the Doc are in hopes the baby will be a girl." The nurse was there to care for Mrs. Hagerthy.

One Saturday after the chores were finished, Lottie asked if I would just as soon go down to the river and find a few fiddleheads for dinner. "Gee Lottie," I said, "I'm awfully busy getting ready for my tests; however, I will go for I like fiddlehead greens myself." I took a pail and went down to the river and had not searched very long before I found a fine patch of fiddleheads just the right size to pick. They were three to six inches high and the curl was at its best. Soon the pail was filled to the brim. I hurried back home. There wasn't anyone around to tell me what to do with the fiddleheads so I turned them into the iron sink plugged the drain and filled it up with water so as to wash the greens. While washing the greens, I heard footsteps behind me. The nurse had appeared and was looking around when she suddenly fainted dead away. She fell sprawling on the floor and became as "white as a ghost."

I ran to the living room and hollered for the Doctor but received no answer. Then I hustled to the laundry room where Lottie usually worked during most of each Saturday forenoon. No one was there. I asked myself, "What shall I do?" Something seemed to say "Throw some cold water in her face." I got a basin of water and a couple of wash cloths, got down on my knees beside the nurse and was applying wet cloths on her face when Lottie appeared. My, wasn't Lottie excited. "What is going on? What are you up to?" She wanted to know. Miss Mutty was coming out of the faint as I answered Lottie's question. "Oh, this woman just fainted She will be okay now."

In a short time, Miss Mutty felt like getting up. Lottie and I helped her to a chair. She said, "This boy has filled the sink with those awful snakes. Please take them away." This was why she fainted; she thought the fiddleheads were snakes. I listened for some ten minutes while Lottie convinced her they were not snakes but fiddleheads that we were going to cook for dinner.

At dinner everyone had a hearty laugh. The Doctor allowed, "Well, Phinagin passed that test. Now, I'm sure that he will make a good doctor some day."

During the days before graduation, I studied very hard and late most every night so I could pass all of the tests. When graduation time came, I was honored to be the class valedictorian. The fact that I graduated with the highest ranks in my class pleased Dr. and Mrs. Hagerthy very much.

As I've mentioned before, when I first went to live with the Hagerthy's they had two young sons. Besides Dana, the boy who died from ptomaine poisoning, there was Bert, who was only about three months old at the time. Not yet old enough to sit in the high chair, this little fellow was a cute youngster and before the end of my first school year at the Hagerthy's he was old enough to be put on the floor. Many times I was left to babysit and he and I would have a good time playing until he became tired and dozed off to sleep.

As he grew older, we had many good times playing together. When I graduated from high school in 1915, Bert had grown to be a stocky boy and seemed like a brother. I'd come in from outside and dress the little tyke in my cap, scarf etc. The Doctor always was amused at this.

As I explained earlier, Miss Mutty's presence in the Hagerthy household was due to the fact that Mrs. Hagerthy was expecting a baby soon. The Doctor and Belle were hoping the baby would be a girl. The baby born to the Hagerthy's was a girl and we were all saddened by the fact she lived only briefly.

I have mentioned only a few of the many trips and experiences that took place while I lived with the Hagerthy's. This was time well spent. I learned to "rough it" and learned to work with the poor and the sick. I learned of the many hardships people had to endure in the early part of the century. I feel that this experience was perhaps as good as a college education for it has helped me all down through the years.

I could not help but mention some of the trials Dr. Hagerthy endured to attend to his patients no matter where they lived or who they were. He never seemed to fear for his own safety. I have always felt that the Doctor never had an equal in the state as a general practitioner and country doctor. I have known of several cases where he, with the assistance of a nurse or another doctor, has operated for appendicitis by the light of a kerosene lamp with the patient lying on the dining room table of their own home. Many times, the recovery of a patient was no less than a miracle.

Yes, Dr. Hagerthy was the most dedicated and outstanding country doctor of all times.

The Doctor maintained a pharmacy of his own so that his patients would never want for the proper kind of medicine which he would prescribe.

He always wanted to establish a hospital in Ashland. None of the existing buildings could be fixed up to comply with the state laws pertaining to fire escapes etc. After open roads, it was easier to go to the hospital in Presque Isle and the need for a hospital in Ashland was not as great. Still Dr. Hagerthy always dreamed of having a hospital in Ashland and I dreamed of working with him.

Doctor Hagerthy's Last Call

It was September 26, 1941 that Dr. Hagerthy made his last call to Castle Hill. It was in the early evening when Dr. Hagerthy drove in at my home and asked me to come along and have a ride with him "just like you used to." I inquired as to where he was going. His reply was, "Down to Ike York's." "Okay, I will go along with you." I said. When we arrived at Ike's, the Doctor said to me, "Bring in my 'pill box', just as you used to sometimes."

The Doctor sat in a chair beside Mrs. York's bed and went through the usual examination. After awhile he asked for a little warm water in a tea cup. Then he prepared a hypo and injected it in Mrs. York's arm. Some pain pills were left and Mrs. York and Ike were assured that she would have a much more comfortable night than she had experienced the night before. When the Doctor was ready to leave, he handed me his 'pill box' and requested that I put it back in the car.

After we were in the car and ready to leave, Ike and the Doctor had some conversation regarding Mrs. York's condition. The Doctor said, "Your wife and I are about worn out, Ike. There isn't much that can be done. All you can do is care for her the best you can and hope for the best."

As we drove back to my home, I made the statement, "You look so tired tonight. Why are you down here?" He answered, "Oh, you know, it is all in the line of duty." He then said, "I am happy that you came along with me. I'm reminded of the many times that we rode together years ago. Keep up the good work, Phinagin; I understand you are doing a good job for the town of Castle Hill."

On the return trip home, the Doctor stopped at my brother Luther's and left some medicine that he had promised to mail the next day. No record of this was made because the Doctor would not take any pay. Mrs. Hagerthy's records showed that his last call in Castle Hill was to York's. After the Doctor returned home, he was so fatigued that Mrs. Hagerthy helped him to bed. Shortly after, the phone rang. There was another call. As Mrs. Hagerthy told me later, she didn't intend for the Doctor to know about this call. However, he suspected something, got up, put on his bathrobe and inquired, "Who was calling?" Mrs. Hagerthy said she had to tell him that it was James McAlphine calling about his father. "Oh yes," he said, "I was expecting Jim to call. I was over this afternoon and his father is very sick. I just have to go."

Mrs. Hagerthy told me that she could not talk him out of going. The Doctor told her who to call and said, "Have him either come with his car or come and drive mine and I'll go." Very much against Mrs. Hagerthy's will the Doctor was driven four miles over on the Portage

Lake Road to Albert McAlphine's. Mr. McAlphine passed away that night.

The Doctor had made his last call. When he returned home, he was helped into the house and Mrs. Hagerthy helped him into bed again. He became very ill before morning. Doctors were called from Presque Isle. It was the second day after when my cousin Hazen Walker, the mail carrier at that time, stopped at my home and informed me of the Doctor's condition. Hazen stated that he would keep me informed from day to day. I was informed that oxygen was being administered and that the Doctor's condition had not improved.

After another day had passed, I phoned Hagerthy's and inquired of his condition and also if he could have company. The lady who answered the phone informed me that the Doctor's condition was still serious and he was not having company.

On October 4th, through Hazen, I learned Doctor Hagerthy had passed away the day before, Oct. 3, 1941, at the age of 62. I attended the Doctor's funeral which was held at his home, in his office, just where he wanted it to be.

After the funeral, Mrs. Hagerthy asked me to stay awhile for she wanted to tell me something. She told me it made the Doctor very happy to have me go along with him on his last call to Castle Hill. She stated, "The Doctor thought the world of you and has regretted for many years that he could not have arranged for a hospital and have you work with him right here in Ashland."

The going had been rough for the Doctor; however, I was glad that he lived to see open roads for some two or three years. Now patients could be taken to the Presque Isle hospital if necessary, which was a blessing to all.

Chapter 7

Ashland

My first year in Ashland, I did not get around to see much of anything, except the power house at Big Machias and the starch factory. I did see the log drive a couple of times coming down the Machias river and better still saw the main drive coming down the Aroostook River. I did sometimes stop at the covered bridge and observe how it was made. It was fastened together with wooden pins.

The Ashland House hotel burned during the time I was at Penn Craig's but I do not remember seeing it. I understand it was a large hotel and always a very busy place, especially when the woodsmen were going and coming from the logging camps.

The years that I was with Dr, Hagerthy things changed. I had an opportunity to learn of many other places. There were four blacksmith shops in Ashland: "Bill" Hopper's, Charles Orcutt's, Walter McKay's, and Charles Stewart's. Their principal business was shoeing horses, but they also repaired wagons and equipment for the farmers.

There were two churches in town: The Congregational and the Episcopal. There was a large Catholic Church at Sheridan and another on the Old Presque Isle Road. These were always filled to capacity on Sundays. Besides the high school building up on the hill, there was a school building just north of Bridgham's store for the lower grades. Mrs. Mansur, the dentist's wife, taught there. There were many rural schools. Three of them were on the Old Presque Isle Road. The names of these were the Walker School, which was the first out from Ashland Village. Next, beyond Alder Brook, was the Thornton School and last was the Hill School. There was the South School at Squa Pan and at Sheridan there was a school building with several rooms to take care of the many children of the families living there. There was a school building two miles out on the Masardis Road. I believe this one was referred to as the Trafton School. There was another school building out on Worcester Ridge, on the New Presque Isle Road.

The Exchange Hotel was operated by Elmer Howard and his sister, a Mrs. Wheeler. Another hotel was the Union House on Station Hill, owned and managed by "Ed" Junkins and Charles Sleeper. These were always filled to capacity.

Mr. Jim Adams operated a first class harness shop where double and single harnesses were made and repaired. Several men were employed there year round.

There was an Opera House on the corner of Main and Exchange Streets. Mose Smargonsky had a clothing store beneath the Opera House. Another clothing store, owned by Amos Koslosky, was on the other corner diagonally across the square. There wasn't a bank in Ashland at that time.

"Mack" Morin purchased hides and skins of fur bearing animals. This was a good business at that time and brought a lot of money to regular trappers as well as to farm boys, who managed to catch fox, mink, and weasels. Mr. Morin always said, "I'm paying the 'top price'."

The Ashland Grange Store was doing a large volume of business with groceries and feed. Fred Coffin and Ruel Stevens were employed to manage the store. The Grange Hall was above the store. There was a dining room in the basement, where Grange dinners were served many times each year.

Willis Bridgham owned a grocery store (the A&P store is now at that location). He kept a couple of teams busy each day delivering groceries. One team was used in Ashland and one was making trips to Sheridan.

By 1913, a new high school building had been built nearer the center of town. The old high school building was purchased by Charles Brooks for the Oddfellow Lodge and moved down on the lot where the Ashland House Hotel stood before it burned. Most of these old landmarks are now but a memory.

A new concrete bridge was built across the Aroostook River and came into use in 1929. The old covered bridge was dismantled at that time.

The years I lived with the Doctor I had an opportunity to see and often visit the saw mills. There was one at Masardis, another at Portage and the largest one at Sheridan. There were several smaller mills. Dr. George Knowland and his brother, Charles, owned and operated one at the end of the Fenderson Road. There was one over in Garfield and Walter McKay had another out a mile on the Old Presque Isle Road. All of these mills were very busy the year round. The Sheridan mill employed several hundred men and Sheridan was a good sized village all by itself. There was the large Catholic Church, an Opera House, many stores, a post office and a good sized school building. Sheridan was a booming place. While on calls down there with the Doctor, I often had time to hitch the horse and watch the mill being operated. One thing that always impressed me very much was to see men riding the carriage carrying the logs to be sawed. There were two or three of them dogging the logs so they would not roll. The carriage moved back and forth very fast and the men just swung back and forth on it all day long.

It was my good fortune to live in Ashland during some of the years when industry there was at its best.

Ashland Co.'s Mill, Ashland, Maine.

Chapter 8

Teaching At the Hill School

After graduating from Ashland High School, I came back to my father's to help on the farm. It was understood that Dr. Hagerthy would come for me on weekends to mow his lawn and pick up around the premises. Helping on the farm was very interesting as I was older now and could do more of the heavy work.

About two weeks later, Mr. Russell, the Superintendent of Schools in Ashland, phoned and stated that he would like very much to have me teach at the Hill School this next year. This was a complete surprise for I had never dreamed of teaching school. After some conversations, I explained that I was rather young to teach, since my nineteenth birthday would not be until August 15$^{th.}$ Mr. Russell said he would drive down and see me and talk the matter over with my parents.

He came and made quite a lengthy visit. He explained that the School Committee in Ashland had considered me for a teacher and he hoped I would accept an appointment to teach. He stated that the salary would be $9.00 per week and, since the Hill School was not far from home, I could stay at home. My parents allowed that if I wanted to try teaching, I could do the chores for my board and have all of the money to keep.

I told Mr. Russell I would try teaching and inquired about a permit or certificate to teach. He allowed he would secure the examination papers and give the test himself at his office. He requested that I borrow some books from Mrs. Mansur, an experienced teacher in the lower grades, also some material from Mrs. Andrews, a teacher of many years, and before school began in September, to spend a day reviewing the work with each of them.

Only a short time after the Superintendent and I had talked things over, he phoned and stated that the examination papers were at his office and for me to come at a designated day and take the examination. I drove to town with the horse and buggy and took the examination on the day set. About the 10th of August, the certificate came certifying that I was qualified to teach in the elementary schools of the State of Maine. The certificate was signed by Payson Smith, then State Superintendent of Public Schools.

I spent a day reviewing studies with Mrs. Mansur at her school room. On another day, I did likewise with Mrs. Andrews. This proved to be very interesting and I was off to a good start with teaching methods of the various classes.

Between Castle Hill town line and the old Ashland town line on the State Road, lies a section of what was formerly Sheridan Plantation. The distance was approximately five miles. At the turn of the century, this area was thickly settled. The homes, with the exception of a very few, were constructed of logs or hewn timbers.

The people were industrious, hard working men and women. The men found employment in the lumber camps during the winter months and followed up the log drives on the rivers in the spring time. The lumber mills at Sheridan village were booming and many of the men found employment there during the summer months. Others worked on farms in Ashland, Presque Isle, Mapleton, etc. Potatoes were dug with hand diggers at that time and many of these laborers had become professional at digging potatoes and were in great demand at harvest time. I well remember picking potatoes behind those fellows. My father would hire two, or perhaps four some years, to dig his potatoes. The men, working in pairs, brought the potatoes into windrows between them as they dug. They always sang songs as they worked. Sometimes one would sing alone and sometimes they would sing together. Really, those were happy days for them. Their wages were $1.00 per day for ten hours of work. A good digger never bruised the potatoes and always got them all out of the ground. Many of the laborers chewed tobacco, some smoked corn cob pipes. Many mornings, before the harvest was completed, the dirt would be frozen enough to make a crust and much care had to be taken until the sun got up enough to thaw the dirt.

Many times during digging, we would see the wild geese flying south. The laborers would then talk about getting back to the lumber camps for the winter.

The women folks were equally as industrious as the men. For what they had to do with, one could not help but marvel at their ingenuity. In nearly every home, one would find a spinning wheel and a rocking chair. Some kept a few sheep for their wool. The wool was washed, carded and spun into yarn in the homes. Sometimes old woolen clothing was washed, picked all apart and carded into rolls to be spun into yarn. This required a lot of work; however, the savings meant a great deal to those people. Most of the women made and cared for a vegetable garden. Hens were kept, as well as a hog to butcher in the fall and a cow for milk. A good part of their living was derived this way.

There was a large Catholic Church built, about half way from one town line to the other, on a hill that overlooked the area. There was a large bell on the church that could be heard for miles. Every Sunday, the families went to the Church to worship. It was always packed in those early years of this century.

It was always fascinating to pass by the homes when the weather was warm. The doors of the houses would be open and there would be a mother or grandmother rocking away, smoking her TD pipe (the TD pipes were made of clay) and either knitting or spinning yarn.

All of the wells were dug by hand in those days and stoned up with rocks. The pails of water were cranked up on a rope. Those who did not have a well walked quite a distance to a spring. Sometimes several families got water from the same spring. Kerosene lamps were used for many years until the Maine Public Service Co. purchased the George Moores Electric Co. of Ashland. The electric line was constructed through this area in the 1940's. Telephone service was available about 1908.

There were several farmers in this area that operated in a small way. Some of them were Johnny Cloukey, William Clark, Simeon Goslin, Peter Carney and Simon Beaulieu. "Dick" Charette owned a pair of oxen that he used on the land he had cleared. In winter, he would haul out fuel wood. In summer, he often went down to the Castel Hill area to purchase hay. It was quite a curiosity for us youngsters to see this man coming with a load of hay. He walked in front of the oxen and used a goad stick to team them with.

Many of those who kept a cow had cleared a piece of land and raised enough hay for their own use. Not many of the laborers had a barn, just a hovel for the cow. Hay was stacked around a pole. It usually kept very well in the stack.

Deer were plentiful in those days and each family was allowed two each year. Fuel was cut and stacked in wigwam style to season. This was sawed or chopped with an axe into stove lengths as it was needed. Every home was a hospital. All babies were born in the homes at that time.

As the boys reached the age of thirteen or fourteen, they would go to work in the lumber camps. The girls were taught to be good cooks. They often were hired by families in the village of Ashland or other nearby towns, until they eventually married and had homes of their own.

Each home had its own outhouse sitting well in view of the highway. The only mail service was to the Post Office in Ashland village, some six or seven miles away.

Not many of the older people could read or write. Some had never attended school. Of the younger married couples, some had attended school for short periods of time, perhaps two or three years at the most, but after leaving school had not practiced reading, etc. and had forgotten most of what they had learned.

It was here in this community that I began teaching, the winter of 1915 and 1916 when I was but nineteen years old. The folks in this area were a French speaking people, with the exception of the Charles Anderson family. The Anderson children were permitted to attend the McLellan School in Castle Hill without paying tuition.

Tom Carney owned a blacksmith's shop and did the horse shoeing and repair work for everyone for miles around. Tom learned the trade by working for William Hopper, a blacksmith in the village.

Peter Carney, Jr. had been away to a barber school and had recently set up shop near his father's home. There were two grocery stores located in the area of the Hill School. Mrs. William Clark had a store directly across the road from the school house. Joseph Carney and his wife operated a grocery store about a half mile nearer Ashland village.

Having been born and lived near here, I knew nearly all of the parents of the children and they were happy to learn that I had accepted the job of teaching here.

When it came time in September to open school, Mr. Russell gave me permission to spend a day with Ervin Rafford, who was teaching in Sheridan village. Because he taught both French and

English pupils; this was a day well spent observing his way and method of teaching.

The first day at the Hill School was very interesting, although, I must admit, I was very nervous. Most of the day was devoted to getting acquainted with the pupils, distributing the books and assigning lessons for the next day. Fifty-four children registered that day. With the exception of perhaps one or two, all of the children were under twelve years of age. The Superintendent came and brought some paper and pencils. With suggestions from the older pupils, a schedule was made and we were ready for the next day. We would open school with me reading a verse from the Bible, and then we would all repeat the Lord's Prayer, which they already knew very well. They would then sing one or two songs. I didn't know the first thing about music, however, the children did very well. There were about eight little folks who could not speak a word of English. If some understood a few words of English, they were so bashful at first, that I could not learn if they were able to or not. I learned from the older children that it was the usual practice of the previous teacher to let the beginners just sit and listen and soon they would learn a few English words. The idea of children sitting there all day and just learn by observing, did not appeal to me at all.

After a few days, I brought pictures of domestic animals, of vehicles, buildings, etc. and tried to be at school a few minutes early to tack these on one of the blackboards. For the first quarter hour, we would have the beginners take the recitation seats. In about a week, many of them had learned their A B C's and numbers. All of these little folks became very interested and it was not hard to keep them busy, in one way or another, all day long.

One thing that disturbed me was the attendance. Out of the fifty-four registered, the average attendance was around thirty-five. There were many reasons that kept them from attending regularly. In some cases, they lacked proper clothing and the weather was too cold for them to be out of doors. After conferring with some of the parents, I found these situations had existed for many years and nothing could be done about it. Even if a truant officer had been called in, perhaps not much could be done, so I just made the best of the situation and worked harder to help those who could not attend regularly.

Me and the Students I taught at the Hill School in Frenchville

From the beginning, I suggested that the whole school take a nature walk during the last period on Fridays. This did wonders for the children. They learned about different species of trees, about the birds and much about those that migrated South in the fall. On Fridays, when the weather was not good and we could not go out, we would have a review of the things that we had talked about on our previous nature walks. By the last of October, we had to abandon the nature walks until warm weather came in the spring.

Things went along well during the winter months. We had to gather around the big box stove most every morning until the school room became warm. There were no double windows back in those days and a fire was not kept at night. Many times, after a heavy wind, there was snow to be brushed out in the morning from around the door and from around some of the windows.

The fathers and older brothers of the children worked in the lumber camps in the winter months and brought lice home. Many of the pupils just couldn't keep free of lice no matter how hard they tried. During the Christmas vacation, I spent a few days at my father's lumber camp up by Beaver Brook. By the time vacation was over, I too had become lousy. My mother had me change my clothes two or three times each week until I got rid of the lice.

When spring came, I had become very much interested in teaching. We resumed our nature walks and the children learned about the bees, butterflies, and flowers.

The pupils did real well with the examination I prepared for them to take at the closing of the school year.

Chapter 9

Summer School

After the closing of the Hill School for the summer, I made arrangements to attend the summer session at the Normal School in Presque Isle. This was a six week course and the year was 1916. There were perhaps sixty or more girls and women teachers attending but only one other boy besides myself. His name was George E. Martin from Eagle Lake.

It seems that we each were required to study seven subjects. It was not difficult to choose six but the seventh was a sticker for us boys. Finally we agreed to take cooking, providing we could work together. Although sometimes the women folks would joke about our cooking, we made out very well. We learned to cook some and enjoyed it.

On the closing day of summer school, Mr. Merrriman, the principal, announced, "Food has been prepared for a picnic at Echo Lake today. Transportation is being arranged. Be sure and bring your top coats or jackets." I roomed at Mrs. Hayden's home over on Blake Street and had to hustle back for my coat. George roomed on another street and went for his top coat. About ten o'clock, a man employed at the Taylor Livery Stable came with several teams, some single and a couple double, with two seated wagons and one buckboard with four seats. It was quite a sight to see the teams arrive, one tied behind the other. This fellow came along with us to drive the buckboard team and Mr. Merriman assigned some women to drive each of the other teams. Mr. Martin and I had seats with the driver of the buckboard.

We arrived at Echo Lake and enjoyed a nice picnic dinner. Mr. Merriman had arranged for the use of a few boats for those who cared for a boat ride. George and I stayed with the fellow from the Taylor Stable and cared for the horses.

After a couple of hours, Mr. Merriman announced that the teams would soon be ready to take us all back to the school building. Soon all were ready, except a boat load of girls on the other side of the lake. Mr. Merriman requested that all teams wait until the boat load returned. While waiting, George and I decided we would invite a couple of girls to come along with us in one of the two seated wagons. George hollowed his hands and called, "Room here for two. Come aboard and let's go." Avis Walker climbed in for one and she was trying to beckon to another when I stood up in the wagon to say something. At that moment, the horse backed up and I plunged forward, fell over the dashboard and broke off one of the thills. It was a lucky thing for us that the horse was kind and no one was hurt. Avis jumped out. The women gave us quite a ribbing about this. George and I got a halter rope, tied up the broken thill and rode back to school alone.

When we all had arrived back, Mr. Merriman said perhaps we men folk had better drive some of the teams back through town. When we arrived at the stable, I asked Mr. Merriman to have Mr. Taylor have the thill repaired and send me the bill. Mr. Merriman surprised me. He whispered in my ear, "Oh, forget it. This will be included in the total bill."

The six weeks at summer school were very interesting and helpful. Where I had already taught a year, the subjects seemed to mean more to me as I was really interested in teaching by this time and felt that I would be able to be a better teacher during the coming year.

After returning from summer school, the folks at home felt my younger brother, Byron, could do the chores and if I continued to teach perhaps I should pay Mother board. Teachers living away from home were paying $2.50 to $3.00 per week for board. The sticker was the salary; only $10.00 per week.

My father had arranged to lumber again this next winter. He stated perhaps there wouldn't be much of a future financially in teaching, and that he would be paying $60.00 per month plus board and I could come along and work for him. A voice seemed to say "Better forget the school…you can do better."

A few weeks before the time for school to open, I wrote the Superintendent, Mr. Russell, to inform him that I had decided not to return to teach. He phoned and pleaded for me to reconsider. He stated, "Your record was so good. I am disappointed and the people will be too when they hear you will not be back." I explained that my father was paying $60.00 per month, plus board, at his lumber camp, that my younger brother was old enough to do the chores so I wouldn't be doing them for my board this year, that I'd have to pay board out of my $10.00 salary and perhaps it would be wise to help my father.

I got busy and helped harvest the crops. After the potatoes were harvested, my father started me toting camp supplies from Ashland. The team that he gave me to use was one purchased from Alf Trafton. The horse's names were Champ and Harry. This was a pair that Mr. Trafton had, at one time, used in the horse pulling contests at the Presque Isle annual fairs. This was a wonderful team to use. They were slow but strong and steady on the tote roads. A trip was made to Ashland in one day and then it would take two days to divide the load and take the supplies to the camp, which was about three miles from home on the other side of the river.

While the water was low in the river, I could ford with the loads. Later a bateau was used to boat the bales of hay, bags of grain, barrels of flour, pork, and molasses and cartons of other supplies to be used at the camp.

After the river froze over, this team was kept at the camp and I "hot yarded" logs with them. This was taking the logs from the stump and yarding them out beside a road where several could be loaded on a sled for hauling to the landing on the river. This winter, most of the logs we were cutting were not too far away from the river or Beaver Brook and were hauled on one bobsled. This was termed "dragging".

I had passed my twentieth birthday in August and was roughing it with a lumber crew, sleeping on a bed made of fir boughs and eating wholesome camp food. It agreed with me and I began putting on weight.

This life came to a halt about the middle of December when it was my lot to become a pioneer.

Chapter 10

The Mail Line

During spring vacation of the year I was teaching at the Hill School, I went to see the lawyer in Ashland village and explained about the many things lacking in the Hill School District. He allowed there wasn't much he could do to help the situation. He said, "You will just have to keep on and make the best of it." "No matter, Mr. Waldron," I replied, "We do not see alike. I'm not satisfied for things to continue on as they are out there." I felt the answer to some of the problems was to have a mail line. I said to Mr. Waldron, "If you will draft a petition for me, I'll spend all of this week seeing how many people would be willing to patronize an R.F.D. mail line and would purchase a mail box."

A petition was drafted and several copies made. Mr. Waldron charged me a dollar and I was on my way. Every home around the loop was very much in favor of a mail line. The loop, as I have called it, took us down through the French settlement, the State Road in Castle Hill as far as the Advent Church, across the Turner Road, left on the Dudley Road as far as the Haystack Road and then thirteen miles by way of Haystack Mountain and the Wooster settlement back to the Post Office in Ashland. Some of this area was already served by the carrier from Mapleton and it appeared this might make it harder to get this mail route established.

I took the petition to Mr. Greenwood, the Post Master, and asked him to forward it to the proper U.S. Post Office Officials for their consideration. The head of every family on the loop had signed this petition and we all waited for a reply from Washington.

During potato digging time, Mr. Greenwood, Postmaster in Ashland, phoned saying that a Post Office Inspector was at the Post Office and wanted us to go along with him over the proposed route for R.F.D. #2 out of Ashland. I explained that my only way to Ashland would be by horse and wagon and it would take me some time to get there, so Mr. Greenwood stated he would bring his car and pick me up as they came along.

Mr. Greenwood arrived with the Inspector. They had a wheel (a meter) hitched behind the car to measure the distance with. The Inspector complimented us for getting on the ball and requesting mail service for the many families living in this area. He kept taking notes and checking the mileage as we continued on and back to the Post Office.

When we arrived at the Post Office it was a different story. This man's attitude had changed from what it was, after he had covered the first eight miles. He said, "Summing up my inspection, it is very doubtful that the U.S. Post Office Dept. will consider granting your petition for several reasons. First, the distance is 29.2 miles and a large percentage of the patrons live on the first seven miles of the route. I find there is more than four miles of this proposed route already covered by R.F.D. Mail Service out of Mapleton and there is a stretch of woods, nearly four miles long, without any families at all. Really, I feel the physical features of this route will not warrant the petition being granted."

Mr. Greenwood made a plea that consideration be given to the petition in Washington and that we be notified of the verdict. I explained that I had taught school out in that area the past winter, that my home had always been there, that even at my home, we had to drive three miles to the Moran Corner where my father had a mail box at that point connecting with the R.F.D. #1 from Mapleton. Also that, although the physical features of the route were perhaps different than on the average route, there were at least the average number of families to warrant a trial route for at least one year. I also said, "I'm sure a mail line will help with the education of the children, for catalogs and other mail will be coming all the time. If the petition that you have is not granted, we will come back with another seeking a Post Office out about seven miles in the French Settlement. Then it will be necessary for the government to employ a route carrier to service that Post Office and many people will still be without mail service around the loop."

"Well, fellows," he said, "I've done my duty in checking on the petition. I'll return to Washington and make my report. I will also have the department consider the attitude that you have taken relative to this." There wasn't any train out until the next day, so the man wished us good luck and went to the Exchange Hotel for the night.

Mr. Greenwood appeared quite depressed over the statements this man had made and wondered if we would ever hear anything further. He drove me back to my home in Castle Hill. I said something like this, "Cheer up. Where there is a will there is a way. Trying was never beat. We will keep trying and eventually find a way to help, especially those living in the French settlement."

About the middle of December (1916) word came that the petition for R.F.D. #2 out of Ashland had been granted. Mr. Greenwood insisted that I come at once and help get things underway. I hesitated, however my father allowed that as I had instituted the idea perhaps I'd better help. He stated, "We all will benefit by having the mail at the door."

I learned at the Post Office, that the mail service would begin on January 1st, that we would be on a trial basis for one year with delivery every other day and that the carrier would receive $60.00 per month. The salary made me "squirm" yet someone just had to be the beginner.

The first thing to do was to cover the route and take orders for mail boxes. The best price was found in a mail order catalog where we could purchase mail boxes for $1.00 each. Mr. Greenwood allowed that I could charge $1.50 each for the mail boxes, and then I'd have something for taking the orders. It took me about three days to cover the route taking orders for the mail boxes and requesting that everyone get a mail box post ready. These posts had to be located on the right hand side of the highway near the driveways. For those living on the left, their posts had to be on the opposite side of the road from their driveways.

Everyone on the route ordered a mail box. Many paid at the time. Others were to pay when the boxes were delivered. I believe Mr. Greenwood telephoned the order in because it was not long before the mail boxes arrived.

I explained to Dr. Hagerthy about the petition for a mail line being granted and wondered if I could make my headquarters with him. "Sure," he said, "Come on, we will work out some kind of a deal." I arranged to do Dr. Hagerthy's chores for my board. On my days off, it would be okay with him if I found some extra work at one of the stores. I was to purchase the grain for the horse I would be using and he would furnish the hay. A horse was found at the Grange Store, one that had been used to make deliveries with. The cost of the horse was $150.00. My father signed a note with me so I could purchase it. I also purchased a pung, a fur robe, a fur overcoat and a harness heavy enough to haul mail with.

It took a few days to deliver the mail boxes and collect from those who had not paid. Each family was told to have the boxes erected and placed so that I could drive close to them.

January 1st, 1917, arrived and I became the first carrier on R.F.D. #2 out of Ashland. Every patron was happy and each tried their best to meet me at mail time or have their mail boxes shoveled out so I could get to them. The first winter was rather rough. We had a lot of snow and the "snow plow" in those days before open roads, was a wing type plow hauled by horses and used after storms to clear drifts and break track. This plow would push snow so that it was almost impossible for the patron to have his mail box shoveled out all of the time; however, we made the best of the situation. I fastened an extension on the reins so I could hold the horse and wade through the snow to deliver the mail to the boxes. Many days, my feet and legs would be soaking wet by the time I returned to the Post Office.

If I remember correctly, the schedule was to depart from the Post Office at seven o'clock and return at four o'clock. It was not often that this worked out, almost every day I would be late returning.

It was always necessary to watch for "turn out places" since most of the teams I would meet were double teams and often loaded with wood, potatoes or lumber and could not turn out for me for fear of getting stuck.

All in all things worked out well. In the spring, when the snow was mostly gone, I had to purchase a wagon. The wagon was used until the roads were well dried and smoothed up, then I bought a small second hand car for $250.00. (This I managed to pay for by making monthly payments.)

During the summer months, I managed to find enough extra work to make the payments on the car and have some extra money. I managed to do all of the work that Dr. Hagerthy had for me around his home. Mr. Bridgham let me work in his grocery store and this was sure a boost. My wages there were $5.00 per week, if I remember correctly.

This is me delivering mail.

Fall came and it was necessary to change back to the wagon. When snow came (which was early back in those days) I changed again to the pung.

About the middle of December, word came from the Post Office Department in Washington, D.C. that the reports were very satisfactory and that daily mail service was granted and was to begin January 1st, 1918. This was good news for the patrons on the route. Those who were subscribers to a daily paper would be getting their papers every day. Many of those who hadn't been getting the paper, subscribed to it.

Although this daily mail service was good and pleased all of the patrons on the route, it was a financial setback for me. The new salary would be $100.00 per month. It meant that I would not have time to work at the store anymore. I had to purchase another horse. I got along fine with one horse when delivering mail every other day but it would be too much for one horse to make the trip daily. Arrangements were made with Sanford Dudley, who lived about halfway round the route, to care for one of my horses. I would change horses there and continue on with a fresh horse. The charge was $1.00 per day. He furnished hay and I purchased my own grain. This was very reasonable, for often, when he was not too busy, he would change the horses for me while I ate dinner. Mrs. Dudley charged me fifty cents for a good warm dinner.

This second winter on the mail line was pretty rugged. We had an awful lot of cold weather. I bought all kinds of mittens and gloves; still I suffered with the cold. At every mail box, it was necessary to remove the mitten on my right hand. My hand would be damp and nearly freeze before getting away to go on to the next mail box.

Mrs. Briggs, Frank Tarr's aunt, would often bring out a cookie or a doughnut for me to lunch on. One day, she noticed my hand was sort of numb as I fumbled getting their mail out of the mail bag. I explained that my hand would get warm and become moist and when I removed the mitten, which had a leather cover, the cold would get the best of it. Mrs. Briggs said, "I think there is something better to wear on your hands than that arrangement for delivering mail. A couple of days later, she presented me with a pair of black mittens, knit single. Her explanation was that my hands would not become sweaty or moist in those mittens and they would be dry most of the time unless it was raining. The mittens, knit single, proved out so well that I paid the lady to knit a couple more pair.

The snow drifts were so bad that often the harness would break or some part of the pung. This cost money. However, I'd console myself by saying "Such was and still is…This is the life of a Pioneer."

The winter wore away and spring time came again.

Chapter 11

Serving In the Medical Corps of The U.S. Army

During April, 1917, the United States entered into war against Germany. The news soon spread around that men would be given a chance to enlist in the Army, and if there became a shortage of volunteers, it would be necessary to have a draft to fill Maine's quota. A Recruiting Officer came to Ashland, soon after war was declared, to receive enlistments.

The first day the Recruiting Officer was at Ashland happened to be on one of my off days from the mail line. I was twenty years of age at the time. I went to the Town Hall more out of curiosity than anything else to see what was taking place. My, what a large group of boys there were there. I knew many of them for they had attended Ashland High School at the same time I had.

Among the group that day was Walter Brennan, who was employed as a timekeeper at one of the Ashland Lumber camps at or near Big Machias Lake. Mr. Brennan enlisted that day and we soon learned he had gone right along to France with very little training. Walter Brennan served during the "scrap" with Germany. After the war was over he returned to the United States, got a job in a bank and spent his leisure time at Radio City, New York, doing odd jobs connected with show business, such as driving horses in scenes for silent movies. As time went on, Mr. Brennan became so interested in show business that he gave up his job in the bank and moved to California. He eventually became one of America's most famous actors.

Before the day was over, I enlisted along with the others. Since I was employed by the Civil Service, I was given papers to be completed by the Postmaster. Civil Service employees were exempt from military duty at this time. I was also given papers to be completed by my parents as I was under twenty-one years of age. These forms were never completed. Mr. Greenwood, the Postmaster, insisted that I continue with the mail line until it became better established. My parents hesitated to approve of my enlistment and Dr. Hagerthy urged me to forget the Army and continue with the mail line.

A year later, about May 1st, 1918, a ruling was issued and a draft was to be held soon. There was a fellow, named Charles Boyce, who was keeping company with the nurse who had been employed to care for Dr. Hagerthy's mother, who was an invalid at the Doctor's home. Charles and I sat down one evening, after I had returned from the mail line, and talked the situation over. He was 34 years old and came within the draft age. I had passed my 21st birthday and would also be included in the draft, since Civil Service employees were no longer exempt. We each vowed we would not be drafted and decided to enlist.

If I remember correctly, Mr. Boyce was employed by the Bangor & Aroostook Railroad Company and applied for a leave of absence. He and Mrs. Shepard, the nurse, were married. I hustled around and found someone interested in taking over the mail line and purchasing some of the equipment that I had used. One horse, along with the equipment I did not sell, was taken down to my father's.

On June 1st, 1918, Charles Boyce and I said good-by to our folks and began our trip to Fort Slocum, New York, where we would be inducted into the Army. I had enlisted in the Medical Corp, Mr. Boyce with the Engineers. We left Ashland on the early train and arrived in Bangor late in the afternoon. We were to stay at the Y.M.C.A. overnight and a troupe train would be made up the next morning for our trip to Fort Slocum.

My Aunt May Morrison had learned I would be on that train and she was waiting to meet me. She asked the Recruiting Officer for permission for Mr. Boyce and me to stay at her home overnight. He gave her permission, providing she would guarantee that we would be back at the depot by a certain time the next morning. Mr. Boyce said, "You go along with your aunt, I'll stay with the fellows at the Y.M.C.A."

I enjoyed the night with my folks. I was called very early the next morning so as to be on time to catch the troupe train. My Aunt May had me back at the time agreed on; however, the train had just pulled out. The Recruiting Officer was very much disturbed. He allowed he had called the roll and my name was checked off. There was some commotion around the depot for a few minutes until things were straightened out. An excursion train was being made up to go to Boston. It was scheduled to be in Portland at the same time as the troupe train. I was put on this excursion train, not knowing just how I would make connections with the troupe train. However, when the excursion train arrived at the Portland station, a Recruiting Officer came aboard and called for "PHINEAS ELLIS." He shouted, "IS THERE A PHINEAS ELLIS ABOARD?" He repeated this several times until I made myself known. "Oh, good," he said, "Your train is waiting out here in the yard. You come along and ride with your buddies to Fort Slocum." The cars in which we rode to New York were regular box cars with benches around the sides. What a tiresome day it was.

We arrived at Fort Slocum that night. Roll call was taken. We were given some supper at a mess hall and then assigned to a barracks for the night. I'll never think differently than that a laxative had been included in the supper, for many of us spent most of the night in the latrine.

Next morning, after breakfast, we were screened, separated, and assigned to the various jobs for which we had enlisted. It was a problem to find Mr. Boyce again so we could bid each other goodbye. I did not see him again until after the war was over.

Some 2,300 men were inducted into the service that day at Fort Slocum. We each were given several shots and none knew just when or where we were going from there. Recruits were coming and going daily. After a couple of days, I wished there was something to do besides just standing around waiting. One day I met an Officer out in the yard and told him how I felt. The Officer said, "Well, well, sir, this is a coincidence. I am out here right now looking for some husky fellow who would like to work until his time comes to leave this camp for another." This fellow took me down to the kitchen and put me to work. Work was a good name for it. I washed pots, pans, and kettles for several days.

After several days, those of us who were in the Medical Corps were sent by boat to Fort Myer, Arlington, Virginia. This was a splendid day and I enjoyed the scenery. We passed close by the Statue of Liberty and as we continued, our attention was called to places of interest along the way.

At Fort Myer, I was assigned for training at the post hospital. The training consisted of learning how to perform the many duties that we might be called on to do in case we ever got to the battlefield. One of the first things we were told was to maintain a clean personal appearance at all times. There were drills in ambulance work, first aid, stretcher bearing, and in cleaning and caring for the hospital and operating rooms. We had drills in how to prepare food and work in a diet kitchen. We learned how to keep records. We were drilled on making beds, caring for the sick and injured, and performing ward service duties. We worked in the morgue, at times, preparing the bodies to be returned home.

Me and a buddy in our Army uniforms.

The bodies of the men who died at the camp were embalmed, furnished with a new uniform and a suitable coffin. A search was made of the post records to locate a man from the same area of the country as the deceased to accompany the body back home. A new flag was always sent to be presented to the parents or next of kin.

I enjoyed the training at Fort Myer. I continued performing all of these different duties until September, when one Thursday afternoon, the Camp Officers received word to clear the camp of all trainees to make room for more. We were all given a chance to go home and see our folks "because some may never return from 'Over There'."

It was difficult for the clerks to determine just what was best for me. It was explained that I could leave on the early train Friday morning and arrive at Ashland, Maine by Saturday noon and that I could hop the train early Monday morning at Ashland and be back in camp by Wednesday morning. The cost of the trip would be one cent per mile and there would be the expenses of buying lunches. I checked my money and found I did not have enough for the trip. One fellow in the office said, "Oh, go ahead just the same. Your folks will be so happy to see you that they will furnish you with train fare for the return trip." I agreed with him and decided I'd better take the trip.

I left Fort Myer early Friday morning. It was a continuous ride. I changed trains in Boston and again at Portland, Maine. I arrived at Ashland around noon on Saturday and phoned my parents informing them of my arrival. I told them I could stay until the early train left on Monday morning. The folks owned a car at this time and said they would come for me, but Dr. Hagerthy came along and offered to drive me down to Castle Hill. He allowed that he could make the trip while my father was cranking his overland car. The Doctor was about right. It didn't seem more than twenty minutes and the eight miles to Castle Hill were made.

I was awfully hungry and so happy to be back home so I could have some good home cooking like no one but one's mother could make. Those hot buttermilk biscuits and those home baked beans sure tasted good. It was so good to have dairy cream again. It was not served in the Army.

The telephone rang and Mother answered. "Oh yes," she said, "He is home." She then turned to me and said, "Dr. Ellis is wanted on the phone." I took the call. It was Mrs. Wood, the same lady who had taught our Sunday school. Only a few months ago, I was delivering mail to her home.

Before I had a chance to say anything, she insisted that I come right down and treat her leg. Mother explained, "Mrs. Wood has a bad leg sore, sometimes people call it a fever sore." I hesitated to go because, as I said to Mother, "I'm not a Doctor. I don't know a thing about treating leg sores." "Well, go along," Mother said, "It will please the old lady to see you anyway."

I took my father's car and drove to Mrs. Wood's home. She was happy to see me and addressed me as Dr. Ellis. I couldn't explain to her that I was not a Doctor, just a Medic in the Medical Corps of the U.S. Army, for she just didn't give me the chance to make the explanation. She told me that she "suffered everything" with a bad leg sore. The sore was uncovered and what a mess it was. She asked me to dress the sore. She stated that she had taken medicine prescribed by the doctors but the medicine didn't help much, if any. I told her the best I could do would be to administer first aid. "Well, go ahead and do what you can," she said, "I'll die before long unless I get some relief from that awful pain, twenty-four hours a day, seven days a week." I agreed to dress the sore and perhaps it would bring some relief.

It definitely appeared, right from the start that cleanliness was lacking. I took off my coat, found a clean pillow case, stripped it up to make bandages, got soap and hot water and "Dr. Ellis" began to practice on a real case. Mrs. Wood had creolin and iodine that I could use. I put the creolin in the hot water and washed the sore several times until it appeared all of the pus had been washed off along with fragments of decayed flesh. After this was done, I insisted that the sore be exposed to the air until it had completely dried around it. When it was dry, I applied the iodine. Not on the sore but on the flesh around it. Next, because I didn't have sterilized gauze, I scorched some of the pillowcase strips on the stove and proceeded to bandage Mrs. Wood's sore leg.

As I took my leave, she thanked me and predicted that some day I'd be a famous doctor and help many people in many ways. I told her the first aid would give her some relief and requested she remove the bandages each day and have someone clean and care for the sore as I had done. I thanked her for giving me a chance to "practice" and hoped the time spent would pay dividends.

Several weeks later, Mother wrote that Mrs. Wood had asked her to thank me for helping with her troubles and that the sore had completely healed.

I spent a quiet Sunday with my parents. I enjoyed telling them about the different places I had seen and especially about the training I received at Fort Myer and I "showed off" my uniform. Mother gave me $10.00 so I would have enough money for train fare back to camp and some left over to get me by until pay day. The pay was $30.00 per month with $7.50 deducted for insurance.

Monday morning came. I said good-by to my mother, and my father drove me to the train. Everyone was very sad. All understood that I might be shipped overseas when I returned to camp and, as the war was at its height, might never return. Dr. and Mrs. Hagerthy came to the train that morning to say good-by and see me off.

It was a long and tiresome ride back to camp. I arrived at Washington, D.C. the next evening and later arrived at Alexandria, Va., which was close to Fort Myer. It was very late at night. No taxi was available at that hour, so I waited at the depot until Wednesday morning. I then got a ride over to the camp and found the hospital area to be like a ghost town. I found the Post Commander and he told me the boys had all been shipped out the day before. I felt disappointed, but Sgt. Ellingson said, "There were enough Medics to fill the quota requested without you but your turn will come soon."

It seemed rather lonesome. Buddies that I had become acquainted with were gone. New recruits were coming daily. A bad epidemic of the flu struck and I helped as much as I could in the sick wards, with the diets and in the morgue. It was not very pleasant working in the morgue but the base undertaker and embalmer needed help to prepare the bodies to return home and I took my turn. Many boys died with the flu. One morning, when I was assigned to help, there were six in the morgue all at one time.

In October I was transferred to Camp Eustis, Virginia, and assigned for duty with the 57th Ammunition Train, a group scheduled to go overseas. For several days we were drilled as in overseas duty. We were issued packs weighing seventy pounds and each morning we marched back some six miles. At this point we medics rested most of each day and the Company drilled with the "big guns," my, what a racket. The "big guns" were about three miles behind us and the shells were directed to the area where we tented at night. As the shells went over us, a sound was made that made the chills run up and down my spine.

This drilling lasted for some two weeks. We were all getting used to the racket. This was part of the training for Medics and others to prepare us for duty "Over There."

November 11th came. About half of the soldiers (part of the Company) were loaded on a ship and headed for France. The other half of the Company, to which I was attached, was prepared to sail on November 12th.

When we woke the morning of the 12th, sirens were blowing, guns were sounding out on the drill fields and we were all confused as to what was going on. By mid-forenoon word got around that the Armistice had been signed and the war was over. By the afternoon of Nov. 12, 1918, it seemed the whole world had gone BATTY. An ambulance was brought out on the field. A dummy Kaiser was fastened on a pole which was spiked on top. Then the ambulance was pushed out on a wharf and dumped into the ocean.

Much property was destroyed that day as the group celebrated the "Ending of the War." Many of us were disappointed about not having made the trip overseas, yet we were happy to learn that "It was all over, over there."

From this day, November 12th, until a few days before Christmas, every day seemed like a month. There was nothing to do in the line of training. We Medics had little to do except for a little first aid from time to time. A few days before Christmas we were broken up as a group. Myself and others from Northern New England were sent to Camp Devens, Massachusetts.

Each of us was given a chance to continue on in the Service, if we cared to, and make it a career. I chose to return to Castle Hill, Maine, and arrived home just in time for Christmas dinner.

Chapter 12

Back Home and the Collins Lumber Company

It was January of 1919 and I was back home from the Army wondering just what to do next. The Postmaster coaxed me to return as mail carrier. He stated, "The job is yours if you want it." I turned him down because reports were good about the acting carrier and he was said to be "okay."

Mr. Bridgham contacted me and stated, "The offer is still good for you to become a partner with my son in the grocery store." My folks feared that I would have to hire a lot of money to become a partner. Mr. Bridgham allowed that if I did not want to become a partner he would pay me each week what I had received in the Army. This was $30.00. I thought this offer over and turned it down because my father and brother, Byron, were cutting rough pulp wood at $4.00 per cord and allowed I could come along and perhaps earn even more than $30.00 per week.

My mother coaxed me to work at home for awhile at least. She said, "You have been away for some time and we would love to have you at home." I agreed perhaps this would be better in the long run and went to work with my father and brother.

The Castle Hill town meeting was held in March and I attended. I was elected 3rd Selectman. This was the beginning of my political career. That spring I tackled farming along with my father and brother. I became very interested in the combination of farming and municipal work. I got along fine until fall came and the plowing was done. Then came the time to decide what work I should find to do for the winter. My father had accepted a job with the Collin's Lumber Co. of Caribou. He was to take charge of the lumber operation at Squa Pan Lake.

A long lumber mill was being built there and I was invited to come to the camp for Thanksgiving dinner. There were openings there for most any kind of job, relative to logging, that I might be interested in. Mr. Collins suggested that I do the marking of the lumber at the mill as it was being sawed. The pay would be $78.00 per month, plus

Me (right) and the Cook in front of the woods camp.

board. This was an attractive offer so I accepted the job. I found the work very interesting but it was very cold working at the mill during the severe cold days. I took time in the evenings to post tally for the day. I also spent many evenings helping the cook, Bert Randall, and the cookee (cook's assistant), John Archer, catch up on washing dishes and preparing dinner buckets for the woods crews. There were approximately seventy men employed in the mill and woods crews. I never got tired and worked each day as long as there was anything to do.

A good first aid kit was brought in for me to use. This made my work more interesting. After a time my wages were increased to $91.00 per month, an increase of fifty cents each working day.

When the weather was awfully cold, the sleds, loaded heavily, coming from the yards, would "grind." That is, there seemed to be a lot of friction between the cold steel of the sled runners and the frosty snow on the logging road. To overcome this, the roads were iced. A water tank was constructed of matched lumber so that it would not leak. The tank was fastened on a set of bobsleds and taken to the water hole to be filled. Here, at the Collins' camp, there was a natural spring, several feet deep and it did not freeze over even in the coldest weather.

The water tank was about 12' long and had baffle boards about 1/3 of the way from each end. The baffle boards extended down to about 6" from the bottom of the box-like structure. The top part of each end was boarded over. The center section was left open so water could be dumped into the tank. A gin-pole was fastened to one side of the open section. A pulley was fastened to the top of the pole through which a wire rope extended from the front of the sleds, down to a bale fastened on the end of a pork barrel. Also fastened to the barrel was a piece of wood used as a handle to tip the barrel into the water hole to fill it. It only took a jiffy to fill the barrel. The fellow tending the barrel, at the water hole, would holler "Go!" The teamster, who had one horse unhitched from the team, would lead it out a few feet. This brought the barrel of water up a trough-like slide to the top of the water tank. The fellow at the top of the tank would grab the handle fastened to the barrel as it came to the top. He would then holler, "Whoa." The horse would stop and the barrel was tipped over the side of the tank and the water dumped in. The teamster would then back-up the horse. This would allow the barrel to return to the spring. This continued until several hundred gallons of water was loaded. After the tank was filled, the horse that was used was returned to the pole and hitched up with the other horse. The load of water was then brought out on the main hauling road. Holes had been bored in each bottom corner, at the rear of the tank, in which cedar plugs were driven. The woods boss was usually around and decided where to start spreading the water. He would pull the plugs and holler "Go." The water sort of sprayed down on the road just about where the sled runners would pass. This procedure was called "Icing the Roads." Much larger loads could be hauled over a good iced road. In very cold weather, this was a usual morning chore that sometimes lasted until well along into the forenoon.

One morning when it was decided to "Ice the Road," the mill hadn't started operating yet as there was trouble getting the motors started. I had helped with the loading of the water tank several times in the past, so this particular morning Wilson Collins, son of the owner, asked me to come along with him since I could not work at my usual job without the motors running. "Okay, I'll go," I answered, "What's up?" "Well," he said, "I want to learn all about working in the woods, tricks used, etc. I am going to help ice the logging road this morning and your father says for me to bring you along because you have had experience filling the tank and I haven't."

He and I followed the team out to the water hole, which was about one quarter of a mile from the camp. The teamster put the water tank in position to be filled. We got all set to go. I gave Wilson Collins his choice. He could fill the barrel at the spring or climb up on the tank and empty the water. He allowed he'd rather stay on the ground for his first lesson.

Poles had been laid all around the spring with boughs placed over them. Snow had been shoveled onto these boughs and allowed to freeze. This formed a walk on which the person filling the barrel could stand. I explained to Wilson Collins that we should keep our mittens dry and take great care not to get splashed with water.

Everything was going along good. The loading was about completed when a blood curdling call echoed through the frosty air. "HELP! HELP! HELP!" I didn't realize what had happened for a couple of seconds but when I looked down, Wilson had vanished. I jumped down off the tank and began hollering "HELP! HELP! HELP!" The water had thawed up through the boughs enough so that Wilson Collins, who was quite heavy, had fallen through. There he was, with one arm up over the poles and his face just about at water level. By the time I reached him, Mr. Leavitt, the teamster, came around and began hollering "HELP! OH, HELP! OH, HELP!" Our shouts must have sounded weird echoing out over the ridges that awfully cold frosty morning.

Mr. Leavitt and I managed to pull Wilson up out of the water. About this time, my father came running, all out of breath, to see what was going on. He saw at a glance what had happened and shouted, "Run, boy! Run to the camp! For your dear-life, run like Hell!"

That morning, Wilson had put on a pair of cotton overalls and in seconds, after he was pulled from the spring, they had frozen stiff. Father gave him a push and kept shouting, "Run and run like Hell!" Wilson said, "I can't run, Jap. I can't run because my clothes are frozen stiff." Father grabbed a stick of wood or a limb from a tree that was lying there and shouted, "You will run or get the damnedest flogging you ever got. Now run for your life!" Wilson geared up and

My father, Jasper Ellis, far left, Woods Boss for the S.W. Collins Lumber Company with his crew.

made record time to the camp, with my father running behind him with the stick shouting, "Run, boy, run!" all of the way.

Mr. Leavitt went to spread what water we had loaded and I followed him to pull the plugs when he gave the word. By the time I arrived back to camp, Wilson had been stripped of all his clothing and was bundled up by the stove getting warm. He had the chills for a time but came out of it okay. My father's quick actions had saved his life. Even if we had taken him back with the team, he would have most certainly frozen before we reached camp. Keeping his body moving was the only way he could have come out of this all right.

Wilson allowed that "Lumbering is not all sunshine and history has been made when a 'Baptism' takes place in the logging camps of Maine."

Some of the more humorous fellows inquired of me, "Are you sure you quoted the proper scripture when this act took place?"

I'd like to mention here the history of the Collins' Lumber Company. The Collins' Lumber Company dates back to 1844 when Samual W. Collins (1811-1899) organized the S. W. Collins' Lumber Company at Caribou, Maine. At that time, Caribou was called Llyndon and the population was 297. The Company continued to expand and grow down through the years.

After the death of Samual, his youngest son, Herschel Douglas Collins, took the reins and continued to manage the business. Herschel passed away on December 30, 1936. At this time, Samual Wilson

Collins, only son of Herschel, became manager of the Lumber Company.

Herschel had lumbered at Squa Pan Lake for a couple of years. The lumber cut was shipped by train to the Caribou Mill. In 1919, Mr. Collins conceived the idea that it would be to some advantage to build another mill at Squa Pan and increase his cuttings as there was a vast lumber area there from which stumpage could be bought.

In the summer and fall of 1919, a long lumber mill was built near Walker Siding. Extra crews were busy cutting logs to supply both mills.

The Squa Pan Mill began operating the latter part of November, 1919. The power used was a combination of steam and gasoline engines. The output, while I was marking at the mill, was 14,000 F.B.M. (feet board measure) per day.

Much of the lumber sawed here was shipped direct to the consumer; however, the cedar, hardwood, and some of the pine was shipped by the Bangor & Aroostook Railroad Co. to the Caribou mill for further processing.

Chapter 13

The Mapleton Local

I continued on, working everyday at the Collins Mill, until town meeting time in March. The town reports had been prepared by M.A. Dudley, Chairman of the Board, and F.J. Porter, 2nd Selectman. As 3rd Selectman it was necessary that I attend, but I returned to camp the day after and continued marking at the mill. About the first of April, the wood cutting crews were discharged. As there was considerable lumber yet to be sawed, I stayed on for some time.

After the mill closed for the summer, I came home and agreed to help with the farming. I spent quite a lot of the money that I had earned. I had the harnesses repaired and purchased some new equipment, including a set of army wagon wheels for the gigger wagon. I helped get the crop planted. Things were going fine when the Postmaster requested that I return to the mail line. I turned down his offer because I had promised to help with the farming.

Next, Mr. Bridgham contacted me again to see if he could interest me in becoming a partner with his son Hadley, or, if I preferred wages, he would pay me $1,800 per year. This, too, I let pass. I informed him that I had agreed to help at home through the farming season.

About July, the Directors of the Mapleton Local of the Aroostook Federation of Farmers came to see if I would be interested in being manager for the Local. They explained the Local had purchased the grist mill property and were in the process of building a new mill. The plans were to ship potatoes, handle fertilizer, cement, all kinds of feed, etc. My work would include the office work and supervising the men who would be hired to do the manual labor. They allowed that, at the start, I could set my own salary. This deal looked very attractive. After talking the offer over with my folks, I accepted at a salary of $1850.00 per year.

I reported for work in July of 1920. At the beginning, no system of bookkeeping had been installed. I tried to arrange and prepare a system similar to what we had learned in the commercial course in high school. This did not work out very well so, after a couple of months, we employed the Shean Accounting Service of Presque Isle to set up a good foolproof system of accounting suitable for the business. It was separated into three parts; milling, potatoes, and other sales including fertilizer, cement, spraying material, etc. This system proved to be very satisfactory and good accurate monthly reports could be prepared for the directors.

At the time I came to work, time was very precious. Mr. Frank Chandler, former owner of the mill which had burned, had been employed to construct the new building. New machinery had been ordered and a millwright from the machinery company was due to arrive any day. It was necessary to rush the whole program for the wheat harvest would begin the latter part of August. Farmers would be expecting to get some of their wheat made into flour as soon as possible. The new building had been closed in by the time the millwright came and the machinery arrived. Installation went along fine. I had some time to help with getting the machinery installed.

About the first of September, the directors met and reviewed what had been done. They informed me it soon would be time to ship potatoes and the orders would be coming from the Federation's main office at Caribou. I learned the shipping procedure as quickly as possible. The plans were to ship from three loading places: Mapleton, State Road Siding, and Brennan Siding. Box cars had to be rented from the railroad and wood lining placed inside to prevent frost claims in winter. Stoves were purchased to be used to heat the cars going to Boston, Yonkers, New York, and other destinations. A fireman went along with the car loads of potatoes. Several shippers would employ the fireman and each one would pay his part. Usually the fireman would have four or five cars of potatoes to look after. The directors estimated the number of cars that we might need for the season. Seasoned wood was purchased and, in very cold spells, about one-half of a cord was placed in each car for the fireman's use. If ever the supply did not last for the trip we would always hear about it, but, if any wood was unused, word never came back to us as to what had become of it.

A potato house was rented at each loading point and a foreman was hired to do the loading. Grading potatoes was not practiced.

Potatoes were loaded in bulk and, much of the time, just as they came from the field. We stood a very good chance of having a "come-back" but things worked out well this first year, no claims except for frost damage which sometimes occurred.

The second year we tried to do better. The potatoes were put in sacks and we had tags printed to be fastened to them. The tags had consecutive numbers. A record was made of the numbers. This way we would know just where to place the claim if any came back. I would have the buyer state the numbers on the bag or bags in which he had found potatoes that were damaged or of a poor grade. As time went on, grading became a must and State Inspectors checked the cars before they left.

If I remember correctly, more than one hundred cars of potatoes were shipped in 1920-21, about the same in 1921-22, and around two hundred cars in 1922-23.

I had mastered the accounting part of the business and when my work was all caught up I'd go out into the mill and work with the miller. Frank Chandler, former owner of the grist mill was employed as miller. After a few months, he would leave me alone to do the milling while he went home for supper or to the barber shop. By the end of the first year, I had just about mastered the milling business. I had learned to repair the silks on the reels and could change the tension of the rolls that crushed the wheat. Some grists were harder or softer than others and it was necessary to adjust the rolls to get as much flour as possible from the bran. The bran was the outside of the wheat kernel.

The farmers would start bringing their wheat to the mill after harvest, as soon as it was dry enough. Usually a small portion of the crop was brought in first, so as to get flour to use through potato digging time. Later, when cold weather came, the balance of their wheat crops was brought to the mill. Sometimes the wheat was brought in barrels, which I liked, and other times in old bags. Each load was known as a grist. The grist was taken in and weighed. A charge of twenty cents was made for each bushel of sixty pounds. A large set of scales, which were set level with and in the floor, were used. After the whole grist was weighed, the wheat was dumped into a hopper which was constructed under the floor. From the hopper the wheat was taken by a bucket conveyor to the third floor of the building. Magnets were built into the conveyors to pick up any steel or iron particles that may have gotten into the wheat. Even a small nail would raise the dickens with the silk reels if it should get that far. Sometimes we found nails, beater teeth from the thrashing machine, wrenches, and small tools. One day the magnets picked up a four pound axe. This could have caused considerable damage if it had passed by the magnets. I remember scolding the farmer whose wheat and axe it was. His only comment was, "Thank you, thank you so much. I remember purchasing the axe last fall but had forgotten I had hidden it in a barrel of wheat."

After the wheat was conveyed to the top floor of the building it passed through a large fanning mill where the straw, chaff, and very light wheat kernels were blown out. Next, the wheat passed through a scalper, a machine that removed any loose hulls that may have been left. Now that the wheat had been cleaned of chaff, straw, etc., it was taken to another large hopper on the second floor of the building. From here it was conveyed through various chutes and elevators in the process of becoming the finished product.

In the final process, the wheat passed through a series of silk covered reels. There were three reels and two sets of rolls, if I remember correctly. This machine was very compact. It was eight feet wide, about eight or nine feet high and approximately twelve feet long. The silk covered reels were about thirty inches in diameter and revolved continuously. As the wheat came down through a chute, it was crushed in the first set of rolls (two iron rollers). The hull was removed as it passed along through one of the reels. If the customer wanted the hard wheat germ, as it was called, it could be taken from the conveyor as it passed along to the next set of rolls where it would be crushed finer. This wheat germ was cream of wheat, just like we purchase in the stores. As a rule, the farmer would only want a few pounds of the cream of wheat. In large grists we could take out ten pounds or so if he desired. As the crushed wheat passed through the second set of rolls it was crushed again and another grade could be removed. This grade was called middlings, known to the consumer as graham flour. From the second reel the wheat went to the third reel. A very fine silk covered the last reel and from this the fine white flour was conveyed to the bagger. Sometimes the farmer brought his own bags but we always had new seamless bags to sell.

A feed grinder was always ready to grind feed, such as oats mixed with corn. A hopper had been built on the second floor to hold whole corn which was purchased to grind with feed. Many times a farmer would buy as much as a ton of the corn to feed his hogs and horses. Oats were purchased too, but not as often as corn. Every farmer planned to raise enough oats to last him through the season.

After the potato shipping season was over in the spring of 1923, the grist mill was sold to Orin Winslow. Mr. Winslow was one of the directors at the time. He had helped us some at the mill and enjoyed the work. The Maine Potato Growers Exchange had been organized so the Federation of Farmers organization ceased shipping potatoes. I was told the Local would not need me anymore; however, the directors recommended me to the new organization: The Maine Potato Growers Exchange.

My three years as manager of the Mapleton Local were busy years. We were in operation during some of the booming years in this farming area. The grist mill and the feed mill played a very important part in the livelihood of the community. As I check back in the records of the town reports for one of those years (1921) the inventory showed a listing of 212 cows, 328 horses and 67 other kinds of livestock in the town of Castle Hill. For the same year there were 328 cows, 478 horses and 211 other livestock in the town of Mapleton.

The area that we served went far beyond these two towns. Grist and feed to be ground came from Chapman, Washburn, Ashland, Masardis, Portage and Oxbow. There was a grist mill at Caribou serving that area; however, we milled for the greater part of the Presque Isle area because we had a more modern mill.

Every weekday from the latter part of August through the winter months, up until May at least, we were humping all through the day and sometimes far into the night. The summer months were almost as busy with cleaning the grist mill, installing new silks on the reels, checking the buckets in the elevators, etc. Several car loads of spraying material was handled each summer as well as several car loads of cement.

After the shipping season for potatoes was over each year, the lined cars were returned, the linings removed and stored away to be used another year.

Receiving orders for potatoes from the main Federation office at Caribou, placing orders with our local buyers at each loading point, making payrolls, keeping time sheets, making bank deposits, and preparing bills of lading was all part of my work. The experience I received working for the Local at Mapleton during those years has been of much value to me.

The directors of the Mapleton Local, while I was working there, were E.M. Turner, President, Harry Hughes, Treasurer, Halsted Foss, Secretary, F.M. Dudley, George R. Cook (who was succeeded by Orin Winslow) and Charles Chandler. They were a fine group to work with and it was a sad day for me when their final meeting was held.

When I first went to Mapleton as manager for the Local, it was necessary for me to make arrangements for board and room. Robert Dudley and his wife learned of this and offered me a room in their home until I could find a permanent place. They suggested that I eat at the restaurant. "Lonny" Wilcox owned and operated a restaurant and he served the finest of food at reasonable prices. "Lonny" did his own cooking and the price for what we call a three course dinner was only fifty cents. A good hearty dinner like "Lonny" served would cost a person several times that amount today.

After a few weeks a sign, room for rent, was posted at Sarah Waddell's home just across the street from the grist mill. I hired the room and moved my clothes from Dudleys to Waddells. I told the Waddells my stay might be a long one because I was employed as manager of the Mapleton Local of the Aroostook Federation of Farmers. I learned there were 23 Locals in the organization and this one was number 5.

Some time in August "Ed" Flannigan passed away. He owned a nice little home on the south side of the street in Mapleton. His heirs were a son, Charles Flannigan, who was living in Skowhegan, Maine, and a daughter, Mrs. Maude Chandler. After the funeral was over brother and sister got together and divided the estate. Charles Flannigan wanted to sell his share in the house. They agreed on a price and Mrs. Chandler bought her brother's share. School was to begin in September which was only a very few weeks away. Mr. and Mrs. Chandler came to house clean and make repairs and decided to set up housekeeping there for their children, the ones who were in high school, so they would not have to drive a team four miles to school.

There was a lot of room in the house and my sister Dorcas arranged to board with the Chandlers. Not long after school began the son, Lawrence, asked me, “Why don’t you come and stay with us?” This seemed like a good idea and I had an interview with Mrs. Chandler. I asked her what she would charge me for room and board. She stated, “I’ll board you for seven dollars a week and perhaps Dorcas will do your washing.” Boy, what a surprise that was. I’d been having my washing done at “Mame” Judkins and was paying twenty-five cents per week and I’d also have a savings of at least five dollars a week in board and room. So late in September or early October I moved from Waddells over to Chandlers. This arrangement lasted until June of 1922. At this time the daughter, Mildred Chandler, graduated from high school and her brother Lawrence decided to drop out of school. Mrs. Chandler received a good offer for this home and sold it. Dorcas returned home to Castle Hill.

It occurred to me that perhaps I should do something so Dorcas could finish high school. She would be a senior in the fall. I learned that my brother Luther and my sister Opal were ready for high school but mother said, “Due to finances we won’t be able to send them.” Now that Mrs. Chandler had sold the house in Mapleton, I had to make some arrangements to stay myself. I located an apartment where we could all stay and made this suggestion to my parents, “I will take this apartment that has enough room for the four of us. I’ll pay the rent and you can furnish what you can in the line of vegetables and cooked food. I’ll provide the balance of what is needed and they can all go to high school.” This arrangement was agreed upon and I rented the apartment. Things worked out very well and Dorcas graduated with her class in June of 1923.

Chapter 14

The Vacation

One day during the summer of 1922 I was up to my home for dinner. Father permitted me to take his car back to Mapleton. He stated, “Keep it for a few days and perhaps you can look around when you have time and find a good buy on a secondhand car.” I did not have a car and only got around to places that I could walk to unless I was invited to ride with others.

About this time Frank Chandler had purchased a new four cylinder Buick. I told him I might buy a good used car and he began to discourage me from even thinking about buying a used car. One day, when there was time to lock up the mill for an hour or so, Frank insisted I come for a ride in his Buick. I tacked a note on the office door (this was unusual for I’d never done this before in all of the time I was employed at the mill) saying Frank and I have gone to Presque Isle and will return soon.

I went to the bank in Presque Isle and made a deposit for the Local. Next, as I remember, Frank and I purchased some hardware, that was needed at the mill, at A.M. Smith’s Hardware Store.

When we were ready to return to Mapleton, Frank said, “Come along with me and I’ll introduce you to the folks at Bean’s Garage. They may have another Buick like this one and perhaps you can arrange to purchase it.” At Bean’s Garage Frank introduced me to Fred Loring, a salesman for Mr. Bean. Mr. Loring stated that the price of a car like this “Buick Four” was $1,207.00. I had just ridden in Frank Chandler’s car and admitted that I would like to own one but I did not have enough money saved to buy it and asked if perhaps he might have a good used car that I could pay for. Mr. Loring asked if I was employed and if so where and how much was my salary. After I answered his questions, he said, “Mr. Ellis, you shouldn’t even think of buying a used car. I can sell this car for one half down and we’ll arrange for you to pay monthly payments on the balance.” I inquired, “Do I have to have someone sign the note with me?” He answered, “No, your own personal signature is sufficient.” We decided to close the deal right then and there. I went back to the bank and drew enough from my checking account to pay half of the price of the car. I signed the note and drove the car back to Mapleton. We returned to the mill and I thanked Frank for the ride and for getting me interested in purchasing a new car rather than fooling around with a secondhand one. Frank said, "You made a good deal today and one for which you will never be sorry."

The next weekend I managed to return my father's car and "show off" the Buick. My Mother had prepared a special Sunday dinner, perhaps because I was home. After dinner I said to Mother, "Two years have passed since I went to Mapleton to work. I haven't had a break, except I've managed to attend Grange on a few Saturday evenings and have attended Church most every Sunday. I do not remember of you ever having a vacation. I still have some money saved. Now what do you say, let's take a vacation? I'll drive you down to Bangor and we will visit Aunt May." Mother said she would like to make a suggestion. "Well," I said, "What is the suggestion?" She said, "It seems to me you should take Byron along. He has never been to Bangor and neither has he had what we might call a vacation. Why don't you invite Mildred Chandler and Byron perhaps will invite Josephine Welts to come along and I'll be the chaperone." I answered, "Well, that seems like a grand idea if it is okay with the girls."

Before driving back to Mapleton that afternoon, I stopped by Chandlers and talked with Mrs. Chandler about Mother's suggestion. "Why that would be wonderful," she said, "Perhaps Mildred would like to go along." I found Mildred and broke the news to her about buying the Buick, about having dinner up home and about the plans for a vacation. "I have talked with your mother," I said, "and she is willing for you to go if you care to." While Mildred was pondering in her mind about the trip, I said, "If you care to join us on this vacation, it will be a graduation present for you." She answered, "Yes, I would enjoy the trip."

I phoned back and told my mother, "We will start our vacation next Sunday. Mildred has agreed to come along. Have Byron ready and there will be room for Miss Welts if she cares to come."

Sunday morning came. We all met at Mother's home and got an early start. It was about 160 miles to Bangor by the road we used at that time, and after some nine hours we arrived at Morrisons. It was a wonderful summer day. The car seemed to have a good rhythmic sound when driving at 22 to 24 miles per hour, so I tried to keep at that speed all day. When we arrived I hardly knew what to say or do. Ralph Morrison, a brother of Aunt May's husband Charles Morrison, lived there and he had a large family. Aunt May said, "Now don't fret. You and Byron can sleep in the sugar camp up in the grove and I'll tuck the others in somewhere." After supper, Mother and Aunt May made plans so that we could visit as many places as possible in a week. It was decided before bed time that there would be three trips. Each trip would take two days and we would be back here every other night.

Early Monday morning everyone was up and ready to leave. We drove all day, stopping briefly at Waterville, Auburn, and Augusta. We also spent some time at Old Orchard. Aunt May was our guide and we were having a very interesting trip. Late in the afternoon we discussed as to where we would "tie-up" for the night. I told the group I would like to treat them to hotel accommodations. This would be a new experience for all of us. We drove to Portland and looked around for awhile. We spotted a hotel close by where we had parked and decided to stay there. Aunt May knew the ropes about registering at a hotel so she agreed to go ahead and make the arrangements. She did a splendid job. Byron and I were assigned to a small room and the others had a room large enough to accommodate the four of them. The next morning, we had breakfast at the hotel, I paid the bills and we were on our return trip to Bangor. As I remember, we returned to Bangor mostly by another route. The weather was fine both days, the car worked perfectly and each and everyone allowed this was a wonderful experience visiting so many cities on a two day tour.

Wednesday morning arrived. Mother and Aunt May had planned that we would drive to Lubec and spend the night at Aunt Nell's. Aunt Nell was Mrs. George Kelly, an aunt to Mother and Aunt May. We saw many new places on our way down. Aunt Nell and her husband were happy to see us when we arrived.

Byron and I were given a clam hoe and a bushel basket. Aunt Nell showed us the way to the clam flats. She also told us how to dig clams. We found this very interesting and filled the basket nearly full of clams in an hour or two. The clams were steamed for supper and relished by all.

Before retiring for the night, Uncle George and Aunt Nell told us of their many experiences down through the years and of events that had taken place around the seacoast where they lived. The home was small so blankets were spread out on the floors and we all tucked in for the night. Sleeping here on the floor was very different from the soft beds at the hotel two nights before.

Morning came. Byron and I arose early, explored their small farm and spent some time down by the ocean before being called for breakfast. After breakfast, we took our leave and returned to Bangor by another route. This trip too was wonderful both going and coming.

Friday morning Byron and I got up early to observe how a dairy farm was operated. The Morrison brothers, Ralph, Archie, and Uncle Charles owned and operated it on shares. The business had been started by their father. There were perhaps some fifty cows being milked. A milking machine was used. The manure was loaded in a bucket which was on a cable fastened to a trolley. The bucket passed by behind the cows and when it was filled it was pushed out on the cable, a hundred feet or so from the barn and automatically dumped. The outer end of the cable was just a bit higher so that when the bucket had tripped and emptied it would return by itself. This amused my brother and me very much.

After the chores were finished and breakfast was over, Aunt May told us Uncle Charles was taking the day off and he would take his car, divide the load, and we would go to Lead Mountain to do some fishing and spend the night there. Uncle Charles and Aunt May had camped there many times before because fishing was one of Uncle Charles' favorite pastimes. It seems that we arrived at the lake soon after dinner time. There were boats there and Uncle Charles had brought along plenty of fishing tackle. It was a pleasant afternoon to be out on the lake but the fish were not biting very good. What few were caught were cooked for supper over an open fire and divided among the seven of us. During the evening, Uncle Charles entertained us with a few songs and many stories. After awhile it appeared we were getting tired so Uncle Charles, who had been a bugler in the Army (World War I), brought out his bugle and sounded taps. Someone in the group inquired, "What does that mean?" Having heard this every night while in the Army, I quickly answered, "That means time to go to bed."

There was a barn nearby filled with hay. Mother and Aunt May had placed the blankets, which had been brought along, and we were all assigned to our resting places for the night. I'll always remember how restful it was camping out there by the lake in this old hay barn.

Morning came and Uncle Charles was up first, just about daybreak, and sounded reveille. He took Byron and me out fishing until the women folk were up and had prepared breakfast over an open fire. The fish were not biting and it was decided not to fish anymore. After breakfast, Aunt May and Uncle Charles planned a return route back to Bangor. We arrived about mid-afternoon.

I checked the car all over to see if everything was in order for our return trip home. I saw that there was water in the radiator as well as in the battery. I checked the crank case, added a little oil, greased the fittings, etc. After noting that everything was in order, we loaded some things to be brought back with us.

We got up extra early Sunday morning and left as soon as we could for home. We arrived back in Castle Hill late in the afternoon all rather tired. Everyone couldn't seem to thank me enough for taking them along on such a vacation as they had never had before. After leaving the others at Mother's, I drove Mildred to her home. She thanked me for such a lovely graduation present and said, "This has been such a wonderful trip." Mrs. Chandler seemed very happy that we had returned safe and sound. She also thanked me for Mildred's "graduation present." I returned to my room in Mapleton, had a much needed bath, went to the restaurant for supper and began making plans for the summer's work at the mill.

Chapter 15

A Decision Of Once In a Lifetime

Summer of 1923 arrived. The Mapleton Local had sold the grist mill and I agreed to go over and work for the new co-operative, the Maine Potato Growers Exchange. I began wondering very seriously if it wasn't time for me to find a lifetime partner.

There was a grocery store near the grist mill owned by Chester Cook, a bachelor. I used to stop by once in awhile to purchase a candy bar, chewing gum, or something else to nibble on and I often kidded Chester about being a bachelor. He would always have a very good reason for not having married and he'd explain why it was not worth while for a man to marry. At this time, I paid a visit to Chester's store and, as he was alone, I told him I'd soon be leaving Mapleton and working for the new potato organization which was making their headquarters at Caribou. "Now, Chester," I said, "Wouldn't it be wise of me to find a partner, get married and settle down?" Chester answered something like this, "Everyone for himself and the devil for us all. I've told you before how I feel about marriage but your life is your own and I shouldn't try to influence you one way or the other."

This was next to my last week at Mapleton. I thought day and night of what might work out best for me. The only one that I wanted to explain my thoughts to was Mildred Chandler. I joined the Grange in 1914 and had been acquainted with her ever since. I also had known her father and mother all of the intervening years. Mr. Chandler had been Road Commissioner and I had worked under him. When I served as Selectman for the Town of Castle Hill in 1920 and again in 1921, I was Chairman of the Board and he often had taken orders from me. When I was with the Mapleton Local, he was a director and I, in turn, had received orders from him. At this time, I felt the Chandler family had had a chance to size me up.

Saturday came and I made up my mind to shave, clean up, and drive over to the Chandler's State Road home. After work, I hurried down to the barber shop for a shave but found only one barber, Tom Bishop, on duty. The shop was full of waiting customers and he assured me he could not possibly get to me that evening. I went back to my room, got out the old straight razor and, being careful not to make too many nicks, I shaved myself, changed into clean clothes, and drove over to the State Road with the idea in mind of talking over with Mildred the thoughts I had of the future years.

Mildred was sitting out in the hammock and asked me to come and rest for awhile. There never was a more perfect day than this one. The fields were green and, as we sat there admiring the beauty of nature, we could hear the birds singing in the near-by trees. We talked about most everything and especially my new job. Suddenly I became very quiet. Mildred noticed this and inquired, "Are you ill?" "No," I replied. I still was very quiet. "Are you sure you are all right?" she asked. I finally got up enough nerve to ask, "Mildred, will you marry me?" At this point, Mildred became speechless and we sat there for a time in silence.

After awhile, she said, "It will be hard to leave home at this time because Mother needs my help but I will talk things over with her. You come over for supper next Saturday and I'll give you my answer."

Next Saturday came. I had met with Mr. Chandler during the week and talked with him about it. I said, "Perhaps it would be wise to have a wife to share the ups and downs of life with me." Mr. Chandler did not object in the least, in fact he said, "I'm sure you and Mildred could make life's journey together a very happy one. Whatever plans you care to make will be agreeable with Maude and me." Before driving over for supper, I saw to it that I was barbered and had my clothes pressed. When I arrived, Mrs. Chandler was sitting out in the hammock resting. "Come and rest for awhile," she said, "Mildred is getting supper on the table. It will soon be ready." In a short time, we heard the call, "Supper is ready."

What a banquet Mildred had prepared. It occurred to me I had heard many times "The way to a man's heart is through his stomach." We enjoyed the supper. Mrs. Chandler said to Mildred, "You need to rest. You have been working hard all day. You and Phin go out and rest in the hammock."

We went out to the hammock and Mildred said, "Phin, here is my answer to your question. Yes, I'll marry you." At this time we began to make plans for the future.

Mildred Chandler and Phineas Ellis, August 22, 1923.

As summer went by plans were made for our wedding. It was to be held on August 22nd at the Chandler home. The great day arrived. The Rev. David Jones of the Mapleton Baptist Church came over and "tied the knot." After the wedding ceremony, a reception was given by Mildred's parents. What a wonderful evening it was. Many friends and relatives came. Many presents were received, some of which are still being used. The food, the homemade ice cream, and such friendly greetings will never be forgotten.

The next few days were spent at the Chandler cottage at Portage Lake. Mr. Dinsmore, a friend of the Chandler's, came with his motor boat and gave us a ride each day. Mildred was lucky and caught a salmon up Fish River on one of the trips. There were no scales available to weigh the salmon on, so, for the record, we measured it. It was twenty three and one half inches long.

Prior to our marriage, I had arranged for an apartment on Bridge Street in Caribou. The rent was $25.00 per month. The apartment was furnished and we were to pay our own light and fuel bills. There were several apartments in the building but I always felt we had the best one. It was on the ground floor and had three rooms and a pantry. I furnished wood for our cook stove and paid for my share of the coal used in the furnace. There was an old shed not being used and, without extra charge, I was permitted to fix it up and house my car there.

After our few days at Portage, we began life's journey together at Caribou.

Mrs. Augusta Armstrong, a widow and a corsetiere, owned the house in which we lived. It was a very large house and besides the several apartments she rented, she had her business office and living quarters in the front of the same house. Mrs. Armstrong made special corsets for certain patients referred to her by Doctors all over the County. She was very good to us and we continued to live there for the two years that I was employed in Caribou.

Mildred and I sat down and tried to figure out a budget that would make our money go as far as possible. At the end of the first and second weeks, I got a shave at the barber shop so as to be looking my best for Sunday. The money spent in this way was listed in our expenditures. At the end of the second week Mildred asked me if I could shave myself. I replied, "Yes." "Well, perhaps we can make some savings here," she said, "Each time that you shave yourself give me the amount that you usually pay the barber and I'll put it away." She also stated, "Anytime you feel that you have made a savings on a purchase, give me the difference. The savings may be very helpful some day."

The months passed. I became very interested in my work with the Exchange and Mildred kept the home fires burning. A few times she said, "If only I had a sewing machine we could save even more." A few days before Christmas I came home with my check and said, "Now Mildred I feel I can afford a good Christmas present for you. Name over some things you would like to have and we will go shopping." "No Phin," she said, "We will not go shopping tonight. You have already made me a wonderful Christmas present." "How come?" I asked. She answered, "I priced the sewing machines over at Morgan's Furniture Store awhile back and they had one that I liked. Today I counted the savings and found we had $30.00, the price of the machine, so I went over and bought it from Mr. Morgan and it has already been delivered." She went over and uncovered it saying, "This is my Christmas present from you and I am so happy with it." What a surprise this was and it all came about by saving a little money each week to be used for something useful. Over fifty years have passed and the sewing machine is still going strong. The savings that we made in the fall months of 1923 have multiplied many times over by having the sewing machine.

Although we were getting along fine, life in the village was not the same as back on the farm. Sometimes I'd wonder what we would ever do if the "co-op" did not succeed. One time, when we had our car out of storage, (spring of 1924) and the snow was all off, we visited my parents for a day. My father mentioned that he had a feeling the Exchange would "not make a go of it." He said, "If that should be the case perhaps you should be thinking ahead as to what to do." This gave Mildred and me something to think about. There was a small unoccupied piece of land near my Uncle Jim's home. One day we decided that buying this land might be a good "bet" should the Exchange "fold up" sometime.

On one trip over to my father's home I inquired about this idle lot known as the "Will Turner place." Father went down with us to look the place over. He informed us he felt quite sure Dr. Dobson, now of Presque Isle, had become owner of the lot by a foreclosed mortgage. Father stated, "Perhaps you could buy it and have a place to come to when you tire of working out for someone else. Why don't you see Dr. Dobson and see how much he wants for it. If I remember correctly, he mentioned having about $600 tied up in the place."

Mildred and I came over one Sunday, looked the place over again and decided it would be well to consider saving to buy it but first we wanted to see how much the Doctor wanted for it. There were no buildings on the lot except a little old shed. The land had not been tilled for awhile. There was quite a lot of wood land out back and we daydreamed of having some lumber cut and building us a home here. This, we agreed, would be a goal to look forward to and began saving for it.

While working at my job I often thought of going back to the farm. One day the Exchange had an errand for me to do at Houlton. I left Caribou about seven o'clock and, as I drove along, something seemed to say, "Why not see Dr. Dobson and perhaps you can make some sort of a deal for that piece of land." I arrived at Presque Isle and as I passed Dr. Dobson's office, which was right on the main street, I noticed the Doctor just coming out his walk.

I drove in and asked if he could spare me a minute or two. "Well yes Phin," he answered. "What do you have on your mind?" I said, "My wife and I might not always want to live in the village. We understand that you own the Will Turner lot up in Castle Hill. Would you sell it and if so how much would you want for it?" He answered, "Boy, Phin, I have been thinking that I'd like to sell the place and the price I have in mind is $2,000." I thanked him and started to walk away. "Wouldn't you be interested in the lot at that price?" the Dr. asked. "No Doctor," I replied, "I am not interested in buying the place at that price. I saw you coming down your walk and thought I'd inquire as to how much you wanted for it." "Well, Phin, have you been thinking it over seriously and have you looked the place over?" he asked. I told him that we had looked the place over and it appealed to us as a place we could improve and perhaps we could build us a home there. I explained that the land had not been tilled for some time. I also said, "I have cruised the wood land with my father and it appears there is enough lumber suitable to build a house with and perhaps enough more to build a barn which will be a must if I should farm there. My father mentioned he remembered of you telling him one time of having about $600 tied up in the place." I explained that I was working for the "co-op" at Caribou for about $30.00 per week and hardly felt I could ever save $2000 with which to purchase the place and at the same time be able to build a home. The Doctor piped in, "How much would you be willing to pay? You must have some figure in mind. How much money have you saved that you could use toward this deal should we make a deal this morning?" I said perhaps Mrs. Ellis had some savings but I did not know how much and before I could go on the Doctor interrupted asking again, "How much money would you be willing to pay for the lot?" I answered, "I'll be willing that you get your investment back plus a fair rate of interest. Perhaps that would be around $800." The Doctor inquired, how much money do you have in your pocket this morning?" I took out my wallet and showed him that I had only $60.00 in bills. "Well," said the Doctor, "I guess we can make a deal for $800 right here this morning if you want to part with the $60.00." He continued on saying, "Come on, let's go. I'm needed at the hospital but you come along and as we pass by Charles Daggett's law office I'll instruct him as what to do about making out the necessary papers."

At Mr. Daggett's office Dr. Dobson hurriedly explained, "I'm selling a piece of land up in Castle Hill to Mr. Ellis for $800. He will pay $60.00 today. Make the balance of the payments $25.00 per month. Skip a month now and then in case he might need more time. Make the balance of the note due in two years and the rate of interest six percent. I'll bring my deed in at noon for you to go by. Have the papers ready for this fellow as soon as possible after dinner. He is on his way to Houlton and if he returns before you close shop this afternoon, close the deal."

The Doctor allowed he was a half hour late for his appointment at the hospital but added, "That is okay this time." I went on to Houlton and hurried up with the work assigned for me that day. When noon time came I found a restaurant and was about ready to order lunch when it occurred to me that perhaps I did not have enough money. I checked my wallet and found that, besides the $60.00, I had some change. I spent what change I had on a light lunch. I finished my work in Houlton and returned to Presque Isle in time to see Mr. Daggett before he closed his office. I paid the $60.00, as promised, took the notes along for Mildred to sign and promised to return them the next day. I arrived back in Caribou in time for supper and had made a deal which Mildred approved of. I said to Mildred, "It's been a long time since I've been so hungry" and explained the reason for it was lack of money with which to buy a regular dinner.

The summer of 1924 went by quickly. We took a ride over to Castle Hill most every Sunday to visit our folks and we always stopped at the little farm and made plans for the future. During the summer we managed to save quite a sum of money. I was paid seven cents per mile for the use of my car, when using it for working for the Exchange, and Mildred put this away for improvements on our little farm.

About the latter part of August, I had the feeling we might be leaving Caribou before too many years and decided to begin improving the land and perhaps plant a few potatoes the next year. I had my Uncle Jim look over the land. I wanted to see if it could be plowed and fixed up so a few potatoes could be planted in 1925. "Why, sure Sonny (as I was called by him) I will plow all of the land that is suitable for potatoes for you for $30.00," Uncle Jim said. I thought for a few minutes about the seed and fertilizer that I would be needing but decided "nothing ventured, nothing gained" and told my Uncle Jim, "Go ahead and plow the ground that you feel is or can be made suitable for planting potatoes on next year."

During the fall Uncle Jim and his son, Fred, plowed up the land and, boy, they did a fine job. Uncle Jim saw to it that all of the sods were turned over and the loose rocks were thrown up on top. Before cold weather arrived Mildred came and looked the place over. I made the statement to her that day, "Those ridges of dirt (plowed ground) on this land look like a gold mine to me." Mildred said, "I do hope it will turn out to be that way."

Back in the spring of 1924, Mrs. Armstrong gave me permission to plant a garden out back of the house. I spaded up some of the area and planted it. We harvested quite a few vegetables which helped with the food budget.

In the spring of 1925, I arranged for a man to bring over a load of barn yard manure and plow and harrow the whole area. The area was not very large and this fellow charged me seven dollars. This seemed like a lot of money, yet it took about one half of a day to bring the manure and do the job. I do think this little patch of ground produced more than I had ever seen grown on a similar area. This same spring (1925), I also managed to have some potatoes planted on our little farm. I had measured the plowed land and found it contained about six acres. I purchased enough certified seed to plant the six acres and bought about six tons of fertilizer. My father and Uncle Jim found the time to prepare the ground and plant the potatoes for me.

As summer passed, they too looked after the cultivating and hoeing. Joe Ellis (one of Uncle Jim's sons) did some much needed hand weeding. I remember of paying Joe at the rate of $4.00 per day for his work but do not remember how much the other charges were.

August came and the Exchange called it "Quits."

Chapter 16

My Experiences with The Maine Potato Growers Exchange

I've told about my personal life while with the Maine Potato Growers Exchange and now I'm going to write abut the origin of the Exchange and some of my experiences while working for them.

In 1922, Congress passed a bill entitled the Capper-Volstead Act permitting farmers to form co-operatives to collectively market their products. During the fall and winter of 1922-23, a young corporation attorney came to Aroostook County and held several meetings explaining to the potato growers the substance of the bill. This man's name was Aaron Shapiro. Mr. Shapiro was attempting to form co-operatives among the potato growers all over the United States to regulate supply and demand in the markets and bring a reasonable profit to the farmers.

Meetings were held in several parts of the County and it was decided to organize under the name of the Maine Potato Growers Exchange.

The enthusiasm was so great that similar meetings were held and co-operatives were formed, among the potato growers, all over the United States. Here in our potato growing area, Mr. Herbert Foss, a potato grower and also principal of the Fort Fairfield High School, became so enthused that he volunteered to donate his time to the organization of the Exchange. He firmly believed this plan would bring to an end the uncertainty of realizing a profit each year for the potato crops.

Mr. Foss was a real orator and could explain in detail about contracts that were to be signed. He was chosen President and General Manager of the new co-operative.

Andrew J. Beck of Washburn was elected Business Manager. "Jack" was a young lawyer and president of the Washburn Trust Company, a bank which he had founded.

Harry Umphrey was elected Sales Manager of the Table Stock Division. Harry was one of the larger potato growers in Aroostook and perhaps the largest shipper of table stock potatoes. His reputation with the buyers, in various markets, would certainly make this Exchange a decided success in a few years.

Ray Hews was elected Sales Manager of the Seed Stock Division. Ray owned and operated a seed farm in Easton. He was a graduate of the University of Maine, had learned and practiced planting seed potatoes the "tuber unit way" and had studied potato planting diseases, rogueing, and spraying. Ray's knowledge of the whole potato business seemed unlimited.

Edward (Deak) Morton was elected Chairman of Publicity and Field Representative. Deak had served the County as County Agent. He, like Mr. Hews, knew all of the angles of the potato business and would be "worth his weight in gold" as one of the Directors.

Ray Geary of Caribou was elected Office Manager and Treasurer. Ray, a Public Accountant and an expert in setting up bookkeeping systems, organized the office staff and prepared forms that would be needed in the several departments.

With the Board of Directors that were elected it would seem the Co-operative could not help but succeed. A building was rented at Caribou and early in the summer of 1923 plans were completed to "get going" with the 1923 crop of potatoes.

As I've mentioned before, I made the decision to go to work for the new organization as my employment with the Mapleton Local was coming to an end.

July 1st, 1923 came and I began working for the new co-operative at Caribou. Fred Loring, who had been a salesman for the L.S. Bean Co. selling Buick cars, also reported for work the same day. He had resigned from Bean's and stated he wanted to be a little closer to the potato industry in Aroostook. We were to work under Ray Hews for the summer.

The first day, Mr. Hews briefed Fred and me as to what he wanted us to do. He said, "I have arranged for Dr. Schultz, at the State Farm, in Presque Isle, to teach you about the potato diseases and how to detect them in the growing plants." Fred and I went directly to the State Farm. Dr. Schultz was waiting and asked us to be seated. He said he would explain all about what Mr. Hews wanted us to learn.

This lecture lasted for more than an hour, and then he drove us to the fields in his pickup. We were shown how to detect the diseases. After an hour or so we were told, "It is lunch time. I'll expect you boys to return in an hour and a half and we will continue on with the instructions."

Fred and I drove into town for lunch. I had my Buick and Fred recalled the day I had purchased it. He stated, "Boy, how well you have kept it."

After lunch, Dr. Schultz took us out to the fields again. After a couple of hours he said, "Perhaps it is time for you fellows to return to your office and write up your notes. Be back here tomorrow morning, as soon as the dew is off the plants, and we will work together again."

Even though I was a farm boy, little did I know about potato diseases. I can remember Dr. Schultz repeating over and over again, "This is mosaic, this is blackleg, this is leaf roll and this is rhizatonia." The potato plants at the State Farm were nearly free of disease so we often traveled some distance between diseased plants.

The next day Fred took his car, a Buick just like mine, and, as we were driving, we compared notes on what we had learned the day before. Dr. Schultz took us to the fields for further instruction. He gave us each a stick with which to point out diseased plants. I walked between two rows on his left and Fred between two rows on his right. He walked between the two rows in the middle. If Dr. Schultz found a diseased plant first, he would stop and name the disease. If either of us found a diseased plant, we were to stop and point to it with the stick. Dr. Schultz would tell us if we were in error and, if not in error as to the plant being diseased he would name the disease and we would pass along.

About eleven thirty, he suggested we break for lunch and return at one. We returned and went through the same procedure again for about two hours. "Now, boys," he said, "Go to your office, write up your notes and return again tomorrow."

The third day at the State Farm, Dr. Schultz gave us each a notebook and said, "Now, boys, we will work this way today. We will proceed in the same formation as yesterday. Count one hundred hills of potatoes in one of the rows as you pass. Watch for diseased plants as you go along. The number of diseased plants found will be the percentage of plant disease. List each disease, as you find it, under the proper title and when we have finished in this field you will know just what the percentage of each plant disease is."

Before lunch on this third day, we were working on just one variety of potatoes. After lunch, Dr. Schultz took us to fields where different varieties were growing. By the end of the day, it seemed as if I could spot a diseased plant several feet away.

Dr. Schultz said to us, "I'm sure that you boys can inspect the potato fields that Mr. Hews wants you to and make reports, such as he will need in selling seed potatoes for the organization for which you are working." Fred and I returned to the Caribou office. We found it easy to make a good report relating to potato plant diseases.

The next two days, Mr. Hews drove us around the county pointing out where members lived. Once in a while, Mr. Hews would stop at some potato field near the highway and, together, we would count one hundred hills in a row and find the percentage of disease in this field. We found this very interesting and when Friday night came, Fred and I were duly qualified Potato Inspectors.

The lessons learned this week were very valuable to me in the following years when I was raising potatoes.

Monday morning came and we were told to inspect all of the potato fields of the many members throughout Aroostook County. This was done on days when weather permitted. My, what a job it was. The first time around all of the fields had to be inspected, but fields in which we found more than 5% plant disease were omitted on the next inspection. These fields of potatoes that failed to pass the 5% test were sold as table stock. Many fields did not pass, so the next time around there were less growers to call on. This second time around, a record of the disease percentage had to be kept of each variety and of the location of the fields.

Before we finished, time was running out. The potato plants were beginning to wither and it became more difficult to detect the diseases. Many of the growers had begun to do some digging. As the potato harvest got underway, Mr. Hews had his office staff summarize the reports we had given him.

All through the harvest, we were kept busy checking the potatoes of the fields that had passed inspection for seed. The potato growers were very cooperative in permitting us to inspect their fields and places of storage.

I will always remember how nice the people up in the Stockholm and New Sweden area were. It was my good fortune to be in that area several times during the potato harvest, about mid-afternoon. The women folk would come to the fields with hot coffee and doughnuts or cookies. A few potato barrels would be turned bottoms up and a tablecloth spread out. The farmer would halt digging and have the crew gather around for a lunch. My, what a treat this was and a new experience for me, too. I'll always remember the coffee as being the best I ever tasted. A few times, I talked with the pickers after the lunch. They all agreed "this is a nice thing for the farmer to do. It gives us a rest and the coffee perks us up so we can pick without tiring all the remainder of the afternoon."

After the potato harvest was over, in the fall of 1923, I was assigned to work in the office, under Ray Geary, during the winter months.

Spring came and the official office records showed that many of the growers were short on deliveries of their potatoes to the Exchange. The Directors felt it would be necessary to check with the members and see why so many variations in delivery occurred. At this time, Fred Loring, a boy named Dave Hoyt, and I were sent out to cover the entire area and report, as soon as possible, as to what was taking place.

We covered the entire area, as we had done the past summer and fall and found many shortages. Many complained about shrinkage. Many had "jumped" their contracts in order that their families might not want for food. We discovered that non-members were selling potatoes for more money than the net returns were to the members. It would appear, from our study and reports brought back, that many growers were getting "cold feet."

Most all of the members gave us fairly honest reports; however, there were several cases where we were sent back to make demand of delivery and tag bins in which potatoes were found. From our reports, the Directors discovered many cases where a Replevin Writ should be issued and a Deputy Sheriff assigned to go and take possession of the balance of the crop found. This act sort of weakened the morale of the growers. It indicated that the non-member farmers had the advantage over the members of the Co-operative and sort of dampened the courage of the faithful and loyal members.

The 1923 crop was marketed and having faith that the Co-operative would succeed, as had been explained by Shapiro, plans went forward to make an honest try again. Even though the potato growers outside of the Exchange had some advantage over the members, the returns for their crops were not too satisfactory and many decided to join the Exchange and help make a "go" of it.

Summer of 1924 arrived. The planting season was over and it was time to go through the same procedure of inspecting the potatoes as in the previous year. Forms were furnished to Fred Loring, Dave Hoyt and myself. We were to check with all of the member growers and find out how many acres each had planted, as well as what varieties and whether potatoes were being grown for table stock or seed. We were kept busy checking in these various ways until about July 10th. At this time, we inspected the fields of seed growers to determine the supply of seed potatoes that would be available for the next shipping season.

Fred, Dave Hoyt and I had tried to make careful and detailed reports of the number of acres of potatoes planted as well as the acres inspected which qualified for seed. Twenty-five dollars per acre had been advanced to members to help them harvest their crops.

The farmers had forgotten the trials of the previous year. Everyone lived in the hopes of making a profit "this year." The creditors and banks were solidly behind the potato growers and thought that the co-operative way of marketing, under the Shapiro plan, would work out very well in the end.

Fall came and shipping started off with a "Bang," but the market was not as good as expected.

Reports would come to the office that "so and so" was selling a load of potatoes outside of the Exchange. Then one of us three field men was delegated to check on the report. If found true, we were to demand delivery of all the crop, for in some cases, growers with thirty acres of potatoes had received an advance of $750, so it became very important to keep a close watch on delivery. One million dollars had been hired to help the growers over the "hump" of harvesting and no chances to lose should be taken.

Checking on cases where the farmer was "stepping out" on his contract was interesting but, in some instances, not very pleasant.

One interesting case that had been assigned to me was in North Caribou. A man had been reported as selling to independent shippers. I checked and found this to be so. I went to see this man, inquired about his crop and asked why he had jumped his contract with the Exchange. This fellow had an awful hard luck story about his need for money to pay bills with, etc. As I remember, he had raised ten acres of potatoes and drawn $250 to help with the harvesting. A check with the buyer of the potatoes already sold indicated it was time to put a clamp in the balance of the crop in storage. The reports I had returned to the office, in this case, didn't seem to add up, so a Replevin Writ was obtained and given to a Deputy Sheriff. He was to go and seize the balance of the crop.

Jarve Kelley, a Deputy Sheriff, was assigned to the case and I went along to show him where this grower lived. We arrived at the cellar, where the potatoes were stored, with trucks in which to haul away the balance of the crop or at least enough to cover the digging advance.

Mr. Kelley served the papers on the grower and then opened the cellar door. To our surprise, the cellar was "cleaned out" with the exception of a few barrels for the family to eat. Mr. Kelley argued for some time. As I listened, the fellow told this story. He said he had harvested a very small crop and the potatoes were not keeping very good, so he had notified the Exchange of the situation and had been advised to "hold on for awhile and maybe the market will improve and there will be a profit for you."

Mr. Kelley took me to one side and pretended to give me "hell" for bringing him out on a "Tom Fools errand." Here, in his presence, I went over the data I had brought along and told him there was something "certainly fishy" about this whole deal. As we stood out by one of the trucks that had come along to haul away the potatoes, I happened to notice the house was much longer than the area we had inspected and found empty. I called the Sheriff's attention to this. "Well, that is strange," he said, "Let's go back in and look around."

Our inspection showed there was a false wall in the cellar. Mr. Kelley said, "Well, I'll be damned!" He looked around, found an axe and a peavey, went back into the cellar and made a hole in the false wall disclosing a few hundred barrels of the finest table stock potatoes.

The potatoes were all removed that day and Mr. Kelley reported his findings to the office. He told them at the office, "This Ellis is a better detective than I am a sheriff. If you have any more cases for me, I'll expect him to come along for he has an eye like a hawk."

During the fall and winter of 1924-25, many cases were referred to Fred, Dave, and myself to investigate for one reason or another. In most cases, a satisfactory settlement or explanation was made that satisfied the Directors of the Exchange.

There was one case on the Washburn Road, however, which became a real problem to solve. The farmer had a nice farm and grew and harvested potatoes of the finest quality. He had reported that fifty acres of potatoes had been planted and our inspection reports showed that approximately fifty acres had been inspected. This man had drawn $1,250 in advance.

The complaint was that he had sold a whole bin of potatoes, which had been stored at the railroad siding, to an independent potato buyer. I checked and found where the potatoes had been stored. The buyer admitted he had purchased and shipped them. He stated, "The potatoes were of the finest grade and quality and I was not aware the farmer had done anything wrong."

The farmer advised me not to worry about the digging advance for he had harvested a bumper crop and could refund the $1,250 without any trouble. He took me to the basement of his barn and several hundred barrels of potatoes appeared to be stored there. He said, "I also have a large quantity stored in my house cellar."

A report of my findings was made to the office. The inspection notes, the report of the potatoes harvested by the grower, and the fact that some five hundred barrels had been sold, just didn't sound right to the Directors. It was decided to obtain a Replevin Writ.

Mr. Kelley took the writ and proceeded to take possession of the balance of the crop.

The house cellar was described as being very deep, yet the outside measurements indicated it would not hold the amount of potatoes reported to be there. These potatoes were to be taken out first. The farmer did not object in the least. He said, "You fellows have a job to do. Go right ahead."

We found the cellar was not as deep as described. The potatoes had been turned down from holes in the floor above. A furnace, with a large metal jacket, was found all covered over with potatoes. We were very disappointed to find only about half as many potatoes as we were led to believe were stored there.

Mr. Kelley became very frustrated. Next, we went to the barn basement and began to remove the potatoes found there. Mr. Kelley said, "Looks as though we can make up for the shortage found in the house cellar." He instructed the truck driver, and the men employed to help, to "hurry, for we do not want to leave a 'keeper' here for the night."

About an hour later, we got the surprise of a lifetime. The potatoes stored here had been dumped down through holes in the plank floor above. After potatoes from the front of the bin were removed, a basement full of machinery was found. Mr. Kelley was angry by this time and wanted to see the farmer but we were informed he had gone away for the day and would not be returning until supper time.

By mid-afternoon the potatoes found were hauled away and the reports, when summarized, indicated that not half of the acreage, as reported, had been planted. Our reports did not show how many acres had been measured. This was something that had not been questioned before.

Mr. Bernard Archibald, the attorney for the Exchange, was called in to decide what to do in a case as serious as this one appeared to be. He instructed the Directors of the Exchange to have the potato land measured. If I remember correctly, Mr. Henry Lamoreau was with us at the time. It was ordered that this land be measured and measured accurately. A steel 100 foot long tape was used.

The farmer came to the field where he had planted the potatoes and said, "You fellows go right ahead and I'm sure everything will come out okay." After a few hours, we were able to find only eighteen acres of land where potatoes had been grown that year. We were puzzled to know where our error was as our records showed approximately fifty acres had been inspected. We learned we had inspected potatoes on another farm which he claimed he owned.

We made a check at the office and went back to locate the other farm. It proved to be over on another road and occupied by another man. The crop here had been harvested and hauled away. The fellow living here allowed that he had seen "some man" inspecting potatoes back in the summer but hadn't thought anything of it because the farmer we were investigating had a mortgage on the land and he thought perhaps it was him who was having the potatoes inspected for some reason or other. We were advised that the farmer we were checking on had no interest in the crop and neither was it under contract with the Exchange.

Mr. Archibald stated, "This is definitely an embezzlement case and must be taken to court." The Grand Jury was in session and proceedings were started at once while there was still time to have the case tried in the 1924 November term of court. The farmer was indicted for embezzlement and Mr. Archibald, as attorney for the Exchange, presented the case which seemed to be fair and accurate in every detail.

It was brought out that the farmer had drawn $1,250 for a digging advance on fifty acres but only eighteen had been planted and of the 2,000 barrels that had been harvested, more than half of them had been sold and not a cent was refunded to the Exchange.

Mr. Hamilton, an able lawyer, was employed by the farmer. At no time during the trial did he dispute anything that was said. After awhile, Mr. Archibald stated, "The plaintiff now rests the case" and Mr. Hamilton presented the side of the defense.

Every detail that had been presented was gone over carefully and in not one single statement was a discrepancy mentioned. This seemed to be an odd situation for us to be in so the defendant was questioned again. At this point, the Judge did the questioning.

Do you say Mr. (x) that you planted fifty acres of potatoes this past farming season?" he asked. The farmer answered, "Yes that is correct." The Judge continued on with, "Do you admit that you were paid a digging advance of $25 per acre to help with the harvesting?" "That is correct," said the farmer. "Are the measurements, as shown on the blackboard, drawn by Mr. Ellis, of the several fields correct?" the Judge asked. "Yes," the farmer answered. The Judge said, "It appears that your attorney has failed to note an error in the statements of the witnesses for the Exchange. Can you explain just where the difference is that has caused you to be brought to Court?" "Yes", stated Mr. (x), "There was another field right up here (he went to the blackboard and made a drawing) that they did not measure." "How many acres are in that field?" asked the Judge. "Well," answered the farmer, "I never have measured it exactly but have paid men for reaping grain there and it always has been considered 32 acres. That is what I paid for reaping grain there." "Thank you, Mr. (x)," said the Judge, "Now Mr. Hamilton, do you have any further comments?" "No," answered Mr. Hamilton, "I visited Mr. (x)'s farm before coming to court and believe this man's farm contains the number of acres that has been listed as measured plus the 32 acres that was not measured."

Mr. Henry Lamoreau, of the Exchange, had sworn that my statements and drawings were correct. Mr. Archibald said, "I do not remember of, in all my years practicing law, such a peculiar case as this."

The attorney for the Exchange took about one half hour to present the case to the jury and the lawyer for the defendant took about five minutes, dwelling wholly on the field that had not been measured. Not a word was brought up as to what sort of a field this was or whether there had been any crop taken from it this year of 1924. The Judge addressed the jury briefly and they were ushered to the jury room.

Suppertime arrived and a recess was called until seven o'clock. After supper, we, who were representing the Exchange, were waiting patiently to hear the verdict of the jury. The jury returned and the verdict was "Not Guilty."

Just imagine how "sheepish" we felt.

The defendant had told of a field that had not been measured and there had not been a contradiction at any time during the trial. This field was a hay field and there may have been twenty acres, more or less, on it. We never knew for it had not been measured by any of us field men.

I never learned what part of the $1,250 digging advance was recovered in this case. Neither did I learn how or what sort of a settlement was made with Mr. Bean for the potatoes we had taken, for after the potatoes were hauled from the house cellar and barn basement, a representative of the L.S. Bean Company arrived and said his employer was holding a claim on those potatoes. The Exchange was threatened with a law suit.

I have often wondered just where this farmer went after he died.

There was another case the following spring in which a very large acreage was involved. I helped the Sheriff recover the balance of the crop found. It seemed that in this case the farmer mortgaged his property and made good the loss to the Exchange.

With the closing of the 1924-25 shipping season, the Directors of the Maine Potato Growers Exchange voted to call it "quits."

Mr. Shapiro's plan had failed. Not because of poor management but because the Exchange just couldn't regulate the flow of potatoes to the market. The fact that a large percentage of the potato growers were not members of the Exchange and marketed through independent buyers made it difficult to even begin to control "supply and demand." The return, in the final months, only netted the grower about 25¢ per barrel.

The best of the Aroostook County potato growers, managed by the ablest men connected with the various phases of growing, marketing and handling finances, had displayed an honest effort for more than two years and now they allowed that "This plan to raise the standard of living in the potato growing areas of Maine, as well as in other parts of the U.S., has failed."

The old saying is "Where there is life, there is hope" so the next year a miracle seemed to happen. Creditors still had faith in Aroostook County, the potato industry, and in the rugged tillers of the soil. The supply was not too great and the demand was much better. Around $4.00 per barrel was received in the fall and increased to more than $9.00 in the spring, bringing new courage to the potato farmer. His credit was restored as many delinquent accounts were paid off.

Chapter 17

Back To Castle Hill

Here, at this time, I felt like the prodigal son. I was out of work and wondering what to do. My father came to our rescue. He allowed we had better move home. He and Byron came with the truck and moved us over to his home in Castle Hill. He stated, "You have your potatoes to look after and get harvested. We'll call it exchanged work, you help us get our crop taken care of and we will help you with yours. Mildred can help your mother and she can pick potatoes if she cares to. After the fall work has been finished, I will be working for the Collins' Lumber Company again and you can work in the woods this winter and save your earnings towards building a home down on your lot." This was a wonderful deal for us. Although I was as "soft as a pumpkin" I went to doing hard work again and soon got hardened up to doing the many farm tasks.

I helped with the grain harvest. My father had an old "Gray" separator to thresh grain with. It was powered by a gasoline engine. After the grain was taken care of it was time to haul out manure. Back in 1911 this was a job that I did not care for, however, at this time, (1925) I was happy to have the job to do. After the spreading of manure was finished it was time to get ready for the potato harvest. Due to lack of money new barrels could not be purchased, so we bought some cleats and extra hoops for the bottoms of the old barrels. All of the old potato barrels were repaired, as well as the machinery, to be used during the harvest.

About September 10th, the potato buyers opened up their warehouses and began buying. The price started off at about $4.00 per 165 pound barrel. My, what a difference from last year when at the close of the shipping season only 25¢ per barrel was received. My father and brothers had about thirty acres to harvest and, with my six acres, we knew we would have to make the most of every minute. We had to dig, store, and market and we wanted to sell as many as we could right out of the field.

Things were working out just perfectly. Father had placed his first crop mortgage this year. He was getting it about all paid. The home cellar (used for storage) was filled to the limit and the only outlet left was to keep selling. We had a Chevrolet truck with a body that held sixteen barrels each load. Byron was driving truck. He had to work hard and put in long days in order to market six or seven loads per day.

About the first of October, there came a "blizzard of a snow storm." I had about one and one half acres of Spaulding Rose potatoes left to dig. The folks at home had about seven or eight acres. The snow covered the potato rows right over level. Now what should we do? The yield was 100 or more barrels per acre and at the present price, here was about $5,000 worth of our potato crop buried under the snow. In about two days the storm abated. None of us could rest easy just wondering what the outcome would be. My father seemed completely discouraged and wanted to call it quits with farming and not plant again in the spring. I coaxed him into reconsidering.

After the storm was over, I drove down to the State Road Siding to see if there was any storage available should we be able to dig later. The first man I wanted to see was Bernard Kenney. Mr. Kenney was buying potatoes for some dealer and he said, "Perhaps I may be able to help you. The potatoes are apt to be very muddy if you can dig them later." He wanted to know how many acres we had left to dig. When I told him, he said, "Spaulding Rose potatoes are bringing a premium price over the other white varieties. On the acre and a half that you have, try your best to get them out if the snow goes off." He had an empty bin and allowed the potatoes could be turned down there to dry and when dry, he would ship them for me.

I hurried home and explained to my father and brothers about what I had been doing all of the morning. My father said, "I'm going to get ready for the woods. The chances of getting those potatoes out of the ground are very poor."

It was noontime. We had dinner and I said, as Dr. Hagerthy used to say many times, "Where there is life there is hope." I continued on with, "So, let's get a shovel and one of the old hand hoe diggers, bring the truck and some barrels and let's go down and make a test on the Spaulding Rose potatoes." Everyone agreed to make a try. We made a test by shoveling off the snow. The ground had not frozen and neither had the snow melted to cause the potatoes to be muddy. Boy, what a surprise it was to all of us. I stated, "I'll shovel off the snow if you all will pitch in and help with the rest of the work." Everybody said, "It is worth a try so let's get started." I shoveled, my father began digging and everyone became interested. Those big Spaulding Rose were coming out almost dry and at the rate of more than 100 barrels per acre. As I remember, we managed to get two truck loads that afternoon and got things ready for the next day. Mr. Kenney sent word back "Those potatoes are of the best. Make an effort to get them all out."

That night, my father allowed he could dig the potatoes by hand in a few days if I'd shovel off the snow. I said, "It is hard work digging by hand so let's go to Frenchville and find a man to come and help with the digging." The name Simon Beaulieu was suggested for he had been an expert at digging potatoes by hand in the years gone by. Simon still had potatoes in the ground but he could not quite see shoveling off the snow. He allowed he would come anyway and help for a day.

When daylight came the next morning, we were all there ready to see if the rest of the potatoes could be salvaged. I brought along a horse and a stone drag to bring the potatoes out of the field with. About three barrels at a time could be brought to an area where the truck could be loaded. I peeled off my coat and began shoveling. The weather was cool and the snow was not melting. This made things better for us. I managed to keep enough snow cleared off so that Father and Mr. Beaulieu could keep digging. Byron drove the truck and hauled the potatoes to the siding. The other brothers, Alonzo and Luther, picked potatoes and hauled them with the horse to the barnyard, which had been cleared of snow the day before, and loaded the truck.

It was a surprise to see how nice things worked out, although I was almost petered out when we got out all of those potatoes. We had dug more than 150 barrels in less than two days. Mr. Kenney dumped them into a bin to dry some more. In a few days, he sent word for me to come down to the siding. I drove down and he showed me how good the potatoes looked. He stated, "You old time farmers up there know just how to manage when things get really tough. There is not much waste as I can see. I can get you about $6.00 per barrel. How does that sound?" That sounded so good. I just said, "Mr. Kenney, you use your own judgment. Sell them all for the best price that you can and take out your pay or commission for all of your bother."

A few days later I drove to the siding and found that Mr. Kenney had sold the potatoes. He deducted his pay for handling them and gave me a check for nearly $1,000. I never felt richer and felt it had been a wise move returning to the farm.

About the time we finished digging the Spaulding Rose, the weather changed. It began to rain. I felt sort of guilty because I hadn't suggested we dig some of Father's potatoes instead of mine. The rain took off all of the snow and the sun shone. It seemed brighter than ever before. The weather continued to be very good for several days. This was a wonderful Indian summer. As soon as the soil had dried, we tackled digging my father's potatoes with the horse drawn digger. It was at least two days longer before the ground was dry enough to go in the fields again with the truck so the stone drag was once more brought in to use. A pair of horses was used and about five barrels of potatoes could be hauled on the drag at one time. They were hauled to the edge of the field or the farm road and loaded on the truck or wagon. Byron hauled all he could to the siding with the truck each day. We hauled potatoes in with the wagon and dumped them in every nook and corner. The basement of the barn was papered up with sheathing paper, to keep out the frost, and potatoes were stored there temporarily until they could be hauled to market.

In a few days, more than 800 barrels of those "gold nuggets" were harvested. The market had improved from day to day. The crop mortgage had all been paid off. A good supply of provisions had been brought in for the winter. There were some 700 barrels of potatoes stored in the home cellar. I had a small bin containing 49 barrels of round whites stored there, too.

What a change in the morale of my father and brothers in such a short time. It was often mentioned, "It is a good thing that Phin was here to encourage us to 'not give up.'"

During the next few days, in which the weather continued to be good, plowing was done to get ready for the 1926 crop. Then, if I remember correctly, Byron drove truck and my father and I cleaned out the potatoes that were in cold "storage." The market held good.

Some round whites sold for better than $5.00 per barrel. We all pitched in and cut some ten cords of hard wood for winter use here at home.

One day, in the latter part of October, Mr. Collins of Caribou came and had a talk with my father about getting started in the woods. Stumpage had been obtained on the so called "Mile Block" right here in Castle Hill. A day was set to "get going." Several local woodsmen, living in the French settlement, were hired and, for several days, a few drove from Caribou each day to help build the camp and a hovel. These men were all experienced lumberjacks. In a very few days, a hovel, big enough to accommodate four pair of horses with a lean-to on one side for storing grain and baled hay, was completed. The cook house was ready for use at about the same time. Next, a bunk house, large enough to accommodate about thirty men, was constructed.

There was a space of about twelve feet between the cook house and the bunk house. This space was closed in on one side and covered with a roof. This area was known as the "dingle." Provisions for the winter were stored here. Salt pork was brought in by the barrel and so was molasses. Flour was brought in, several barrels at a time. Sides of beef and salt codfish were brought in by the quintal. Potatoes and other supplies used were kept in the cook house. Tables, made from rough boards, and benches of hewn logs, could easily accommodate thirty to forty men at one time.

About a week from the time we first started, Bert Randall, who had cooked at my father's camps for many winters, came. The lumberjacks moved into the bunk house and I began my duties as the cookee and bookkeeper. The cook and I slept in the cook house in a bunk we had made in one corner of the cook room. Mr. Randall occupied the lower bunk and I took the upper deck. We were provided with two stoves that were placed back to back. Tin stove pipes extended from each stove up through the roof.

The walls of the building were made of round logs and the roofs were made of boards and covered with tarred paper. Spaces between the logs were chinked with moss.

Part of my job was to prepare the fuel wood each day to be used in both the bunk house and in the cook camp. Logs were brought to the camp yard and then I took over. Most every day, Joe Theriault, the filer, would come and help me saw the logs into sixteen inch blocks. This was a great help and sometimes we were assisted by one of the men from the woods crew.

This winter, of 1925-26, worked out well for all of us. There was not very much snow. It was a down hill haul to the river where the logs were piled on brows by the river bank until spring. When the ice melted, they would be rolled into the river and driven to Caribou for processing at the Collins sawmill. This winter proved to be a prosperous one for the Collins' Lumber Company.

Mildred was helping my mother for her board. Things were working out for the best for all of us.

Cutting logs continued on through the winter until about the middle of February. At that time, an unusually heavy snowfall brought the operation to a close and we "broke camp."

I had earned about $350 in wages working in the woods that winter. In addition to our wages, Bert Randall, the cook, Walter Bolstridge, the stumpage scalar, and myself had earned some extra money trapping weasels and mink. The pelts of those fur bearers brought a good price. Mr. Bolstridge had a few traps and I purchased a dozen or so more. Mr. Bolstridge scaled for two other camps up Beaver Brook and had a chance to set traps along the way. Bert Randall claimed to know all the tricks of trapping so his part was to show me how and where to place the traps. Walter did the skinning and stretched the pelts for us. Due to the fact that we handled food, Bert and I could not do this.

Weasels were always around the dingle looking for meat scraps. As for mink, we made our best catches along a little nearby brook or by the river.

I checked the traps around noontime, around four o'clock in the morning with a lantern or after my work at the camp was finished for the day. The amount we received for the weasels varied from $1.00 to $3.50. The mountain weasels, with their black tipped tails, brought in the higher price.

We sold our pelts to Mack Morin of Ashland and he always said, "I'm paying the 'top price.'" Bert Randall and I divided our share of the "take" which was about $50 for each of us. The trapping had been interesting and, as Bert said when we settled up, "Boy Phin, what a fist full of money."

Chapter 18

Family and Farm

Soon after breaking camp, my father suggested that a road be broken out to the back of my lot and that we begin getting out lumber so that Mildred and I could have a home built.

Mildred and I drew up a plan for a bungalow type house, twenty-four by thirty-four feet. A house of this size, with a good stone cellar, would be sufficient for our needs.

Frank Chandler was now devoting all of his time to carpenter work. He looked over our plan and prepared a list of the various dimensions of lumber that would be needed. After looking over his list, I felt it would be best to increase the size of the pieces by one inch. That is to make 8" x 8" sills where he listed 7" x 7". The 2" x 7", I increased to 2" x 8". For rafters, he listed 2" x 4" and this was changed to 2" x 5".

As the snow was very deep, it would be a tough job getting a snow road broken out to where the lumber would be cut. We decided Byron's team would be the best for this job. About the 25th of February, the team was hitched to a bobsled and my father, Byron, and I made a start. The distance out to the back of the lot was about one-half of a mile and our first trip out was very tough. Father stayed out there, cruising out trees, finding roads to reach them and deciding the best and quickest way to cut the lumber needed, while Byron and I made the second trip to break out the snow road. It was rough on the horses making the first trip, but was much easier the second time out. This second trip out, I cut some small bushes and on the way back placed them at intervals along the way so if it should storm, we could easily find the road.

The next day, we began work in dead earnest to cut and haul out the logs. The snow had packed and hardened overnight and we had a pretty good snow road. This time we brought along the second team and my brother, Luther. It was a great day and with Father's know-how, logs were being moved out at a good rate. We chained the logs to a bobsled and dragged out three or more each trip.

A landing place was broken out on the side of the slope where the logs could be piled. It was surprising to see how fast the four of us could get the logs out. The house plan would require some 12,000 board feet and we decided to cut extra, if time and weather permitted, so a goal of 14,000 board feet was set.

After a couple of days, our father made the wise suggestion that we haul potatoes on warm days and cut logs on the cold days. This idea worked out well and we were soon busy with both projects.

Not long after the first of March, it was estimated that we had cut and yarded enough logs to saw out at least 14,000 board feet. About the middle of the month, a pause was taken in hauling potatoes to cut and pack ice for summer use.

At father's home a bin was constructed beneath, and in the shade of a large maple tree. The ice bin was about twelve feet square and some seven feet high. The walls of the bin were made of boards or mill slabs. About a foot of sawdust was placed on the bottom of the bin. Two heavy posts, about three feet apart, were set in one side. This was the "doorway" and was boarded up as the packing took place.

Most years, there would already be a road broken open to the river, where logs or pulp wood had been hauled, that we used. Some years, several neighbors would "join forces" and we'd have an ice cutting bee.

At the river, an area of fifty or seventy-five square feet was cleared of snow and a hole chiseled in one corner. Not having an ice saw, we used the same crosscut saws we used in felling trees, with one handle removed. The ice was cut in twelve or fifteen inch squares and would be, most years, twenty or more inches thick. Cutting ice was slow work even when two or more saws were put into use at the same time.

The cakes of ice were pulled from the water, as fast as they were cut, with large ice tongs. As to how many would be hauled at one time depended on the condition of the road but usually six or eight cakes made up a load. The cakes of ice were "dumped off" at the ice house and, when it was decided that there was plenty to fill the bin, cutting stopped. A summer's supply of ice could be harvested in two or three mornings.

The packing of the ice was always interesting. The cakes were placed close together on the sawdust in the bottom of the bin. An area, of about one foot, was left all around the sides to be filled with sawdust. A layer of ice was placed and the cracks between chinked with snow. A layer of snow was added and water poured over all. Heavy slush (snow and water) was stirred in a pail and, with a shingle, was put in the side cracks between the cakes of ice. This procedure took time but, when completed, there was just one solid cake of ice and it was practically free of air pockets.

Next, a new layer of snow was added, wet down with water and, in the same manner, the second and third layers were packed in the bin. Sawdust was used to fill the areas around the sides of the bin. Sometimes we used sawdust from piles where portable mills had sawed the year before. In these piles, a crust, a few inches thick, had to be broken away and then there was plenty of good fresh sawdust. Other times, we hauled the sawdust from the Mapleton sawmill.

Cutting and packing ice was heavy muscular work but, when summer came, the ice box could be kept full and many savings could be made in the grocery bill. Every Sunday, a freezer of homemade ice cream was made. My, what a tasty treat.

I do not remember just when the packing of ice ended at my father's home, but Mildred and I always had a good supply of ice for summer use until we purchased a refrigerator in 1947. About two years later, we bought an eighteen cubic foot freezer. Each of these appliances helped a great deal in preserving foods and cutting the food budget all through the years.

One day, about the 10th of April, I phoned Mr. Hadley Bragdon of Ashland and asked if he would come sometime this spring, with his portable saw, and saw my lumber. He agreed to come "just as soon as the roads are fit to move on." About this time, we had a storm which left several inches of new snow that enabled Mr. Bragdon to come down with two teams loaded with his mill equipment. We shoveled snow away from the log yard. The mill was set up, leveled and made ready to use. There was not room, here at my place, to stable the horses, but it was a fairly warm day so, covered with horse blankets, they were okay. Mr. Bragdon and his helper had brought their dinner and, along in the afternoon, they returned to Ashland. It was about 11½ miles to his home. I have often thought about how hard people worked, back in those days, to make a living.

It was on a Saturday that the mill equipment was moved down and set up. We told Mr. Bragdon that we would tend the mill, get logs up to the carriage and take away the sawed lumber and slabs. He allowed that, if the weather would permit him to saw, he would be down bright and early Monday morning.

Monday morning came and it was a nice April day. The mill was in operation by nine o'clock. After that first day, sawing began earlier in the morning. Room was made available for Mr. Bragdon and his helper to stay at Father's home until the lumber was sawed. At noon, I would go up to the house and bring down a good warm lunch which Mildred and my mother had prepared.

By the end of the week, the lumber had all been sawed and the necessary planning had been finished. On Saturday, Mr. Bragdon had some of his boys bring down the teams and the mill equipment was loaded and taken back to Ashland to another job that was waiting for him. I had shoveled off a grassy area, near where our house was to be built, and the lumber was properly stacked there so it would season as much as possible before it was time to use it.

After the winter "snow roads" broke up, there were still a few more potatoes to be hauled. We left these to be hauled, after the road had dried and settled, with the truck.

When all the potatoes had been sold, we never felt so rich. I had managed to sell my forty-nine barrels for $9.00 per barrel. My father and brothers sold theirs for about the some price. Mildred and I had $2,300 in the bank. My father purchased new seed and paid cash for the fertilizer to be used on the 1926 crop. We all anxiously waited for the new planting season to begin.

Boy wasn't I busy that summer of 1926. I often thought of what my father had told Penn Craig back in 1911. "We want Phin to go to high school so he won't have to work for a living," and again I'd remind myself of our class motto… "No reward without labor."

By farming time, I had fixed up the old shed that was on my place with some new boards, hauled six tons of fertilizer, arranged for about 30 barrels of certified seconds to use in planting the new crop of potatoes, bought enough good seed oats to plant about two acres and enough wheat to sow one acre. I also bought a little pig and a few garden seeds. Now, Mildred and I were ready again to try our luck as tillers of the soil.

My folks were especially happy this spring. The fertilizer had been bought with cash and there were no bills hanging over. A few new potato barrels had been purchased. What a contrast from the year before when my father was ready to "call it quits."

Planting season came about the usual time and things went along very well. I used three of my six acres of plowed land for grain and three for potatoes. In order to plant six acres of potatoes again this year, I went to the DeMerchant farm, which my father owned, and planted three more acres.

Just as soon as the planting was finished, Chub, the little horse I had used on the mail line, was brought down and kept in the shed. Every minute that I had to spare, Chub was hitched to the stone drag. There had been a house on this place that had burned so a cellar was all dug. My father and brothers had come with pick axes and shovels and we cleaned out the old cellar. We enlarged it enough to make room for a stone wall, all the way around, that would fit our plan for a house of 24 by 34 feet. There were stone walls and rock piles most anywhere from which suitable rocks could be obtained to use in building a cellar wall. With Chub, I hauled rocks after supper and on days when the weather was "not fit" to work in the potatoes.

There was a patch, of an acre or more, where dozens of large flat rocks could be dug up. My brother Luther came often and helped me with these. A pair of horses had to be used. A chain could be hooked around many of the rocks and pulled out by the horses. Others, Luther would shovel the dirt away and we would pry them out.

I had Gus Richardson, a stonemason, come and make an estimate as to whether we had placed enough stones around the cellar for a stone wall. Mr. Richardson allowed we had plenty of the rougher type and suggested I find some flat stones so that he could make a double wall, with an air space, for the underpinning on the three sides. He allowed the fourth side, on the back, didn't matter because it wouldn't show and probably would be banked up more anyway.

Mr. Richardson could not come, at that time, to start work on the cellar walls but he allowed he would come soon. He said, "Have some hydrated lime and cement on hand and plenty of washed sand ready to use."

The sand was hauled from the river, from about where we had cut the ice. Wet sand weighed about 600 to 700 lbs. per barrel and only two or three barrels could be hauled at one time. My father came along on the first trip out and helped find a suitable place to obtain the sand. After that first trip, I went alone. I made several trips so we would be sure to have enough.

Mr. Richardson was very busy that summer with so many jobs that he didn't get started on mine right away. He was building fireplaces for people around Portage Lake. Fireplaces built from stone required a special tact and Mr. Richardson was well qualified to do that kind of masonry work.

"Gus" Burby was also a stonemason and his son-in-law, James Breslette, was his assistant. When Mr. Richardson got around to doing my cellar, he and his brother Frank came. With his permission, I also hired Mr. Burby and his son-in-law to assist. The four of them put up stakes and strings and work began in earnest. Mr. Richardson and his brother, Frank, found the time to come and help with this because Mr. Burby allowed he was not qualified to make an underpinning like we had planned.

A flat wall underpinning, about eighteen inches high, was made using flat rocks with the smooth side outside and the rougher side inside. We found that I did not have enough flat rocks to do a good job, but Mr. Breslette had some at his home and sold them to me. This was a great help. A few trips to his home, about two miles away, and I had hauled enough flat stones to finish the wall.

After grading around the wall, up to the underpinning, the stone wall showed up like a picture. The dead air space between the stones helped to keep out the frost in winter. This was a great way to build a wall. What a wonderful job those old timers did on work of this nature. Here, after 48 years of service, that stone wall, built by those four men, still stands as a monument to their memory.

It was now getting along in July and we were ready for the carpenter. Frank Chandler came, allowed the masons had done a fine job and found the foundation measurements were okay for the house we wanted built. He was busy at the time building a house for Mildred's brother, Lawrence, but he allowed he would be able to build ours before cold weather set in. He told us we would be eating our meals in our new home by the middle of October. How happy Mildred and I were, for we were anxious to be living in a place of our own.

Me with my team, Chub and Bess.

During the summer, things went along on schedule but it was certain that we would need another horse and more machinery before another year.

After Frank Chandler came and began work on the house, I mentioned to him the need of another horse. He said, "I can fix you up. I have a horse, just about the size of yours that I will sell you for $100." The horse was at his son Emmon's home and was only used part of the time. One evening, Frank went with me to look at the horse. I brought it home on a trial basis and fixed up an old harness. The new horse's name was Bess. Chub and Bess worked along so good together, that I paid Frank the $100 and now had my own team.

There wasn't much room in the shed for the team, the pig, and the cow and there wasn't much available space in the back for hay. There was lots of hay on the DeMerchant farm and my father and brothers helped me bring over several loads and stack it. Stacking hay was a new experience for me, however; others, without barns for storage, were doing it, so why couldn't I? Three poles were placed into the ground. Hay was placed around each of these twelve foot high poles. Father showed me what to do. He said, "Keep it well trodden down all the way up and it will keep wonderful. Then find an old piece of something that won't leak water and place it around the pole, at the top of the stack, and you will have just as good hay as we have in the barn." Father pitched hay onto the stack from the wagon. He would say, "Place it out. Don't be afraid…keep treading…pack it down all you can…be careful not to get out far enough to fall off the stack…keep it level and keep treading."

My, but this was interesting. Three good stacks of hay were made and it kept very well. When the space I had for hay inside the shed became empty, I would cut some off the side of one of the stacks and refill it. This worked out fine and I had the choicest of hay, all through the winter, to feed the cow and the horses.

We managed very well with the hoeing and spraying with the three teams. About August 20th, we were harvesting grain. When it was dry enough, the old hand thresher was set up. Part of the grain was threshed in the barn at my father's place so we could save the straw for bedding for the livestock but most of it was threshed right out-of-doors near the grain fields.

From my one acre of wheat, I harvested some twenty bushels. The yield was so good on my two acres of oats that I hardly knew what to do with them. I harvested over 100 bushels and, since I did not have any storage on my place, a bin in the grainery on the home place was made available for me to use.

After the grain was all harvested, it was time to haul out the manure again. I was very happy to get going and used my team to do the job. I forgot all about this chore being a tedious one and how I had despised it back fifteen years ago.

Before the potato harvest was completed, Mr. Chandler had our new home ready for Mildred and I to move into. Cedar shingles had been purchased from a saw mill at Portage Lake and pine clapboards from Bert Flint, of Ashland, who owned and operated a clapboard mill at Little Machias Stream. Mr. Chandler had done a marvelous job and had worked most of the time by himself. He allowed if he could work alone, more would be accomplished in a day.

When Mildred and I moved in, the inside was not finished. We bought a cook stove from the Montgomery Ward catalog for around $40.00. Later, they refunded $4.00 to us, stating the stove had been on sale and we had not taken advantage of the sale. Our table was made by the carpenter, out of rough lumber. A roll of sheathing paper was bought to use, temporarily, on the partitions. With the many dishes, etc. that we had received on our wedding day and with the bedding we acquired while we were living in Caribou, we were "all set" to begin farm life in our new home in Castle Hill.

During the potato harvest, we trucked and sold as many potatoes as we could right out of the fields. The price we received was nothing like we'd received the year before but with a good yield of fine quality potatoes, we all did very well. I stored about 200 barrels of potatoes, to market when spring came, under the new house. My father and brothers had their home cellars filled to the cover.

After the harvest and the plowing was done, a few days were taken off to "batten up" around the buildings for winter. At our new home, I drove stakes and fastened boards and mill slabs all around, about a foot out from the wall, and filled this space with sawdust, right up to the first clapboard. This required a lot of work although, with potatoes in the cellar and new fill all around the wall, it seemed the best thing to do to keep out the frost.

One sunny afternoon, Mildred was out locating a place where we would plant our garden the next spring. She observed me banking the house and complimented me for the good work I was doing and made this statement, "Be sure and make a good banking and have plenty of wood split up and covered for we are going to have company sometime this winter...probably about March." I was curious to learn more about the company, when she added, "Let's hope it will be a boy then you will have some help, in a few years, on the farm."

For many years, it had been the custom, at my home, to get in a good stock of supplies for winter, like salt pork, molasses, beans, and flour. My twenty bushels of wheat was taken to the mill where I used to work and made into flour. Both the white flour and the graham flour were put into new seamless bags and the bran we brought home in a grain sack. From this grist, Mildred stored away more than enough flour to last until the next harvest came along. A few pounds of cream of wheat had been saved out at the mill. This provided us with part of our cereal for the winter. Quite often Mildred made rolls from the graham flour and nothing ever tasted better than graham rolls with fried fresh pork.

When we moved into our home, my father had given us one of his cows. This provided us with milk and cream. Mildred had purchased a churn and butter tray and was making our butter.

It had been the practice, at my home, to butcher on Thanksgiving Day. By this time, it was cold enough to keep the meat in cold storage. Father was working in the woods for Mr. Collins but found the time to be home for Thanksgiving dinner and help butcher the hogs and beef kind. The little pig I had purchased the spring before had grown very big and weighed about 150 pounds when it was dressed out. Most of the pork was taken to Cyr's slaughter house and smoked, providing us with ham and bacon. My, how rich we were when winter set in.

During the winter, my brothers and I cut fuel wood with a drag saw. We sawed it into 16" blocks and piled it near the roadside to season. This was to be sold in the summer and fall.

Winter passed…most of the weather was rough. March came and our "company" arrived on the seventh day of the month. It was a girl and we were both very happy. I allowed it was best that we had a girl and said, "In a short while you will have some much needed help with the housework. My brothers are helping me. This is for the best." Our "company" was named Myrtle.

When the spring of 1927 arrived, my father suggested we "stick our necks out" and replace the old worn-out machinery with new. One bright morning in April, we all went to Washburn with a double team to see about buying new machinery.

Ernest Woodman was a dealer for the International Harvester Machine Co. and we outlined our needs to him. After listing our needs: a tractor, a blower threshing machine, a new truck, a spring tooth harrow for the tractor, and a few smaller tools, Mr. Woodman quoted the price of $6,400. This seemed like quite a lot of money to us, but, if we were to farm, the new machinery was a "must." Father told Mr. Woodman that we would go into a huddle at the restaurant, have lunch, and give further consideration to buying the amount of machinery as listed

While having lunch, Father suggested that we increase our acreage of potatoes to sixty acres, share the crop and purchase the machinery under the name of J.O. Ellis & Sons. This seemed agreeable to all and we returned to Woodman's store to inquire as to what terms of payment could be made.

The terms were something like this, we were to pay $2,400 in cash and make a note for the balance, at 6% interest, to be extended over a three year period. Mr. Woodman allowed that he would like to buy 100 cords of seasoned wood each year. He would pay $8.00 a cord, haul it himself, and we could apply this money on the note; this sounded good so the deal was closed. As soon as the snow was off the roads, Harry Maynard, who was employed by Mr. Woodman, began delivering the machinery.

During this spring of 1927, the partnership farming began. Byron was to have a one-fourth interest and I the same. Our father and the younger brothers were to have one-half interest.

Jasper Ellis (far left) with sons (from l. to r.): Phin, Luther, Alonzo, & Wilson

We all went into a huddle to see who would operate the various machines. I was chosen to operate the 10-20 tractor that we had purchased and was given permission to use the tractor and work for others harrowing when time permitted. The revenue received for this would be applied to the note at Mr. Woodman's.

Byron had married Josephine Welts and they had begun housekeeping in an old house on the DeMerchant farm. The old house would not be suitable for the cold winter months so we all got busy and cut lumber so he could build a new home.

The DeMerchant farm was acquired by my parents from John DeMerchant, who worked for us several years and later made his home with them until the time of his death in the spring of 1926.

After the crop was planted, the same portable mill that had sawed my lumber came and sawed Byron's. During the summer, we all pitched in and helped Byron build a good stone cellar wall. By winter, he was living in his new home. The old house was torn down and some of the lumber saved. It could be used later in many ways. There was a good barn already on the farm. Byron had a good team of horses, of which he was very proud, and was a natural born teamster. He was given a cow, bought a pig and some hens and "set up business" for himself on the DeMerchant farm.

Water, on this farm, was obtained from a hand dug well. It had to be brought up in a pail fastened to a rope. This was a slow process, especially if one was in a hurry. The stock required a lot of water and a barrel or so was needed in the house on wash day. So a well was drilled, near the new house, and a hand pump installed.

In the fall, I began threshing for others when time permitted. The new threshing machine had a blower attached that blew straw up in the lofts of the barns or into stacks in the fields. A machine like this was entirely new to our area and every farmer was anxious to have us thresh for him. I threshed from John Berry's, four miles up on the Ashland Road, down to the Jones' Brothers farm on the State Road, a distance of about seven miles. The machine was kept on the job until snow came and it had to be housed for the winter.

The charge for threshing was six cents per bushel. A good day's work would be 500 to 700 bushels, but, when the grain was good and dry and we were tended good, I have threshed as many as 1000 bushels in one day. The work was very dusty at times; however, the income helped to reduce the amount of the note at Mr. Woodman's.

One of the best features about threshing for our neighbors was the bounteous dinners that were served to the threshers. At no other time would there be more good food served. We had chicken stews, roast pork, good old fashioned vegetable boiled dinners, etc., etc. If prizes had been given for the best dinners, I'd have voted for Mrs. Simon Beaulieu's. I operated the thresher every fall, except one, up to and including the fall of 1946. During these nineteen years, we always threshed at Beaulieu's. Mrs. Beaulieu always had a large kettle of fresh chicken stew with heaps of dumplings in it. About 8:30 or 9 o'clock in the morning, chickens would be flying in all directions with Mrs. Beaulieu in hot pursuit. From the taste of the stew, I'm sure she caught at least two of them.

The winter of 1927-28, we cut fuel wood again to sell. The summer of 1928, everything went right along on schedule. Organized and working together, it seemed we could accomplish more each day.

The winter of 1928-29, we were cutting wood again as usual. During planting time, that spring of 1929, Byron seemed to have contacted a cold. He didn't seem to be recovering so the Doctor was called in. By July 1st, the Doctor had called to see Byron several times and suggested he leave all of the work to others and take a good long rest. Byron had tuberculosis. A bed was placed on the veranda of his home so he could sleep in the open air and get well sooner. This method of treatment did not work out as well as the Doctor thought it should and the State Nurse suggested it would be wise for Byron to get a room at the State Sanatorium in Presque Isle and take treatments from Dr. Carter.

Everything that Dr. Carter could do was done but nothing helped. My brother, Byron, passed away at the Sanatorium on November 4, 1929, at the age of 31. He was survived by his wife, Josephine, and a small daughter, Hope, who was much too young to remember her father.

We had all pitched in that summer to keep up his end of the farm operation and made sure he got his share. His passing was very hard on our father and was equally as sad for Mother and us brothers and sisters.

During the fall of 1929, Dr. Hagerthy called to check on us once in a while. One day, about the first of December, he whispered in my ear, "Phinagin, we are going to bring you a Christmas present and this time, it will be a boy." Christmas time came but the Christmas present didn't arrive until two days later. I inquired of the Doctor, "What is the verdict this time?" He replied, "Damn it, Phinagin, it is another girl." I said, "Well, that is fine. We all will be happy just the same. Mildred will have more help and Myrtle will have a playmate." Our Christmas present was named Elaine.

I was desperately in need of a barn in which to keep the horses, cow, pig, etc. In early 1930, my father allowed it was time for me to be waking up to the idea of building one. My brother and I were cutting fuel wood to season and sell the next winter. My father had been taking charge of a lumber camp for Mr. Collins and they finished hauling logs to the landing about the middle of March.

The barn raising.

He suggested, since I had plenty of lumber on my lot with which to build a barn, that we should break open a snow road and cut it. The weather was good and we all got busy cutting and hauling. In a very short time, we cut and yarded some 18,000 FBM logs, enough to build a 36ft. x 40ft. barn

Later on , Mr. Hadley Bragdon came with his portable mill and sawed the lumber and I hired Mr. Laurel Kennedy, a carpenter noted for his know-how in building barns, to come and tell us how much lumber to cut and in what dimensions. We all helped haul the sawed lumber to the area where the barn was to be built and Mr. Kennedy went to work framing the barn as the lumber was being sawed.

It took only about four days to saw all the lumber we would need. About the first week in May, Mr. Kennedy had finished framing the barn and said, "I will be ready to have a barn raising any day now." A day was set for this and our neighbors and friends were invited to the "bee." Mildred and I arranged to have plenty of food on hand for the old fashioned barn raising. It was understood that the raising would begin at 12 o'clock noon, that we would do as much as we could in the afternoon and enjoy a baked bean supper at 5 o'clock.

About twenty-five men came to help. At the appointed time, Mr. Kennedy began giving orders as to how and where to place the many pieces of lumber. Almost like magic, the barn was erected as far as the rafters. Then Mr. Kennedy took the men who could climb and put them to work on the upper part.

By five o'clock supper was ready. Tables had been arranged out-of-doors and we all enjoyed a traditional barn raising supper. Many of the men complimented Mr. Kennedy on the fine job he had done in framing. There was not a hitch at any time. The auger holes always matched and the wooden pins he had prepared fit just right. I thanked everyone for giving me a lift and all went home happy to think they had an opportunity to participate in another barn raising.

Mildred Ellis with the Ellis children, Myrtle, Elaine, and Malcolm.

This was the last barn raising, that I can remember of, in Castle Hill.

After the barn raising was over, I found I was short on lumber. Andrew McLellan had some cut which he sold to me. As the mill was still there, Mr. Bragdon came and sawed it for me. Andrew was a handy man at carpenter work, so I hired him to help Mr. Kennedy finish boarding and shingling the roof of the barn. I managed to make the stalls and do other inside work myself during the summer.

In that spring of 1930, Byron's widow did not care to continue farming and Father went to the Federal Land Bank and obtained a loan. All of our properties were mortgaged to buy back the farm from Byron's widow.

New arrangements were made about sharing the crops. Luther had been included in on Father's share but he now took over Byron's one-fourth interest. Father continued to have one-half interest. Three other brothers, Alonzo now 16, Forest, 13 and Wilson, 10 were now taking part in Father's interest in the crops. This arrangement continued on until the "cropping season" of 1946.

After the farming began, in the spring of 1933, a girl was hired to assist Mildred with the house work. June 1st arrived and Mildred said, "Better call the Doctor today." I called him on the telephone and he talked with her. I was put back on the phone and the Doctor said, "Better have Mrs. Pulcifer brought over."

Mrs. Pulcifer was a midwife and I made the trip to Mapleton and brought her over. Later in the day, she came out to where I was planting the garden and said, "I have called the Doctor. He will be along shortly."

An hour or so after his arrival, Dr. Hagerthy came running out to the garden, clapping his hands, grinning from ear to ear and said, "You're a lucky man, Phinagin, I'm leaving a boy with you today. Now you will have some help here on the farm. You know, boys grow up fast."

Mildred and I were very happy. She had selected the name Malcolm in hopes the new baby would be a boy. "Okay," I said, "The name Malcolm suits me right to a "T." We called the little fellow "Mackie." Myrtle and Elaine were happy to have a little brother for a playmate.

The last few years of our partnership farming, the government limited the number of acres of potatoes that could be planted. They determined the amount we could plant be the acres of cleared land that each farmer had. This limitation caused our acreage to be set back. There was only six acres for potatoes on my lot and I did not feel it was hardly right for me to cause the others to share their allotted acreage with me. Our son, Malcolm, was fourteen and ready to enter high school. I suggested to my father that Mackie take over a share, of what my six acres would allow, and I would turn all of my interest in the machinery over to them. They could help Mackie get interested in farming and have the returns from what could be grown on the six acres. This was agreeable and I dropped farming to take on the full time job as Town Manager for Mapleton and Castle Hill. My last year farming was 1946.

Malcolm became very interested in farming. Throughout his high school years he was a very active member of the Future Farmers of America. He served as State President of this organization before being named National Vice-President serving the North Atlantic region. Mom and I were very happy to accompany him to the Silver Anniversary Convention of the Future Farmers of America held in Kansas City, Missouri, October 12th through the 15th of 1953.

Family and Farm

Chapter 19

My Political Career

My memories of the old time town meetings, held in Castle Hill, go back to the years before my high school days.

They were always held the last Monday in March. The voters came from all parts of the town to the Grange Hall and put their teams up for the day in the Grange stable. The meetings were held on the ground floor of the hall and dinner was prepared by the women members of the Castle Hill Grange and served in the dining room below. Baked beans were usually the main course and there was always a good supply of homemade bread, dairy butter, salads, pickles, cakes, pies and other goodies. Coffee was steeped in old fashioned tin coffee makers and cream and sugar was never forgotten.

The meeting was called to order at ten o'clock by the town clerk, who then proceeded to read the several articles of the warrant. A moderator was elected to preside at the meeting and was sworn in by the clerk. The next article on the warrant was to elect a town clerk for the ensuing year. The clerk elected was then sworn in by the moderator.

Next came article three, the choosing of all other town officers, and here was when the fireworks began. Many of the voters didn't like how the town business had been carried on during the past year by those in office and came with chips on their shoulders. They aired their grudges, found fault, swore, tongue lashed, ridiculed, etc. This continued right up to dinner time. The moderator had to be a real diplomat to get all of the officers elected before noon.

Dinner was always served at twelve o'clock sharp. The moderator would declare a one hour recess and everyone would file down to the dining room. They would peel off their sweaters or jackets, mingle with each other, shake hands and talk about their problems at home during the past year. Apparently all grievances were forgotten during the lunch hour.

The meeting reconvened, by the call of the moderator, at one o'clock sharp. The afternoon was spent in making appropriations for the officers' salaries, schools, roads, interest, etc. In those days, never was an attempt made to prepare a budget. Each article was discussed separately and the money appropriated would always be the sum approved by the majority of the voters present.

It was in this atmosphere that I began my political career.

It was in 1919, after the First World War, that I was elected Third Selectman. I served with First Selectman, Mel Dudley, and Second Selectman, Flavious Porter. It was always understood that the First Selectman was to be the chairman of the board and his home was where the town records, with the exception of those of the town clerk, were kept. The records show that I received $89.25 as my salary for the first year.

In 1920, at the annual town meeting, I was elected First Selectman. C.G.R. Chandler was elected Second Selectman and Ervin L. Dudley was elected third.

In 1921, I was again elected First Selectman, Mr. Chandler was Second Selectman again and Guilford Smith was elected third.

My salary for the year of 1920 was $200. In 1921 it was $250.

After the town meetings, on the first Monday in April, the Selectmen, who were also assessors, would visit each taxpayer in the town and take inventory. The school census was taken at the same time.

Taking inventory took the better part of three days. I will always cherish the memories of the dinners we had at some of the homes. Two years in a row, it came out just right for us to have dinner at Fred Johnson's. His wife, Fern, put on a dinner that was fit for a king. For fifty cents each, we had all we could eat. One time we ate at my mother's. She also loaded the table with a variety of foods and we ate to our fill.

One day, in each of the three years, Mrs. Granville (Eleanor) Cook was called and told she could expect us for dinner. In 1921, we were about one half hour early arriving at the Cook's home on the Haystack Road. Eleanor suggested that we go to the barn and take inventory while the dinner finished cooking. She said, "Granville is out there doing the chores. By the time you finish, dinner will be cooked and ready to serve piping hot."

Charles, Guilford, and I went to the barn and found Granville feeding the stock their noon meal. It was noticed that the hens had nests in several places. That day I learned Guilford liked to suck eggs. He would pick up an egg, step around a corner out of sight and suck it. He continued doing this all the while we were taking inventory. Granville never noticed what was taking place. Just how many eggs Guilford put under his belt that day will never be known.

As we filed in from the barn, Mrs. Cook said, "Now boys, take off your duds and dinner will be on in about two shakes." She handed Granville a kettle and commanded, "Run back to the barn and gather some eggs." He obeyed her command and went to the barn on the run. He did not return as quickly as Eleanor had hoped so she went to the door and hollered at the top of her voice, "Come on, hurry! Dinner will be cold if you don't get a wiggle on." Granville came hurrying back saying, "Eleanor, I couldn't find a damned egg. Can't figure out what has happened. The hens have been laying good. I just don't understand what has happened today."

Mrs. Cook said, "Well, come boys sit right down at the table. We will eat the ham anyway, eggs or no eggs." Guilford kept his face straight but it must have been quite an effort. He never looked up and before we had finished eating, he began to urge Charles and I to hurry. He said, "You know boys, we still have many places to call today."

Mrs. Cook had prepared a wonderful meal but she kept apologizing for "shortchanging" us on the eggs. We were grateful for all the trouble she had gone to serving us such a fine dinner for fifty cents each. Today, such a meal would cost six times that amount.

I was living and working in Mapleton at the time I was a Selectman. I claimed my father's home as my legal residence. Some of the voters questioned the legality of my being a Selectman in the Town of Castle Hill. In 1922, at the town meeting, I was asked to rule on this matter. I stated, "I can't see any harm being done, but since I'm not a lawyer, it would be better for the voters to settle this grievance."

Mr. Arthur Tarr, one of the outstanding taxpayers in the Town of Castle Hill, was appointed to rule on the question. He served as Tax Collector during my years in office and we were the best of friends. Mr. Tarr stated, "I'm not a lawyer either but this question should be settled to eliminate criticism." Several suggestions were aired and it was decided, after some discussion, that my legal residence would be where I was getting my washing done.

I thanked the voters for making the ruling and thanked them for the opportunity of serving them for the past three years. I continued on by stating, "I get my washing done in Mapleton now. You may proceed to vote and elect the officers for the ensuing year."

My next assignment with town affairs took place in January of 1927, the first year that Mildred and I were living in our new home.

Mr. Webber, then superintendent of schools, drove in one day with his horse and pung. I had known Mr. Webber for some time, but little did I surmise what was up on this day. He blanketed the horse, took off his cap and placed it on the seat of the pung. He took a paper from his pocket and came over to where I was splitting wood. He said, "Mr. Ellis, Mr. John Belyea passed away a few days ago. You will remember that Mr. Belyea was a member of the School Committee. You have been appointed to fill the unexpired term of his office. I am qualified to administer the Oath of Office. Please remove your cap and raise your right hand." I had become a member of the Castle Hill School Board, hardly realizing what was taking place. What a thrill it was to experience such a ceremony, here at my home, on this cold January day.

That year, at the town meeting, I was re-elected as a member of the Castle Hill School Board. I was re-elected each year for the next twenty-seven, altogether serving twenty-eight consecutive years. My experiences as a school teacher in 1915-16 were very helpful to me as I served on this school committee. Each year, after the first two, I was honored to be chosen chairman of the committee.

In the early years, when Castle Hill was still a plantation, the town fathers had seven school buildings, built at locations that were suitable to the areas they served. The McLellan School was located on upper State Road, about one mile east of the Ashland town line. The Moran School was about two miles east of the McLellan School and the Porter School was located two miles from that on the some road. The Richardson School was on the so-called Wade Road, about one half mile north of the State Road. The Dudley School was over on the Waddell Road and the Pyle School was located at the south end of the Turner Road. The seventh was the Haystack School located on the Haystack Road.

By 1927, most of these school buildings were very much in need of repair and some were too small to accommodate the pupils of the district which they served.

At the 1927 annual Castle Hill Town Meeting, money was appropriated to start fixing up some of the school houses. The Moran and the Richardson Schools were badly in need of more room.

After the assessment had been made and we knew the amount of money appropriated would be available, work began. It was hard deciding just what to do in each case. Alonzo Flewelling, who was beginning his life's work as a carpenter, was called in to help decide how, and in what way, to make the money available go the furthest.

That year, an addition was made in the length of the Richardson School building. The Moran School was turned around part way and then an addition in length was added.

In each of the following years, appropriations were made to pay for repairs and upkeep of the school buildings. In later years, with open roads, schools were consolidated.

The Mapleton Community School building was built in 1948. In 1949, all of the rural school buildings were made available to those who were interested in purchasing them.

The McLellan School was purchased by Brighton Alley. His widow, Crystal Alley, still lives there.

The Richardson School building was purchased by Roger Porter. He moved it to his State Road farm and it was used for many years for his hired help. Recently, Roger sold the building to Edwin McLellan. Edwin moved the building to his house lot near the "little church" on the State Road. The building is still being used as a dwelling.

The Porter School building was sold to Harold Wood who used it for many years to house his potato picking crews at harvest time. The building has now fallen into decay. This Porter School was a two story building originally named the Tilley School. Before the Grange Hall was built in 1905, town meetings were held there and the Castle Hill Grange held their meetings in the upper story.

The Pyle School burned in 1946.

The Dudley School was a two story building located on the Waddell Road. The upper story was never used. This building was sold to Forest Dudley, who moved it to his farm on the Dudley Road and used it for his potato picking crews. It was later purchased by Delance Lovely who remodeled it into a two apartment dwelling.

The old Haystack School was replaced by a new building many years ago. The old building was purchased by Mr. Webber, then Superintendent of Schools. He moved it to a house lot on the Hughes Road in Mapleton. It was furnished and used as a dwelling. This remodeled building has changed ownership several times but is still being used. The newer Haystack School building was also remodeled into a dwelling after its sale in 1949.

In the later months of 1929, I began to think that perhaps a term as a Representative in the Maine State Legislature would be interesting. About January 1, 1930, I wrote the Secretary of State at Augusta requesting nomination papers.

The papers arrived and were circulated among the voters of Ashland and the surrounding towns that were in this Legislative District. When the June primaries were over and the votes counted, I found myself to be a loser.

Back in January, while the nomination papers were being circulated, Mr. George Powers called me at my home and congratulated me for making a try to represent this district in state affairs. Mr. Powers had, at one time, been a practicing attorney at Caribou, Maine. Liquor had got the best of him and he had to close his office. This man was often referred to as a tramp lawyer. He walked, back and forth, from Caribou to Ashland and offered to assist his many friends in legal matters. His assistance was greatly appreciated in the Frenchville area as well as in Ashland village. His pay was whatever folks could afford. While this man and I were talking over the pros and cons of one attempting the Legislature, he suggested that I try and get appointed to some state office. He said, "This will help get your name before the voters and your chance of winning an election will be greater. Perhaps, to start, you might get appointed as a Justice of the Peace."

He explained to me just what the procedure would be to obtain a commission as a Justice of the Peace and offered to do the legal work for me. This was to be my first try at something of this nature so I accepted his offer and asked for his help. I asked, "Will there be a fee?" He replied, "Of course there is a deposit required. If you are willing to give me $20.00 I'll attend to it for you." I gave Mr. Powers the $20.00 and he went on his way.

A few weeks passed; I did not hear from Augusta or see Mr. Powers again and began to wonder what had become of the $20.00.

One day, along in the spring, my appointment came in the mail. It was signed by William Tudor Gardiner, Governor of the State of Maine. It was necessary to take this to another Justice to receive the oath of office. This was promptly done. I had the certificate framed and hung on the wall of my home. I was feeling proud to be holding a state office. The appointment was for seven years.

In 1937, I made application for reappointment and learned, at this time, the fee to be sent was $5.00. I had known George Powers since 1915, when I was teaching in the French settlement, and considered him to be a very brilliant man. Now I learned he "knew how to make a living."

The 1937 re-appointment was signed by Lewis O. Barrows, Governor of Maine.

Seven years later, in 1944, my re-appointment certificate was signed by Sumner Sewell, then Governor of Maine. In 1951, the commission was renewed and this time signed by Governor Frederick G. Payne. The 1958 renewal bore the signature of Governor Edmund Muskie.

For thirty-five years I was qualified to help my constituents in many ways. I very much doubt if the total amount received in payment for my services exceeded the original $20.00 paid to Mr. Powers, but I was always happy to help others with their legal problems whenever I could.

In 1956, I let my commissions, as Notary Public and Justice of the Peace, expire.

In 1934, I decided to make another try for Representative to the Legislature and once again obtained nomination papers from the Secretary of State.

This time I was successful and won the election. The towns I was to serve were Ashland, Castle Hill, Masardis, Portage, Garfield, Nashville and Oxbow. The 87th Legislature was to convene on January 2, 1935. It was getting late in December, about time to go to Augusta, and I was without funds. I wanted to take my wife and three children along but there wasn't enough money to pay my own way down.

I'd had a good crop of potatoes and there were many barrels in storage. For several weeks, I had been cutting wood but, to obtain the best price, it had to season during the next summer. We (myself, father, and brothers) were in partnership with the potatoes as well as the wood. Due to the settlement we had to make with my brother Byron's widow, there was a real estate mortgage on all our properties. I talked with my father about selling a few potatoes so I could get my family down to Augusta. He objected on the grounds that, in fairness to all, each would be entitled to sell the same amount, but, with the exception of myself, the others could get along without selling at this time.

My father stated, "I have never known anyone breaking even who went to the Legislature. However, now that you have been elected, perhaps you can hire enough money to get started." This I dreaded to do but thought it was worth a try.

I drove over to Washburn, called at the Washburn Bank and explained my plight to the cashier. The cashier allowed that he could usually grant a small loan but said, "In a case of this kind you will have to see Jack Beck. Mr. Beck is president of this bank. His office is upstairs in this building."

I went up to Mr. Beck's office and again explained the situation I was in. Mr. Beck said he personally was in favor of helping me, but, due to the small pay that Representatives received, perhaps the matter should be taken up at the next director's meeting. "When will the next director's meeting be held?" I asked. He looked at the calendar and stated the date. I thanked him for listening to me and told him I'd leave the family behind and make it down to Augusta someway, perhaps hitchhike. He asked me how long I'd be in town. "Oh, just long enough for the horse to eat its dinner," I replied.

I went to the stable, which was directly across from the bank. The sweat was running down my spine. I wondered if I should try to obtain a loan at some other place. A few minutes later, I heard my name called. I could not see who was calling. A bystander said, "Look, Jack Beck is calling you." I looked his way and he beckoned for me to come over to his office. I wondered what was up and went over to see what he had in mind. He informed me that he had called some of the directors of the bank and they each said, "Go ahead and give Phin a lift." Boy, what a relief. Now I could take the family along with me. I made a loan of $100. The note was for four months at 6% interest.

Arrangements were made with Everett Richardson to come and live in our house and keep it warm for there were potatoes stored in the cellar. He also was to do the barn chores and take my place in the woods, getting out fuel wood. He would be paid $1.00 per day. Now we were ready to embark on a new adventure on January 1st.

Arrangements were made in advance to rent the "Lock" house on Western Avenue in Augusta. Although it was located about a mile from the State House, it was a "good deal." We went down on the train, taking along what clothing could be packed in suitcases. It was late in the day when we arrived.

The Legislature convened at ten o'clock the next day and I received my committee appointments: state schools, state reformatories, and towns. In a few days, I received a check for $54.00 which was to cover our transportation cost for the entire session.

Louis J. Brann was governor in 1935. Nathaniel Tompkins of Houlton was Speaker of the House. Mr. Tompkins had taught in the Dudley School in Castle Hill about the turn of the century. He later became a lawyer. During the winter, he and I sat down several times and discussed doings of the "good old days."

We got along fine all through the session, which ended 11:50 p.m. on April 6th. My salary was $600 for the entire period. I'd managed to send Everett Richardson six dollars each week and had saved enough money to pay the note at the bank. We could not attend many social functions during this winter and I walked home to my dinners every day, rain or shine, except for the very last few days when less time was scheduled for lunch. Mildred could prepare a good meal for the whole family for what a single lunch cost at the State House. Myrtle attended school in Augusta while we were there.

We arrived back at Castle Hill a few days after the Legislature had adjourned. Everett had done a fine job looking after things and my brothers allowed his help in getting out fuel wood, hauling potatoes, etc. had been very satisfactory. The bank note, due May 1st, was paid a week or so ahead of time. Everything had worked out just fine and everyone concerned was happy. Soon we were ready to begin farming for another year.

Me in the State Legislature, 1937.

In 1936, I made another try at serving the Legislature as Representative for the same district. I was successful in getting elected and had ample funds to move the family to Augusta for the winter.

Everett Richardson had married. He and his new wife, Edith, moved into our home January 1st to look after things while we were away. Everett once again did a fine job working in my place with Dad and the boys.

This was the 88th Legislature and it convened on January 6, 1937. My committee appointments were the same as before. Also the salary and mileage were the same.

We rented an unfurnished house that was much closer to the State House than where we had lived in 1935. We bought furniture at a secondhand store and sold it back after the Legislature adjourned. Mildred and I were able to attend more of the social functions. Myrtle and Elaine were both in school this year and had only a short distance to walk.

Lewis O. Barrows was Governor and George E. Hill of Portland was Speaker of the House. Part of my committee work was to inspect the Girls' School at Hallowell, the Women's Reformatory at Skowhegan, and the Men's Reformatory at South Windham. We also visited the mental hospitals in Bangor and Augusta. Each committee in the Legislature is made up of three Senators and seven members of the House of Representatives.

This year, I had time to visit other committee hearings and spend some time in the State Library, which was a fine place to study.

In 1938, I made a try for the Senate but lost out. Perhaps I did not spend enough time campaigning. The area I was to serve covered all of Aroostook County and I was not as well acquainted as some of the other candidates. Aroostook County was entitled to three Senators and sixteen Representatives. George F. Ashby of Fort Fairfield, J. Frederick Burns of Houlton and Harvey A. Tompkins were elected to the three Senate seats.

On January 1st, 1939, I had a longing to return to Augusta. This was a mild winter and we had cut about all the fuel wood that could be prepared to sell the next season. We now had open roads. Lawrence Sharp, a neighbor, had purchased a truck. Lawrence offered to haul out the wood we had cut with his truck. Father was taking charge for Collins again and he was getting logs out of the woods with trucks. He allowed things were going along well although, in the beginning, he had protested and said, "I don't think anything will ever take the place of horses in getting logs out of the woods." I had lost out in my try for the Senate seat, but Mildred and I talked things over and we agreed it would be okay for me to go down for the opening of the 89th session of the Maine Legislature and I might be able to obtain a clerkship on some of the larger committees.

I went down, applied for the Clerkship in the Taxation Committee and was appointed. This paid nearly as much as I received as a Representative. There were several smaller committees that paid less. I inquired about them and soon had more work lined up than I could do. I selected as many committees to clerk for as I felt I could successfully serve. Summing things up, I could earn much more than when I was a Representative.

Mildred stayed at home with the children. Everett and Edith Richardson came to be with them. Edith worked her board. I paid Everett to do the chores and help with getting out and slabbing the wood.

I shopped through the ads in the Kennebec Journal for rooms and meals. I found a good room for four dollars a week and a private home where meals were served. This was not as good as having the family along but I could go home often on week-ends by riding the train at night.

In March, I went home to attend the town meeting and was elected first selectman. I returned to Augusta and completed my duties as clerk for several committees that I clerked for. It was early April when I returned home to assist with town affairs.

About the first week in May of 1939, Hazen Walker, our mail carrier, called in one day and said, "I would like to make a complaint." "Sure," I replied, "Go ahead, I'm listening." "You know, Phin," he said, "There is an awful bad frost hole down on the Turner Road. I got stuck in it yesterday and after getting pulled out I had to drive around by the Waddell Road. Do you suppose the hole could be patched up?" I answered, "Well, Hazen, that same frost hole caused me a lot of trouble way back in 1917. That was 27 years ago. I believe it has been patched every spring since. I have a hunch the taxpayer's money is being wasted in patching it every spring. I promise I'll do my best to find where the source of the trouble lies." "Oh, well," Hazen stated, "I didn't want to cause any trouble. I think a load of gravel might tide us over for another year." I remarked, "If the place isn't made passable by tomorrow, I'll eat my shirt." Hazen was amused by this remark and, before going on his way, said, "I'll see you again tomorrow."

That afternoon, I drove down on the Turner Road to look the situation over. Upon returning, I called Lawrence Chandler and told him about the complaint concerning the frost hole. "What do you suppose we can do to fix it once and for all?" I asked. "That is a big question," answered Lawrence. "Okay, Lawrence," I said, "Instead of bringing a load of gravel in the morning, bring a slush scraper. I'll meet you there and we will pretend that we are pioneers for a day."

We met there the next morning. The team was hitched to the scraper. "Now, Lawrence," I said, "You drive the team and I'll handle the scraper." In jig time we had removed about ten inches of mud from an area of about eight or ten square feet. Now we were standing on icy frozen ground. I said to Lawrence, "It is my opinion that one hundred per cent of our trouble is caused by lack of drainage. Do you agree?" "I agree," He answered. I said, "You are the road commissioner elected by the town but I'd like to make a suggestion." "What is it?" he asked. I answered, "I suggest that you get the old road machine, hire someone with a team to hitch on with you and spend the rest of today ditching this road, especially this area. Smooth over where we have been digging. Perhaps this will dry out enough so the mail carrier can get by today. I'll be back here by quitting time this afternoon and see what you have accomplished."

At 4:30 that afternoon, I returned. Lawrence had done a wonderful job. Water was running in the ditches he had made and the road surface had dried out. "Now, men," I said, "I think lack of drainage is the cause of many of our problems with keeping the roads in repair." Lawrence and the fellow with him agreed. "Now, Lawrence," I said, "I'd like to make another suggestion. The town appropriated $1500 for summer road repair this year. I suggest that it be expended in ditching the roads." "Well," he replied, "Perhaps we will catch hell if we do not do some construction, but you are the 'doctor' so we will do our best." I said, "If, at any time, there is fault found with what you are doing, send the fault finder to me and I'll find out why he is complaining."

Lawrence worked most of the summer ditching. He often stated, “We made a great discovery didn’t we?” There weren’t any complaints about the way he was expending the summer road money. In fact, we received many compliments.

This same summer, there was $1500 of State Aid road money to be expended. There was a very bad stretch of corduroy road, just west of the Welts Brook Bridge that had caused much trouble over the years. It was decided to spend the State funds here and a job was done that has stood up under all sorts of traffic for the past thirty-five years. Here is where Lawrence Chandler made a name for himself in road construction.

Late in the summer of 1939, it looked as if it might be a tough winter with our Poor Account (funds to aid the poor). $2,000 had been appropriated for the year and this was already running low. Back in the winter, while in Augusta, I learned much about W.P.A. funds and learned how other towns had made use of them.

Before winter set in, an application was made to the State of Maine for funds to do a winter road construction project here in Castle Hill. My application for funds was granted. Although winter was a poor time of year to do road construction work, especially in Aroostook County, along in November arrangements were made to begin work where the State Aid project ended in the summer. We were to proceed west, up over the so called DeMerchant Hill. In addition to the federal money, the State would furnish a power shovel.

Fred McConnell came one morning bringing Bruce Magill, who was to be foreman of the project. Mr. McConnell was a civil engineer who represented the State in laying out these projects. Guilford Smith was to represent the State during the construction. We were to employ people who were unemployed and on relief.

I have forgotten the number of hours a man could work or the rate of pay he received but I do know that $14.41 was the maximum amount that one was entitled to earn each week. We took on men from Mapleton, as well as from Castle Hill, and this large crew kept things moving.

We were fortunate not to have too much snow or many bad winds. Roads to the rock piles could be kept open with a road machine and a pair of horses. Many rock piles, from nearby farms, were hauled in and a good stone base was built. Usually the power shovel could handle the grading but on some mornings dynamite was used to break the crust on the old road surface. A kerosene heater was kept going in the power shovel overnight so that it might be warm enough to start easily in the morning.

As Chairman of the Board of Selectmen, I felt it my duty to keep posted on their progress. At the beginning, I tried to be there each day in case some assistance from the town was required or town equipment needed.

It was an inspiration to visit the job and watch the men at work. They really kept busy leveling the rocks and the gravel. Many of them expressed their appreciation to me for having the chance to earn some money for their families.

One incident, that I will always remember, concerned a young fellow by the name of Fred Michaud. In the beginning, stakes were placed along the sides of the road for the engineer to use in getting the project lined up. Mr. McConnell requested that I ask one of the men to assist him with the stakes. I looked the crowd over and picked a young fellow whom I felt would be a good man for the job. Looking back, wondering how I happened to pick that particular fellow, I think it was because he was lacking good warm clothes and looked cold. I asked him his name. He told me he was Fred Michaud from Mapleton and that he had a slip from the Town Manager. He gave me the slip and I introduced him to Mr. McConnell saying, "Here is a man that I'm sure will do a good job for you." Mr. McConnell put Fred to work and I gave the work permission slip to the foreman, Mr. Magill.

Later in the day, I was back on the job to see how things were progressing. Mr. McConnell complimented me for picking out this fellow to help him. "Really, it is wonderful the amount of work we have been able to accomplish. Just watch, Mr. Ellis, this young man will go places during his lifetime. Fred is a real genius," Mr. McConnell stated.

A couple of days later, while I was looking around, Mr. Magill complained, "This Fred Michaud that you and McConnell picked out to help set the stakes and keep the strings in place so as to keep an accurate grade, can't read or write. What in hell am I to do with a man that can't read or write?" I said, "He seems to be on the bounce every minute and not shirking like some of the fellows are. If his work is satisfactory, why condemn him. I insist you keep him on that job until

Mr. McConnell returns anyway. How has his work been so far?" Bruce replied, "Well, okay, but he can't read or write."

In a few days, Mr. McConnell returned. I explained to him that the foreman felt some other man, who could read and write, should be setting the stakes and keeping check of the grade. He stated, "Read or not read, write or not write, that young man is just what I sized him up to be the first day we began work. Michaud is a smart fellow and I will stand behind the work he has been accepted to do."

Fred Michaud continued on the job right up to the end and, never once, did I observe him shirking his duty. He was always on the bounce and helped others every minute he could spare. It appeared that he was learning more and more about road construction every day.

After our W.P.A. project was long over, Fred Michaud was a key man with whatever he was doing. He obtained a job with the Bridge Construction Co. doing their concrete work. He built culvert end walls, small concrete bridges across roadways and did other jobs this company contracted to do.

After the army moved in, the Bridge Construction Company had several contracts with the Government. Fred Michaud always worked on the jobs that had to do with concrete. This man, who had never attended school, was foreman of twenty or more concrete workers.

Down through the years, it has been my good fortune to observe some of this man's work. Since writing and gathering notes for my book, I visited Fred and asked his permission to mention his name. He gave me permission. Then I asked him if he'd explain the secret of his success since he had never learned to read and write. He brought out an armful of books and explained that from the time I introduced him to Fred McConnell in Castle Hill, that cold November day in 1939, he had done all his work by drawing pictures. This man had a complete record of all the jobs that were assigned to him.

The W.P.A. road project, during the winter of 1939, proved to be a great success. Nearly three-fourths of a mile of road was built. This road had a good stone base. Many rock piles were moved from farms making the land more valuable.

When spring came, about the first of April, we had reached the DeMerchant Brook on the west side of the hill. Funds were still available for labor but there was nothing left for materials and a metal culvert would be needed if we were to continue. Fred McConnell, the engineer, and Guilford Smith figured out the size needed. I checked with two companies concerning the cost of a good culvert. The estimate was about the same from each company, $2,000.

Jack Beck of Washburn was serving on the Governor's Council at this time, so I drove over and explained what could be done if we only had a culvert. He said, "Perhaps you will be in luck if you go to Augusta and tell Mr. Woodman, who is Chairman of the Highway Commission, what you have told me." This was an idea but I'd have to work fast or we would have to tie up the project. The next day, I hopped the night train for Augusta. It was about two o'clock in the morning when I arrived. I got a room and rested until time for the Highway Office to open. At that time, I hurried over and told Mr. Woodman of the predicament we were in up in Castle Hill. He asked me to hang around for awhile and perhaps he could come up with something to help us. He made a few calls and said, "Arrangements have been made for your town to have a metal culvert, 5 feet in diameter and 120 feet long. The cost of the culvert is around $2,000 and is being paid for by the State."

Boy, this was a happy day for me. I will always believe that Mr. Woodman had the culvert on its way before I boarded the night train for home. The State had purchased the culvert from Bancroft and Martin of Portland and it was delivered, in sections, the very next day.

My Uncle Jim was an old hand at road construction work and was hired to help install the culvert.

The road project could continue. It was about the middle of April and getting rather muddy for trucking but we were able to keep the men busy until the W.P.A. funds were used up.

I received many compliments for finding a way for the many "bread winners" to support their families through the winter and the town now had a fine section of improved road to use.

In 1941, I again went down to Augusta when the Legislature convened in January and obtained clerkships on the Taxation Committee and several smaller committees.

Mildred and the children remained at home. My brother, Forest, looked after the stock and took my place working in the woods until I returned in April.

During this winter, I learned all I could about the town manager form of government. A few towns had obtained charters and some smaller towns were operating under the Enabling Act. We were doing a fine job our old way but it seemed that more could be accomplished by the town manager system. Other towns were operating under the town manager form of government so I made up my mind, by town meeting time in 1941, to "drop out of the picture" if Castle Hill continued on with the old system.

A suitable article was included in the town report warrant asking the voters to consider adopting the town manager form of government. The article was accepted and I was hired to serve as Town Manager at a salary of $850.

In 1946, I felt I could afford another winter in the Legislature. The towns I served were the same as in 1935 and '37.

Malcolm was in the eighth grade. He came along with us and attended school in Augusta. Elaine was a senior at Aroostook Central Institute in Mars Hill living with the Herman Brewer family. (Castle Hill did not have a high school nor did they, at that time, have bus transportation. The girls had to board out away from home with families who lived within walking distance of a high school. The year Malcolm was a freshman, transportation was provided for Castle Hill students to attend Mapleton High School so he lived at home during his high school years.)

Myrtle had graduated from high school in 1944. She had been in nurses training at a Boston hospital but, this winter, she was back home resting up. This was during the war and there was a shortage of nurses so the student nurses had to attend classes, study and spend many hours working in the hospital. After resting up, she intended to go back to Boston and resume her nursing career. When we moved to Augusta, she came along with us and decided to give up nursing for a career in beauty culture. Dorcas's girl, Dorothy, joined us there and the two girls enrolled in a beauty academy.

The 93rd Legislature convened on Wednesday, January 1, 1947. There were so many things I wanted to do for my district.

We lived very near the State House. By being so close, we felt Mildred could visit more of the sessions than she had in the past years and I'd have more time to devote to legislative duties.

This year the salary had been increased to $800 but the mileage allowance was still $54. My committee appointments for this session were mines and mining, pensions, State School for Boys, State School for Girls, and State Reformatories.

Before the Legislature convened in January, Mr. McGaughy, Superintendent of Schools in the Mapleton, Castle Hill, and Chapman areas, called a meeting of the school committees of each town to consider uniting and forming a community school district. The rural school buildings were in need of repair and it had become more difficult for the teachers to find boarding places in the rural areas. We now had open roads making consolidation possible. At the joint board meeting, it was voted to make an effort to get a bill through the Legislature permitting such an arrangement to be made.

If I remember correctly, the town of Fort Kent was the only town in Maine, at this time, trying out this idea with some of its neighboring towns.

Mr. McGaughy gave considerable thought to such an adventure and prepared a rough draft for me to take to Augusta. This I left with the Reviser of Statutes. A bill was prepared for me to present to the committee of Legal Affairs. A hearing was held before this committee and a group from our district came to support me in presenting our case.

On the day of the hearing, I was prepared to explain the predicament we were in and our reasons why we should unite at this time. Some of those who came down to the hearing also spoke and expressed their opinions as to why it was time to remodel our rural school systems.

The Committee of Legal Affairs gave the bill a favorable report and ordered it passed. The Legislature accepted the "ought to pass" report. Later it was necessary to have an amendment added to the bill making it an emergency measure. Then another amendment was found necessary. This second amendment was that the bill would become law only after each of the three towns (Chapman, Mapleton and Castle Hill), at special town meetings, voted to approve of the bill as passed. Mr. McGaughy followed up on this. By the time I returned home, consideration was being given to the size and type of building needed and it was being decided just how to finance the construction.

During the same winter, I was requested by Ashland to try and do the same for their area. A bill was entered to create the Ashland Area Community School District. We were successful with the passage of the bill and another community school district was born.

S. Wilson Collins, Representative from Caribou, managed to do the same for his constituents and the Caribou School District was formed.

The Selectmen of Ashland requested that I make a try at doing something for their town relative to forming a water and sewer district. A bill was prepared. A strong delegation came down for the hearing held before the Committee on Public Utilities. The bill received a favorable "ought to pass" and the Legislature passed it. Now the Ashland voters were pleased to have permission to begin construction of both their water and sewer systems.

Also in 1947, the town of Ashland wished to have a bill introduced to have the former Sheridan Plantation separated from them. This bill was introduced upon request and many hearings were held before the Towns Committee. Checking all the records available, it was found Sheridan was annexed to Ashland in 1901 by an act of the Legislature. Mr. S.S. Thornton, an Ashland attorney, was representative at that time. In 1901, the Ashland Mill Company, located in Sheridan, was booming and it perhaps looked like a very good deal for Ashland to make this move.

Now, almost half of a century had passed. The mill had burned about 1921. What once had been a busy village was now almost a ghost town. The Towns Committee gave a lot of thought to the bill then gave it an "ought not to pass" report. This was accepted by the Legislature and the bill was not passed.

During this same session of the Legislature, I conceived the idea of having the minimum excise tax increased from $2.00 to $5.00. My argument was that the older model cars were using the roads and wearing them out as much, if not more, than the newer ones. The towns needed the extra revenue to apply to the expense of maintaining the roads. My idea caught on. The other members of the Legislature, The Town Managers, and Selectmen approved and the bill was successfully passed.

In Castle Hill, bears were causing considerable damage to the flocks of sheep and the State had been paying damage claims. I made

Town officials for the town of Castle Hill (from l. to r.): Jasper Ellis, Ivan Sawyer, myself, John Hoffses, and C.G.R. (Charles) Chandler.

an effort to have a bill passed putting a bounty on bears. I presented a very good argument but was not successful. The bear was considered a game animal.

Before leaving for Augusta, for the 93rd Legislature, Maurice Knowles and I were discussing the wonderful scenery we had in Aroostook County. We allowed that it was equal to all, even better than most, other parts of the United States. We talked about how shabby the roadsides looked and nothing was being done to improve them. I suggested that a bill be introduced to the Legislature to create the Aroostook Scenic Highway. If the passage was successful, we would all roll up our sleeves and make this idea a reality.

I presented such a bill and was successful in getting it passed. In the spring of 1947, I became Town Manager of Mapleton, as well as Castle Hill, and did not have the time to follow up on the project dreamed of by Mr. Knowles and myself. The law to develop the landscape and roadsides of Route 11 is still in the statutes. I hope some day this plan will be carried out by someone. Perhaps after I finish this material for my book, I'll go up there, pitch a tent, and get the people organized to improve the "Aroostook Scenic Highway."

That spring of 1947, when I was invited to consider coming to Mapleton and be manager for both towns, I had quite a decision to make. The State Road residents of Mapleton often remarked, "We get the skim milk while those over on the village side of the town always get the cream." In Castle Hill, it was the feeling of many that those living on the State Road were getting more benefits than "we are over here on the south side of the town."

After some consideration, I accepted the challenge and became manager for both towns. I assumed my duties about May 20, 1947. The salary I received was considerably more than the $9.00 per week that I got for teaching school back in 1915-16.

Chapter 20

Hospital Memories

Sometime during the summer of 1910, Mr. Frank White, an attorney from Presque Isle called with horse and wagon at my father's home in Castle Hill. White explained the purpose of his call saying, "I have two thoughts in mind. First, I want to tell everyone of the great need of having a hospital built in Presque Isle. Second, such a venture will cost money." A discussion followed.

"Now Mr. Ellis," Mr. White said, "Can you contribute something to help with the cause?" My father answered, "We are a poor family and cannot give very much." Mr. White stated, "We will be grateful for any amount at all. Just a little folding money will be appreciated and you may pledge to make small payments later if you care to." My father handed him some money, just how much I never knew. Mr. White then inquired, "How far is it back to Presque Isle?" My father answered, "You are sixteen miles from home." Mr. White thanked my father for the contribution and drove away.

One year later, when I entered high school at Ashland, I quite frequently heard someone talking about the hospital being built at Presque Isle.

In the fall of 1912, I entered my sophomore year at Ashland High and began working for Dr. Hagerthy. The Doctor often mentioned the new hospital. Word got around that it would accommodate six patients at one time. The Doctor would say, "This is the beginning. Someday that hospital will grow and grow. It will have to be made larger to take care of the many emergency cases that are bound to happen in such a large area."

About 1914, an addition was built on the original hospital building. Dr. Hagerthy was happy to learn the hospital would now accommodate twelve to fourteen patients.

Dr. Dobson, who had been practicing medicine in Ashland for several years, allowed he wanted to become a surgeon. He went to France to study and Dr. Percy Gilbert took over his practice. While Dr. Dobson was studying in France, war broke out with Germany. He completed his studies but, due to the war, had a difficult time getting back to the United States. When he arrived home from abroad, he sold his home in Ashland, relocated in Presque Isle and began his work as a surgeon.

During the summer of 1916, while attending the Normal School at Presque Isle and boarding at Mrs. Annie Hayden's home on Blake Street, I passed by the hospital to and from school every day. I often wondered if the hospital would expand and accommodate more patients. It was said to be far too small.

When I returned from serving in the Army Medical Corps, a new brick structure was being built. One day, Dr. Hagerthy drove me around by the new hospital. He seemed happy about what was being done. He still insisted, "We will have a hospital of our own in Ashland someday." He would often say, "Phinagin, don't tie yourself down to anything permanent for awhile. We are going to have a little hospital in Ashland and I want you to work with me."

For the next twenty years, I often heard said, "The hospital is filled to capacity all the time." There was always a scramble to get patients admitted. The women, who had served as nurses in their neighborhoods, were giving up on "at home nursing."

In 1937, solariums were added to the brick hospital building. With the coming of open roads, the demand for beds at the hospital was so great that the solariums were converted to accommodate patients. In the years that followed, the need for more beds became worse.

In 1943, I had my appendix removed at the hospital. Dr. Dobson, with the assistance of Dr. Robert Somerville, performed the operation. I was lucky to pull through the ordeal. I was told that I was on the operating table nearly five hours for an operation that was expected to last one half hour or less. The appendix was imbedded in the wall of the intestine and it was after much searching that it was located. I was so sick that a special nurse was assigned to care for me. Miss Alice Oakes was my nurse for about eight or ten days. She had been a telephone operator at Ashland while I attended high school and she remembered me as being "Dr. Hagerthy's chore boy."

During the first few days, I was dreaming most of the time. The nurse would often awaken me and say, "You seem to be having a nightmare or something. Do you remember what the trouble was?"

One time, I remember telling the nurse who was standing by my bed wiping the sweat from my body, "I remember being in sight of the Pearly Gates. There were several angels standing by and then Gabriel blew his trumpet." The nurse inquired, "Is that when you woke up?" "Yes," I answered. She laughed and said, "That was the fire whistle that blew." "Well," I said, "That whistle could raise the dead." "That is right, Mr. Ellis," she said, "No one will die around here as long as the fire station is nearby and that whistle is on top of it."

About the third day, Alice began giving me food. By evening of the same day, she discovered infection had set in and the Doctor was summoned in a hurry. Dr. Dobson arrived and ordered irrigation. The Doctor and Alice stayed by my bedside most of the night. For several days after, broth was all I was fed. I would say, "How many times has this soup been strained." This remark seemed to amuse all who heard me.

During the twenty days I was a patient, several times I jokingly stated, "Someday I'll return and have either the hospital or the fire station moved. The two are a very poor combination."

I soon recovered from the operation and was back to work when winter arrived. Many times, during the next few years, I thought of my stay in the hospital, the close call I had, and of hearing that fire whistle.

In 1952, I was often called to attend the meetings of the hospital trustees. As town manager of Castle Hill and Mapleton, I was becoming more and more interested in hospital affairs.

In 1953, I was made a member of the Building Committee. Perhaps it was thought my experiences down through the years would be helpful in making a better hospital. James Rathbun was President of the Board of Trustees at that time.

The Presque Isle Rotary Club had raised some money, through their radio and TV auctions, to be used for building. The 1953 auction was a great success. All those who were interested in improving conditions at the hospital took a very active part in the bidding and $24,000 was raised. They used as their slogan "Give more to build in `54". When the spring of 1954 arrived, some $40,000 was available for building onto the old hospital.

Hazen Stetson, President of the Maine Public Service Company, and Gerald Shea, owner and manager of the Shea Realty

Company were also members of the Hospital Building Committee. Mr. Stetson was Chairman. Summer came and began fading away and nothing was being done about getting started with the building.

Several times, I toured through the hospital trying to decide, in my own mind, just how the Rotary Auction funds should be used. I observed the crowded conditions and it was obvious the nurses were working under conditions that weren't good. By July, I had made up my mind not to consider spending any of the funds available on the old hospital.

Clyde Johnson, President of the Rotary Club, and James Rathbun approached Mr. Stetson to see what the delay was in getting started. One day in August, Mr. Stetson and Mr. Shea came to my office at Mapleton and allowed we should be getting busy with the hospital project. Mr. Stetson stated, "Officers of the Rotary Club, as well as others, are getting impatient."

I asked Mr. Stetson what ideas he had in mind. He allowed we could at least dig a cellar for a new addition and perhaps get up some frame work before winter. I questioned Gerald in regards to his ideas. He agreed that we should make a start so as not to lose the Rotary Club's support in the future.

About this time Hazen asked me, "What are your ideas? You must have given this some thought." I answered, "Perhaps it would be best for you fellows to tell the Rotary Club that I have decided not to take part in spending their money. Perhaps it would be a wise move for me to resign as a member of the board of Trustees because I'm not taking any part in pouring money down a rat hole." Quick as a flash, both men stated almost in unison, "Oh no, we don't want you to resign," I said, "Okay, just go back and tell the folks involved that we are not spending and wasting the money earned through the auctions."

A heated discussion followed. I expressed my idea that we should have a new hospital on a new site. Mr. Stetson remarked, "It will take a man with a lot of guts to explain an idea of this kind to the Rotary Club and to tell them why the building program should be delayed."

I thought to myself, "You can explain this idea to the Rotary Club, why send word by others." I did some deep thinking then said, "Okay fellows, I'll go and explain to the Club the situation as I see it. Please ask Mr. Johnson or one of the Directors to give me a call."

The following Monday, it was almost noon when I received a call to come over and have lunch with the club. I allowed this was short notice and perhaps I could not make it in time. "Oh, come anyway," I was told, "It will be okay if you are a little late. We want to hear your ideas concerning the hospital." I said, "Okay, I'll leave for Presque Isle as soon as the office girl returns from lunch."

While waiting for her return, I prepared some notes:

1. The old hospital building has served its time.
2. Open roads have resulted in more hospital patients.
3. More people want to use the facilities of the hospital instead of being cared for at home.
4. The Doctors no longer care to visit the homes to treat the sick and injured where many times they had to work under very unsanitary conditions.
5. There are not enough parking spaces around the present hospital, even for the nurses and other employees.
6. Getting the patients away from the fire whistle would be a blessing.
7. Most mothers now want to have their babies at the hospital under sanitary conditions where they will receive good nursing care.
8. It is time for all of the surrounding towns to get together, join hands, and do something constructive.

I was late for dinner but the club had not broken up. For the next half hour I spoke using my notes. I continued on with, "The slogan of last year's auction was to 'give more in `54' and I hesitate to waste any of the money. It is my honest opinion that money spent for building on would be like dumping it down a rat hole."

I thanked the club members for listening and stated, "I am no longer interested in being a trustee if patching up is to be done. It is not good to put new cloth into an old garment. The only way I will continue to be a trustee is if we can work for a new hospital to be located on a new site."

I received many compliments on my speech and someone said, "This man should not be a trustee on the Building Committee, he should be the Administrator of the hospital."

I hurried back to my office in Mapleton. Although I was sort of nervous, I was happy to have expressed my thoughts in the best way I knew how.

The Board of Trustees invited Kenneth Jackson, a local architect, to attend their September meeting. They asked for his professional opinion concerning building an addition on the hospital.

Mr. Jackson stated, "Right off the cuff, I feel it will take at least twice the amount of money available to build even a small addition. At least $60,000 to $75,000 would be needed to make the initial start. However, I will gladly go over, look over the situation and make a more accurate estimate." This was agreeable with the trustees.

Mr. Jackson went to the hospital, reviewed the situation and reported back. He said, "It would cost more to build on than I originally estimated and even with a new addition the old hospital could not adequately provide the facilities required to meet the ever growing demands. It might be wise to consider the suggestion Mr. Ellis made to the Rotary Club in August."

In August, I remember stating, "Perhaps Hill-Burton Funds might be available to us." Mr. Rathbun made and honest effort to get financial help for the hospital from that source but was denied. Mr. Rathbun and Mr. Stetson sought help and assistance form Dr. Dean Fisher. They were unsuccessful in their attempts to have him come to Presque Isle and meet with the Hospital Trustees.

Time passed, October arrived. The Rotary Club scheduled another auction. A meeting of the Trustees was to be held. I hesitated to attend, but I didn't want anyone to think I was a piker so I went and was elected President of the Board. For a brief moment, I wondered if I should refuse but I accepted the position and presided during the remainder of the meeting.

I knew I would have problems to deal with and wondered if holding this position would interfere with my work at Mapleton. During the next month, my mind was dwelling more on the hospital situation than on town affairs. I knew someway had to be found to make a change at the hospital.

One of the things I intended to do at the next meeting was to allow just two hours and no more. It had become a habit in the past for the meetings to last until midnight or after.

A month passed. A meeting was scheduled to begin at seven o'clock. I called the meeting to order and inquired of those present if we had a quorum. It was agreed that we did have a quorum. I stated, "It has been the custom to discuss the many problems concerning the hospital more hours than are needed. You know, fellow members, I live fifteen miles away, I have worked about ten hours in the town office today, have been home, milked the cows, done the chores, ate a hurried supper and arrived in time for this meeting. I have prepared an agenda so we can expedite matters in less time. Tonight we will close shop at nine o'clock sharp. The two hours will be devoted strictly to hospital affairs. Now, let's get on with the meeting and accomplish as much as we can."

Five minutes to nine, I announced, "Time is running out. We have five minutes to conclude our deliberations for the evening. Any items remaining on the agenda will be forwarded to the next meeting."

Believe it or not, after the second meeting of following this schedule, I received calls from the other trustees' wives complimenting me for speeding up the meetings.

The November Rotary Auction was a great success. Everyone had become interested in the hospital situation.

Checking with Mr. Stetson, I found they were still unsuccessful in getting Dr. Fisher to meet with us. I had met Dr. Fisher several times while attending state meetings. Also, while I was a member of the Aroostook County Health Council, he came at my request and spoke to our group.

One day, after our December meeting, a thought came to me. Perhaps I should give Dr. Fisher a ring myself. I telephoned from my office at Mapleton. I informed him that I was now President of the Board of Trustees and explained the purpose of the call. He congratulated me and asked me to stand by for a minute. When he came back on the phone, he said, "I can come January 11th if that is satisfactory." I assured him that date would be just fine and I would arrange a meeting of the Board of Trustees for that evening.

Dr. Fisher came, as agreed, and visited the hospital with Mr. Stetson and myself. Gerald Shea joined us for supper at the hotel. At the evening meeting, Dr. Fisher allowed the building of an addition on the old building would not solve our problems. He told us we had been denied help from the Hill-Burton funds due to two reasons:

1. It is too small a project to be considered.
2. Hill-Burton funds are not allocated for construction or repair on old buildings. He said, "Presque Isle should think in terms of a large addition or construction of a new building at another location. Hill-Burton funds, up to 50% of the cost of the total project, will be available if this community decides to try for a major project."

It was a very interesting evening and we all appreciated Dr. Fisher's remarks. I asked Dr. Fisher to let us know when it would be convenient for the building committee to meet with the State Hospital Board and tell our story to them.

About the middle of March, a letter was received requesting that a representative from our Board of Trustees meet with the Council on April 6th. This was wonderful news. I relayed the message to Mr. Stetson and Mr. Shea. Much excitement prevailed during the next couple weeks. I gathered information concerning the present hospital situation. This, along with the problems at Mapleton and Castle Hill during town meeting time, kept me on the hump.

At the March meeting of the trustees, it was voted that I, as President, appear before the Council at Augusta on April 6th. Mr. Stetson graciously offered his help assembling facts, figures, clippings, etc.

Mr. Stetson and his secretary, Miss White, spent considerable time preparing a summary for me to take to Augusta and I was called in to examine the prepared material.

If I remember correctly, I left Presque Isle by plane on the afternoon of April 5th. The next morning, I visited the State House and met with the heads of several departments that I had become acquainted with back in 1947. At one o'clock, I met with the Council. I was somewhat nervous at first but this soon passed. Dr. Fisher introduced me to the several members of the council. He briefly told of his acquaintance with me and of his visit to our hospital in Presque Isle.

I passed each member a copy of the summary I had brought along and explained why I was there. The question period that followed lasted about an hour. Suddenly the Chairman of the Council looked at the clock and stated, "This has been a very interesting meeting but it must come to a close as we have another one scheduled at this time. Mr. Ellis, we suggest you go rest in the Augusta House lounge. You will be informed of our decision concerning your request for Hill-Burton funds."

Later in the afternoon, a couple of the Council members came to the Augusta House and sat down with me. One of them said, "Mr. Ellis, we have some good news for you. We have agreed to start you off with $300,000 towards a new hospital on a new site. You and your building committee are to see what you can do about raising money in your area."

I was so pleased with the results of this meeting that I couldn't wait to get back to Presque Isle to break the news, so I phoned Mr. Stetson.

There was still time to catch the afternoon plane to Presque Isle. Upon arriving, I got in my car which had been left at the airport and drove home, arriving just in time for supper. I was happy thinking about what had been accomplished today.

Mr. Stetson became very busy following up on the project. He worked with a Mr. Nilson from Dr. Fisher's office in Augusta.

Several months passed. Mr. Stetson was informed by Mr. Nilson that Hedge Westerman, a representative from a firm of hospital consultants, would be coming to evaluate our situation. Also, Mr. Dwight Folsom from a firm of Hospital Finance consultants would be visiting to consider what might be done in raising matching funds in our area.

By October, enough interest had been created for us to make a start. As President of the Board of Trustees, I suggested we set a date for a meeting of representatives from the many towns that the hospital served. I mailed out more than one hundred notices informing people of the meeting to be held at the Community Center on Monday, October 24, at 8:00 p.m.

The entire area was well represented. We had a packed hall. Dr. Giberson spoke for the medical staff. He pointed out the necessity of having a modern hospital located at a more favorable location. Mr. Stetson spoke of our many difficulties in coping with health problems at the present hospital. Hedge Westerman spoke on his recent survey. He allowed he had studied our problems and we were in need of more room. A larger hospital would provide better working conditions for employees and this in turn would result in better patient care. Mr. Dwight Folsom was also present and explained the procedure of organizing a campaign to raise the matching funds. The meeting was interesting and the audience was very attentive. When the speakers finished, the people asked many questions.

At the conclusion of the question and answer period, I explained my connection with the hospital and told of my observations since becoming a trustee. I then stated, "Now, friends and neighbors, residents of the areas served by the Presque Isle General Hospital, let's think seriously for a moment. We have tried to present a clear picture of the situation. Dr. Giberson has presented the needs from the doctor's standpoint. Mr. Stetson has explained very carefully his observations since being associated with the hospital. You have heard the report of Mr. Westerman and Mr. Folsom has informed us what the procedure is to put on a fund raising campaign. Now what is your pleasure? Shall we choose to go forward at this time or will we ask our doctors and hospital staff to struggle on in the present hospital?"

The hour was getting late. I had been on the hump all day at the town office in Mapleton and was becoming very tired. Mrs. Green, secretary of the Board of Trustees, was yawning. She too appeared weary.

Suddenly a gentleman from the audience stood and spoke at length, saying, "The day had come when we must stop, look, and listen. We must consider the need for better health care and provide a larger building for the doctors, nurses and other hospital personnel."

I moved that organization begin tonight. It was seconded by many of the people in the audience. I asked for a show of hands from those in favor. I said, "That is fine but there are a few who have not voted, let's make it unanimous." Every hand went up.

Now it was noticed that those of us who seemed drowsy were wide awake and ready to do business. Frank Smith was elected Chairman of the New Hospital Building Committee, Andrew J. Beck was elected Chairman of the Building Fund and C. Hazen Stetson was elected Chairman of the New Hospital Committee.

I addressed the audience saying, "I want to thank you all for coming. The hopes and dreams I have had since meeting with the Rotary Club in August of 1954 are becoming a reality. Now that this meeting has accomplished its purpose, I will turn the gavel over to Mr. Stetson. He now holds the reins."

In October of 1955, an invitation was extended to me to consider the position of Administrator of the Presque Isle General Hospital. This was a hard decision to make. I had served so many years in the municipal field and had enjoyed helping with the many improvements in my community and things were so friendly all the way. Never had I dreamed of being considered for such a responsible position as administrator. For many days, I considered the offer. After several weeks, I made a decision one morning while sitting on the milking stool, milking the cow out on the farm. The decision I made was "I WILL ACCEPT THE CHALLENGE."

On April 1, 1956, my duties as administrator of the hospital began. For a few days I was very nervous, and then suddenly I discovered that all those fruitful years of experience I had were just what the hospital needed.

During my career in municipal work, I was dealing mainly with people of school age and with the tax-paying group. In the hospital, it went a little further. We dealt with human beings from the cradle to the grave. Daily, I saw newborn babies, people of all ages and from all walks of life, including those who were waiting for the last "Roll Call."

An excerpt taken from the newspaper at that time reads as follows: Ellis takes over as Hospital Administrator. The Chairman of the New Hospital Committee, Hazen Stetson said, "We believe that this is a necessary step in the development of our plans for a new hospital. There have been great advances in medical science in recent years. Hospital facilities and services have become more and more complex. The number of people who require hospital care is increasing steadily. As a result the position of hospital administrator becomes extremely important to the community. It calls for an understanding of the needs and desires of the community. These qualities Mr. Ellis possesses to a unique extent and he has the confidence of the community. Whatever additional detailed knowledge he needs in his new position, he will obtain by his continued studies and discussions with authorities in the hospital field."

Mr. Ellis said that the work as administrator is a real challenge inasmuch as the operation of the present hospital has many problems.

It was an inspiration, as well as a pleasure to have had the opportunity to have been a member of the board of Trustees of the hospital. It was indeed an honor to serve as President of the Board for a year and a half. It was my good fortune to serve as administrator, although it took some time to make the decision as to whether to accept the challenge.

My day began just before the night shift went off duty at 7 a.m. This gave me a chance to say good morning and learn of the problems of the night shift and to say good morning to those who were coming on duty for the 7 a.m. to 3 p.m. shift and then I met the evening shift that came on duty at 3 p.m.

The fund raising campaign was initiated in the summer of 1956. During a six week intensive campaign, total pledges of $600,000 were obtained. This included a contribution of $100,000 from Mr. and Mrs. Wildes, son- in-law and daughter of the late Arthur R. Gould.

It was during the fund raising program that the hospital was re-named the Arthur R. Gould Memorial Hospital. This was done in honor of the late Senator Gould, who, besides being Aroostook's only United States Senator, contributed to the development of Presque Isle and Aroostook County.

The Hill-Burton funds were made available and the old hospital property was sold for $160,000 thus assuring adequate funds.

The Deeves' farm on Academy Street, composed of 30 acres, was purchased by the trustees and was to be the location of the new hospital. Because costs of site acquisition could not be matched by Hill-Burton funds, the farm was acquired by using the grant from the Ford Foundation. The site had ample space for the new building, a parking lot and room for expansion in future years. There was also a wooded area that was to be preserved to isolate the hospital from commercial enterprises.

At a regular meeting of the Board of Trustees, held on May 21, 1957, a motion was duly made and seconded and it was voted that Horton Gilman, Hazen Stetson, and Frank Smith act on behalf of the Trustees in signing necessary forms in connection with plans and construction of the new hospital. Also, it was voted that the President of the Board or the Treasurer of the Board be authorized to act in behalf of the Board on signing necessary forms pertaining to the allocation of federal funds to be used in connection with the building of the new Arthur R. Gould Memorial Hospital.

In July of 1957, at a special meeting of the Board of Trustees, Frank Smith explained the plans in great detail, explaining that small details were still being changed; however, the basic plans were ready for approval. He said the architect's final preliminary drawings would be ready for presentation to the Federal Government on August 15th. It was voted to accept the preliminary plans of the new hospital as submitted by Frank Smith, chairman of the New Hospital Building Committee. Groundbreaking took place April 15, 1958.

From July 1, 1958, we saw many changes. Piles of earth, steel, tiling, wire, conduit, and many other items of building material were assembled so that we could visualize the hew hospital. Frank Smith and Mr. Stetson, of the building committee, gave generously of their time. Yes, many hours, days, and weeks…so that the people of this area, which included some 26,000 to 28,000 people, could enjoy this better hospital in years to come. We are grateful that such big-hearted people would contribute so much of their time and resources to a cause such as this.

From a spark that was kindled back in 1954, to work for a new hospital on a new site, one of the finest and best equipped hospitals to be found anywhere came into being. I was happy to have had the opportunity to play a part in the program. All of the people of the area the hospital serves owe a great deal to the many people who pulled off their coats and gave so generously of their time so that the new hospital could become a reality.

The total floor space was 44,000 square feet. Accommodations for patients: 80 beds and 20 bassinets. Staff: 136 full time and 20 part-time. Total cost was $1,550,000.

The Arthur R. Gould Memorial Hospital is a voluntary, non-profit institution operated by an unpaid Board of Trustees on behalf of the citizens of this part of Aroostook. The new hospital was one of the most modern and best equipped community centers in northern New England with many new features not only for patient care, but for the comfort and convenience of both patients and visitors. It is an attractive brick structure that embraced all the necessary requirements of a modern hospital. It is conveniently located and recessed from the main road. The 30 acre tract of land on which it stands is on Academy Street.

The dedication program was held on Saturday, January 9, 1960, at the Presque Isle High School auditorium. We were honored to have at the dedication ceremonies, Dr. Clifford O.T. Wieden, President of the Aroostook State Teachers College, Fred Warman, President of the City Council, the Honorable John Reed, Governor of Maine, and Dr. Dean H. Fisher, Commissioner of the Maine Dept. of Health and Welfare. C. Hazen Stetson gave an account of how the project was started and Jack Beck explained how it was accomplished. Among other speakers, Dr. Storer Boone, Chief of Staff, spoke on "what the hospital means to all of us." The ceremony was very colorful and the place was packed with people who had supported the idea of a new hospital on a new site all the way.

Tour of inspection of the new building was held on Sunday, January 10, 1960. The hospital, from its limited and meager beginning, was now a $1,550,000 structure. None of this would have been possible without the united efforts of the people of the area. We were all proud of the new hospital.

February 16, 1960 was to be moving day. The change over from the old to the new building was a thrill of a lifetime that many do not have the privilege to experience. We were leaving an institution that had served the area well for nearly half a century; however, the need for more and better medical care outgrew the facilities.

And so began a new era in the life of the hospital. With an able and efficient medical staff, loyal and dedicated employees in all departments, and modern equipment, we moved forward to meet the challenge of the times. We were proud to offer the best in surgical and medical care to the people of the area. The new building was ample in size, of modern design and structure and equipment, and staffed to supply the medical needs of the patients.

Chapter 21

Moving To the New Hospital

About November 1, 1959, the hospital trustees, at a regular meeting, began to make plans to move from the old building to the new. Committees were appointed to oversee the moving. Dr. Boone and Dr. Helfrich were appointed to make arrangements for the moving of the patients. Charles Eber volunteered to bring his farm truck and help move the beds and equipment. I was to see about keeping the pharmacy in order.

Very few supplies were kept on the floors. Several times every hour requests were made, by the doctors or the Superintendent of Nurses, for supplies from the pharmacy. Grace Emack was in charge. She allowed moving her supplies would be very difficult. She would often say "Really, I'm just sick thinking of trying to keep things straight. We have hundreds of items to look after. They are all catalogued and in order on the shelves. It will take a long time to move them. What if the doctors or nurses call for some of the medicines? We will be in an awful fix if things get mixed up."

I assured Mrs. Emack, "Don't worry, we'll find a way." As time went by, I too became a bit nervous. Mrs. Brown, supervisor of nurses, would often state, "I hope the pharmacy supplies don't get mixed up. Hunting for a specific item or a delay in finding a certain pill may affect the recovery of a patient and too much of a delay could cause a death."

One night, I guess I was dreaming, when I heard a voice say, "You are a farmer. Why worry about moving. Get out the potato baskets for Grace to use." When the pharmacy at the hospital was ready, I took Mrs. Emack over to see it. "Now, Grace!" I stated, "Don't worry another minute about moving your stock over here. Let me do the worrying." Twenty potato baskets were purchased. Raymond Bishop, the janitor, brought them to the hospital. As we carried them into the pharmacy, Mrs. Emack inquired, "What is going on?" I explained to her that if she would number all the baskets and make a list of the many items on the shelves when moving day arrived, she could begin filling the baskets. When each basket was full, she could take the scissors and cut the list in the proper place and put it in the basket. I continued on saying, "Before moving day, take your list over to the new pharmacy and label the shelves as you have done here."

February 16th arrived. At nine o'clock, the janitors began loading the baskets on Mr. Eber's truck. Raymond Bishop and his helper were told not to leave the truck unattended, even for a fraction of a minute. Mrs. Emack was to ride in the cab of the truck and be present during the whole operation. Later, Mrs. Emack stated, "That was easy. It is all over with and we worried for nothing. Mr. Ellis, your idea worked out so well I hardly know how to thank you for your suggestion."

The moving of the kitchen equipment was assigned to Vaughn Cole, a Trustee. He had been to the hospital several times to discuss with Mrs. Akeley, the dietitian, just how the task might be accomplished. He allowed he would furnish a truck or two and some men to assist with the lifting of the stoves, ranges, etc. As moving day approached, Mr. Cole became quite concerned over the moving and asked about plumbers. He, Raymond Bushy, and Paul Savard (a new janitor hired to work at the new hospital) discussed the matter. Paul had considerable experience in plumbing and said, "We can do the work ourselves but it will take time. Mrs. Akeley may be held up on account of the confusion of moving, but we will do our best."

I sat down with Mrs. Akeley and asked, "How early in the morning can we begin moving the equipment without interfering too much with the feeding of the patients? What would be the consequences if it took a couple of days to get all the equipment over for you to use?" Her reply was, "Seven o'clock and we'll get by someway."

Mr. Clyde Lynch, owner and manager of Welding Supply, supplied our gas for cooking. The oxygen used in the hospital was also purchased from him. I called him and requested that he stop by at his convenience. He came and we visited the kitchen. I said, "Moving this equipment over to the new hospital could be a sticker. Would it be possible to hire a man or two to help with the moving? Mr. Cole will furnish the trucks." Mr. Lynch replied, "Let's go up to your office. We will talk about the project and I'll give you an estimate of the cost and time required to move." I hoped I wasn't "put on the spot." Mr. Cole had cautioned me not to spend too much. Mr. Lynch asked, "How early in the morning can we start working if we decide to undertake the job?" I answered, "Mrs. Akeley allowed we could begin moving at seven o'clock and if it took a lot of time she'd manage someway." Mr. Lynch would not give me an estimate of the time required to do the job and, as to the cost, he said, "We'll talk about that later." He concluded by saying, "I will bring my own truck and help. Just leave the moving to me."

On moving day, Mr. Lynch came with his truck and helper and parked in back of the hospital. At exactly seven o'clock, Mrs. Akeley called me at my office and said, "Okay to begin moving the kitchen equipment now." I raced down and said, "Okay, Mr. Lynch, you can take over now." They quietly began their work and by nine o'clock, when we were to begin moving the patients, the kitchen equipment and supplies had been moved out. Mrs. Akeley had a few hot plates ready to use in case food was needed for a patient on a special diet.

By eleven o'clock, the kitchen equipment was installed in the new hospital. Mr. Lynch found me and stated, "Tell Mr. Cole there is no charge. This will be our contribution to the good cause for which you are working." Besides the truck and the labor, Mr. Lynch had donated considerable amounts of new pipe. I hardly knew how to express my appreciation for his kindness.

It had been decided to start moving the patients at nine o'clock. I had lost hours of sleep wondering if this part of the moving would be successful. Six ambulances, two from Presque Isle, one from Ashland, one from Mars Hill and two from the Limestone Air Force Base, were warmed and ready at moving time. There were thirty-seven patients to be moved that morning and the weather was not at its best. It was very cold but at least it was not storming.

Dr. Boone and Dr. Helfrich were very concerned and hoped everything would turn out okay. Mrs. Brown and her entire staff were on duty that morning. The other doctors were helping and worrying about the out come of the move. Mrs. Hopping, the Clinic Supervisor, was ready at the emergency entrance of the new hospital to receive the patients.

This moving of the patients was a new experience for nearly everyone. Someone remarked, "Mr. Ellis, you seem to be taking things more calmly than the rest of us." I remembered my training in the Army medical corps and was perhaps better prepared to take the jolt of moving. I also received some experience in moving patients while working with Dr. Hagerthy.

About eight forty-five, Dr. Donahue came hurrying to my office. He seemed quite excited. He said, "Phin, I'm afraid we will have to delay the moving for awhile." "Why?" I asked, "There is to be a delivery very soon," he answered. I looked at my watch and said, "Doctor, tell your patient to wait a few minutes." Several nurses heard my remark and had a great laugh. The Doctor looked puzzled and raced up the stairs. Soon he was back, saying "Time is running out. What are you going to do?" I looked at my watch again and replied, "History is being made here in Presque Isle today. We must keep our schedule. We will start moving the patients at nine o'clock and your patient is to be the first. Have any equipment with you that you might need. Take one nurse with you or more if you think best."

Mrs. Brown and I had a count down. Four minutes to go, three minutes, two minutes, one minute…then Mrs. Brown gave the word, "Mr. Ellis says, ready, let's move!" Dr. Donahue's patient was brought down on a stretcher and placed onto an ambulance. Two nurses hopped in. Dr. Donahue had asked the janitor to place his car behind the ambulance. When the ambulance door was closed, I gave the signal to move on. A member of the State Police rode ahead so there would be no delays. Dr. Donahue followed close behind in his car. It would take at least five minutes to reach the new hospital. Someone standing by said, "Let's pray things go well for Dr. Donahue and his patient."

One ambulance came close behind the other. The nurses, with the help of the doctors, kept the patients coming right along at regular intervals. At ten minutes of ten, the last of the thirty-seven patients were on their way to a new and better hospital. The doctors had followed their patients and not a single nurse was left. By eleven o'clock, the beds and all the usable furniture had been moved. It was a great relief to me. I felt that much of the responsibility of the morning had rested on my shoulders.

Dr. Donahue was very happy. His patient made the trip okay and the new delivery room was christened a very few minutes after nine o'clock. Margaret Brown, wife of Harrison Brown of Easton, had given birth to a fine baby girl, which they named Nancy Marie.

By twelve o'clock, everything was in order and we enjoyed a fine dinner prepared by Mrs. Akeley and her assistants.

The switch board was working perfectly. This system was quite different from that used in the old hospital. Mrs. Neva Dingwall had been on duty there for several days learning the new system. Now she was ready to train the other operators.

As I left for home that afternoon, about five o'clock, Mrs. Brown and Mrs. Hoppin complimented me for keeping my "cool" all day.

Chapter 22

P. S.

I thoroughly enjoyed being hospital administrator. Besides attending to the many things pertaining to my job, I kept in personal contact with the patients. I provided many with newspapers, birthday cakes, and flowers from my garden. I devoted time to meeting relatives and friends of those who reached the end of life's journey.

In August 1961, Charles Eber, President of the Board of Trustees of the A. R. Gould Memorial Hospital announced: "Phineas F. Ellis, present administrator, a former Trustee and President of the Hospital Board, had been appointed to the newly created position of Executive Assistant to the President. Mr. Ellis will have the full responsibility of maintaining a close liaison with the towns that are served by this hospital. It will be his duty to see that the financial burden of maintaining the hospital is more fairly distributed among the towns in this hospital area. Ellis will service building fund pledges and will have general supervision of all public relations. Mr. Ellis' past record as Town Manager and State Legislator will give him the wide experience necessary to fulfill this position. Hollis Irvine will assume the duties of Administrator."

I accepted the appointment with these words: "Another chapter has been written in the history of the Arthur R. Gould Memorial Hospital. It has been a grand experience to have taken part in the management of the hospital, also to have helped with the transfer from the old building to the new. The building committee gave freely and generously of their time, to the extent that they might have neglected their own businesses and even their own health. I believe you are fortunate to have Mr. Irvine succeed me as Administrator. Being young and full of "get up and go" and with more than two years experience here with work that has been closely connected with administration, I'm sure his efforts will be richly rewarded. As Executive Assistant, I am grateful for the opportunity to serve as co-coordinator between the hospital and the various towns which it serves. As we launch forth another year of service with our hospital for the towns and people it serves, let's pull together, play together, and pray together. By virtue of my appointment, as Executive Assistant to the President with the following duties: Public relations with the towns, collecting building fund pledges and public relations with the patients, I will endeavor to fulfill the duties of the position to the best of my ability."

Part three of my assignment had to do with the patients. I continued to visit as many patients as time would permit. I felt this was a very worthwhile thing to do.

Late in 1962, the building fund pledges were just about "cleaned up" and it seemed there wasn't enough left for the Executive Assistant to do to warrant full time employment. I was asked to remain on a part time basis. I was now of retirement age and thought I'd leave the hospital rather than become a part time employee. I retired December 31, 1962.

Mildred and Phineas Ellis, Spring of 1965.

This retirement ended when I was offered the job as head of the Supply Department of the Indian Head Plywood Corp. I really enjoyed working there and stayed for ten and one-half years. Along the last of it, my hearing got bad and this made it rather hard for me and I needed help to handle the toll-calls.

About the middle of July, 1973, I made up my mind to retire in August and told the manager, "I'd like to retire about August 10th." He paused for a moment before replying. "Okay, Phin, we hate to lose you, however, you should have a few years to rest. You have done a marvelous job for us. We all wish you the best of luck." August 10th came and I punched the clock for the last time.

I celebrated my 77th birthday on the 15th of that month. On August 22nd, Mildred and I celebrated our 50th wedding anniversary.

The children were all home and they arranged a "grand program" for Mildred and me. At that family gathering and the following Christmas, the family said, "Why don't you write a book?" I began gathering material and thought if things "shaped up" I'd attempt it. I hesitated to begin but after getting started, it became very interesting. I gathered information from many sources. I'm grateful to those who have responded to my letters and to those who took the time to chat with me and go back in memory to the years gone by.

Phineas and Mildred Ellis, August 23, 1973.

Chapter 23

Premonitions? Perhaps

A Bright Light in the Darkness

I was elected First Selectman for the Town of Castle Hill in March of 1939. In those days the Board of Selectmen had many duties, one of which was "Overseers of the Poor." Seventeen years had passed since I had served on the Board so I endeavored to become acquainted with all the problems in the town.

I was informed that the Elbert Ireland family was living on relief and having a very difficult time. Their home was on the Haystack Road. I had known these people very well in previous years. Mrs. Ireland was the former Effie Roberts. Her father's home was directly across the road from where the Irelands were now living. I had become acquainted with Elbert years ago when he was living with his parents in their home nearer Haystack Mountain.

One night, early in April, I seemed to have a "nightmare" about this family. I awoke with the premonition that I could perhaps do something for them. When morning arrived, I decided to take the time to call on them. They were not prepared for callers and I was afraid I was not welcome. However, I explained my mission (to see just how I could help them) and soon we were acquainted all over again. They remembered that I was the first mail carrier on their mail line.

Their home was a log camp. In spite of the fact that she had little to work with, Mrs. Ireland kept the camp very clean and things were neatly arranged. Mr. Ireland was encased in a plaster cast that went around his entire upper body. He must have been so uncomfortable. He explained that they were living down state when he hurt his back and that this cast had been applied to enable him to move around. He was sitting in a chair mending children's shoes. He said, "We have several children attending school and we find it awfully hard to provide suitable clothing for them."

I said, "I am here to help you in a way you have not experienced since you have been on the relief rolls. I understand you are given a prepared list for groceries, etc. that has been approved by the Selectmen. Today, I will give you an order and you can go to the stores and make your own choices. I believe this will work out better for you." We agreed upon a weekly amount and I promised to increase this amount if they found it necessary.

Before leaving, I said, "I want to tell you I served in the Legislature. While in Augusta, I learned about what the Department of Rehabilitation is doing to help handicapped folks. I believe you would be willing to work at something you could do to provide more for your children and help them finish school." They both became excited about the idea of earning money again as they used to before Mr. Ireland had become disabled.

I returned to my home and wrote to the Department of Rehabilitation in Augusta. I told them there was a very worthy family up here in Castle Hill that qualified for assistance from their department. In a very few days, a representative arrived. I met him in Mapleton and we drove toward the Ireland home. He asked; "What do you have in mind? What do you think they might do to help themselves?" I answered, "Perhaps if a good supply of tools and leather can be furnished we would be off to a good start. This man seems to be an expert cobbler."

We arrived at the camp and Mr. Ireland and this man discussed the families problems from A to Z. Mr. Ireland felt he could earn a lot of money fixing shoes. After a while, the representative asked to be excused saying, "I want to look over the area. Mr. Ellis and I will take a ride and we'll return later."

We drove toward Haystack Mountain for a mile or so, than the man said, "Mr. Ellis, I don't think Mr. Ireland could earn his salt mending shoes. This area is too sparsely populated and a certain percentage would probably forget to pay him." I began to feel guilty for having him come. He continued on saying, "I have an idea that will work. Could we arrange to purchase that old barn that's near the camp where this man lives?" I answered, "It won't be necessary to purchase the barn, it belongs to the town and it could be used in any way that would benefit the Ireland family." "All right," he said, "Here is my suggestion. The Department of Rehabilitation will furnish four angora rabbits, three does and a buck, suitable hutches for them and instructions for their feed and care. The Angora rabbit is known for its fine wool which grows about as long as that on a sheep. They multiply very fast and, in a few months, Mr. Ireland and his whole family will be busy everyday trying to keep up with their work. There is always a ready market for the wool sheared from angora rabbits. New lumber can be purchased to construct new hutches as they are needed." I told him there were partitions inside the barn that could be torn out and used.

We drove back to the Ireland home. The representative explained to them why he would not be in favor of outfitting a shoe shop and told them about the Angora rabbits. Mr. and Mrs. Ireland allowed they would give the rabbits a try.

The man returned to Augusta. Very soon the four rabbits arrived, along with four hutches and instructions for raising them. With these instructions, the family went to work in dead earnest and, in just one year, the family became self-supporting.

My, what a thrill it was to call on this family and see how happy they were. Mr. Ireland still had to endure his cast but he could sit in a chair and shear the rabbits of their wool. Shearing began when the rabbits were only a few months old and each rabbit was sheared several times a year. As I remember, the wool sold for $4.00 or more a pound. Month after month, the business continued to flourish. The family could purchase their own food and clothing to meet their wants and desires.

Mr. Ireland passed away October 4, 1944. On the day of his funeral, after the services, Mrs. Ireland brought her family to my home and thanked me for helping them to become self-supporting. She had each one of the children thank me for making it possible for them to have suitable school clothing they earned by themselves. If ever there was a day in my life that I was rewarded for my faith in people, this was the day.

In March of 1974, while working on my life's story, I thought I would like to write about the Ireland's experience. I found Mrs. Ireland to be living in Naples, Florida. I wrote and asked her permission to mention it. Her permission was granted. I will quote parts of her letter, "Dear Phin…It's been a long time hasn't it?...For twenty years I have been coming to Florida for the winter months…Phin, I want you to know the part you played in our lives is something I will never forget. You helped us, as the saying goes, 'beyond the call of duty.' It was like a bright light in the darkness when you came to our aid…My family is all getting on well and I'm proud of them…"

It is my fondest hope that all of those who read my story will remember, "God helps those that help themselves."

The Case of Estella Wells

From March of 1941 to the spring of 1947, when I was Town Manager only for the town of Castle Hill, my home was the town office and Friday was office day. Most of the other weekdays were spent working on the farm. Days, such as rainy ones, when it was convenient for me to leave the farm, I collected taxes and visited the families who were town cases (receiving relief).

On the morning of March 18, 1945, I left my home early to do some town errands. About a mile and a half from home, as I was passing the home of Jack Wells, I was sure I heard someone calling to me. I stopped the car, got out and looked around but I couldn't see a soul. As I was about to get back in the car, I noticed Jack Wells standing in his doorway. I asked, "Did you holler to me, Jack?" He answered, "No." I got in my car to leave but it would not start. This seemed very odd because it had been starting very well. While checking around the car, my hands got very cold. Mr. Wells again appeared in his doorway and I decided to go inside and get warm.

As I entered, Jack said, "Boy, I've had a tough night. Marm (as he called his wife Stella) is not very well. Gee, I'm glad you stopped, come in and talk with her." A nice wood fire was burning and the house was nice and warm. I went to the bedroom and sat by Mrs. Wells' bed. I inquired, "How are you feeling this morning? Has Jack prepared your breakfast yet?" Perhaps I asked a few more questions before Mrs. Wells aroused and asked, "Are you Joseph?" She smiled and asked again, "Really, aren't you Joseph?" I told her who I was. A strange look came across her face and she said, "I've been waiting for Joseph. Why doesn't he come?"

A few weeks ago, I had stopped by to see how they were getting along and, at that time, she also told me she was waiting to see Joseph. As I listened this time, I had a premonition that I should call Joseph. Joseph Page was Mrs. Wells' son by a former marriage. He was living in Kittery, Maine and employed at Portsmouth Navy Yard.

I assured Mrs. Wells that I would phone Joseph and perhaps he would come. I left the house, hopped in my car and was off. I had forgotten that for some mysterious reason it had not started a short while before. I returned to my home and phoned Joe Page at Kittery. I asked him if he could manage to come up for a few days. He answered, "My God, Phin, I'm so busy I couldn't get off on a bet." Joe and I had been chums for many years and I coaxed him to listen to me for a minute. "Well, go ahead," he said, "I'll listen." I explained, "I called at your mother's home this morning. She keeps asking for you. Now Joe, do me a favor, leave your work today, catch a plane from down there somewhere and come up." There was a period of silence then Joe asked, "Is Mother real sick?" I told him she was and she kept saying, "I'm waiting for Joseph." He answered, "Well, okay, I'll catch a plane and be in Presque Isle this afternoon."

I returned to the Wells' home and told Mrs. Wells, "Joe will be up to see you this afternoon." Her mind seemed to clear and she said, "Thank you Phin, I'll never forget you for this. I've been waiting for Joseph, everyday, for a long time."

Joe Page arrived that afternoon and immediately hired a taxi to drive him from the airport to his mother's home. I later learned that this was one of the best reunions ever witnessed. When Joseph approached his mother's bedside, she at once said, "Why, hello Joseph. Your poor old mother has not been feeling very well lately and I have been waiting and watching everyday for you to come." Her mind completely cleared and Joe and his mother talked about everything for about a half-hour. Suddenly, Joe realized the taxi was waiting for him and said, "Now that you are feeling better, Mother, I'll go back to town, pay the taxi man, have supper and come back later in Harry Rand's car." (Harry Rand's wife and Joe's wife were sisters).

For some reason or other, Joe did not return that evening as he had planned but came back early the next morning only to learn that his mother had passed away at 6:45, just a few minutes before his arrival.

Joe helped his stepfather make the funeral arrangements. Before returning to Kittery, he thanked me for calling him. He said, "How in the world did you know when to call me? I will always remember this kindness of yours until my dying day."

There had been a wonderful reunion between a mother and a son that she had not seen for some time. Mrs. Wells was very happy to have seen him once more before she passed away.

The Passing of My Dad, Jasper O. Ellis

In the last day's of December, 1947, my father became ill and was confined to his bed. As time went on his condition worsened. By the first of January, 1948, it had become necessary for someone to be at his bedside at all times. Four of us "boys" went into a huddle and decided to sit with Dad, one at a time, in six hour shifts.

Each day I was busy working at the Town Office in Mapleton, so I asked if I could sit from midnight until six in the morning. This was okay with my brothers.

During my shift on January 6th, Dad was very restless and his mind wandered a great deal. He kept asking for Dorcas. (Dorcas, my sister, was living in Kittery, Maine.) He kept repeating, "Where is Dorcas? Tell her I must see her. Tell her to come into my room. What is she doing that she can't find a minute to come in?" These questions and more were asked all through the night.

About five thirty in the morning, he dozed off. I fixed up the fires and walked around waiting for six o'clock when one of my brothers would come. During this time, I very clearly heard a voice saying, "Phin, you had better call Dorcas." The voice sounded like my mother's. She had passed away in 1941. I looked around but I was alone. I must confess I was somewhat nervous.

Dad called for me. I went to his bedside and straightened his pillows and blankets. He said, "It is morning and you will soon have to leave to do your chores at home. Before you go, make Dorcas come in." I asked, "Where do you think Dorcas is?" He answered, "She is out there somewhere in another room. Tell her to come in and see me." I replied, "I'll go out and scold her for not coming in."

At six o'clock, I left in a hurry, went to my home and phoned my sister in Kittery. I said, "Dad has been calling for you all night. He wants to see you, can you come?" Dorcas debated as to whether she could leave home at this time. After coaxing, she said, "Okay, I'll come. Meet me at the train in Presque Isle tomorrow noon."

During my next shift, it was the same thing over again. Dad kept asking for Dorcas. He said, "I don't understand why Dorcas does not come in and see me." I kept assuring him that she would be in to see him soon.

The next noon, January 7th, I met my sister at the train and we hurried to our father's house in Castle Hill. Dorcas went immediately to his room. The cloud-like condition, which had bothered Dad for several days, passed in a matter of seconds. Dorcas sat on the side of his bed and they were enjoying a wonderful reunion when I left to return to the Town Office.

That night, after supper, Mildred and I drove up to see how things were going. Dad's mind had completely cleared. Dorcas said, "You boys need not come tonight. I will be his nurse." Dad looked very happy when I left for home.

The next day was January 8th. That afternoon, before it was time to close the office, I received a call saying, "Dad has passed away."

A Happy Day for Nora Joe

Philip Joe was born in Canada and came to Castle Hill, Maine with Joe Paul, a companion, to make potato baskets. They moved into an old vacant log camp, previously occupied by William Porter, and began making baskets. The farmers in the area were very happy to have basket makers living in Castle Hill. Philip and Joe were busy as bees, day in and day out, getting out ash wood (from which good potato baskets were made) and weaving the baskets.

The Brown family lived nearby. The parents had passed on but their two daughters, Nora and Annis, and a son, Lester, lived in the family home. Lester Brown and Philip Joe became great friends. Lester owned a team of horses and he often assisted the men in getting out ash wood or in taking a load of their baskets to town to exchange for groceries. Philip and Nora became the best of friends and eventually they were married. From this union, three wonderful girls and a son were born.

After Philip and Nora's marriage, Joe Paul returned to Canada. Philip remained in Castle Hill. For many years during the summer months, he worked on road construction. I found him to be an honest man, a hard worker, and a true friend. Philip was a professional at making ax handles and made many for me and my brothers during the winters we were cutting hard wood.

When I was serving as Town Manager for Mapleton and Castle Hill, I usually drove by the home of Philip and Nora going to and from my office at Mapleton. One night I was on my way home, thinking seriously about my duties as Town Manager and wondering if I'd accomplished everything I should have that day. Before reaching Philip Joe's home, I had a premonition that Philip wanted to see me. When I arrived at his home, he was out pacing back and forth in his dooryard. I inquired, "Are you feeling well, Philip? It is unusual to see you pacing with your hands folded behind your back."

Philip almost broke down and cried. I hopped out of my car and went to where he was standing saying, "If there is anything I can do for you, speak up. What makes you so down at the heels?" When he recovered his composure, he stated, "I'm alright, Mr. Ellis, it's Nora. She is awfully sick. Come in and see her."

We entered the house and I was shocked at the sight of Nora. She was sitting in a rocking chair looking very pale and her voice was dreadfully weak. I pulled up a chair and began asking questions, "Is there something you would like me to get for you? If there is anything, like obtaining medicine or calling a doctor, that I can do just sing out." Nora allowed that she was too far gone to be helped. She said, "My days are numbered. Soon God will take over and I won't have to suffer any longer."

I questioned her as to what the trouble was and tried to find out how long she had been sick. Nora said, "I can't explain my trouble to you, but it is a condition that has existed ever since Junior was born."

Philip allowed they didn't have the money for a doctor. Nora said, "I have been praying to get better but my prayers have not been answered. I'm getting worse. It got so I can't lie in bed. I have to live here in this chair day and night. I cannot eat much. Tea is about all that tastes good to me."

While they were talking, I was wondering about having her moved to the hospital. The Joe's didn't have a phone. My thoughts went to Peter Richardson, a neighbor. He had a phone. I told Nora, "I'm going to call the hospital from Richardson's. Get ready, get some warm blankets and I'll take you to the hospital myself as soon as I can have a doctor at the emergency room to see you. If the doctor insists, you'll have to stay for a few days." Nora argued a bit about going and asked me whether I thought she might receive some help. "Sure," I said, "You will be as good as new in a short while." I went to the Richardson's, phoned the hospital and made arrangements for a doctor to see Nora.

When Peter learned of my plans to drive the Joe's to Presque Isle, he said, "Gee, Phin, you look tired. I'm not busy. Let me take them. You go home and rest." After I'd finished supper and finished the barn chores, I phoned the Doctor to see how she made out. He said, "Phin, you discovered this case just in time. Mrs. Joe is in bad shape. We have arranged a bed for her. Perhaps it will be necessary to operate. Check with me in the morning. By ten o'clock we will know how things are shaping up."

After ten the next morning, I called the Doctor. He stated, "Things are coming along just fine. Mrs. Joe has already had one operation and it may be necessary to operate again before she goes home. Don't worry. She will be as good as new in a month or so."

Mrs. Joe returned home and became a well woman. Many years have passed and, at this writing, she is still going strong.

I felt well rewarded for the time I spent helping Nora Joe.

The Strange Case of Henry Archer

Henry Archer was a recluse who lived on the Chapman Road in Mapleton, not far from the village.

One morning, soon after arriving at the Town Office, I received a call. The person phoning seemed very excited. I asked, "Is there something wrong?" The woman said, "I'm calling to tell you about Henry Archer. Poor Henry hasn't been seen for several days. My husband went over to his house this morning to find out if something was wrong. He rapped on the door but got no answer. Then he tried the door and it wasn't fastened so he walked in. He found poor Henry very sick. He couldn't even speak, so my husband ran back and told me to call you."

"Where is Laura?" I inquired. Laura was Herman Archer's wife and she sometimes looked after "Uncle Henry." The woman calling said, "I think Laura and her children are visiting down in Brownville with her parents."

I thought it would be wise to call a doctor. Several were called but they were busy. Finally, one agreed to come to Mapleton. I said, "Step on the gas. The person who phoned allowed that Mr. Archer has not been seen out around for several days. He must be awfully sick."

In about twenty minutes, the Doctor arrived at the Town Office. I rode with him to the Archer home. The neighbor was there waiting and we all went inside. The Doctor pulled back the bed clothes and it was obvious the man had not been out of bed for several days. The Doctor made a few tests, took his pulse, tried to take his temperature, and moved his arms around a bit. Then he beckoned for me to come outside. He said, "There isn't a thing I can do. If medication is prescribed, he couldn't take it. It is too late I'm afraid."

As the Doctor drove me back to the Town Office, I asked, "Don't you think this man could recover if he was put in the hospital?" He answered, "No, I think it is too late."

I went into the office and sat wondering what should be done next. I had a premonition that I should go over and check again. I hurried back to the Archer home, entered, pulled a chair up to the bedside and began talking, thinking perhaps Henry could hear but not speak. He seemed to have a bit of warmth under his arms. His pulse was very weak. I kept talking and asking him what I could do for him. After a few minutes, I heard a faint murmur. I kept asking questions and the murmur became audible. I could make out the words Laura. I asked. "Do you want Laura?" Very faintly but audible, he said, "Yes." "Okay," I said, "I'll find Laura for you."

I hurried back to the Town Office and called the Town Manager of Brownville. I told him Laura Archer was wanted. I said, "Her parents live in Brownville and I understand she is visiting with them. I don't know her maiden name, but inquire around and see if you can locate her family. Call me back. This is an emergency case." The Town Manager, I believe his name was Bion Jose, said, "I think I know the family, I'll call you back shortly."

In a very short time, the phone rang. It was a collect toll call and Laura was on the other end of the line. I explained the situation to her. Laura became almost hysterical, repeating, "Oh, my God, Oh, my God." She asked me to hold the line for a minute. She came back on saying, "I have just enough time to catch the bus. I'll be up and look after Uncle Henry this very afternoon."

At five o'clock, I called at the Archer home again. Laura had arrived and had changed the bedding. She said, "Thank you, Mr. Ellis. Uncle Henry is still alive. His bowels have not moved for sometime but I think I can manage. Come over in the morning."

I could not sleep that night, wondering what would have happened if Laura had not arrived. I seemed to hear Dr. Hagerthy saying, "Remember where there is life there is hope."

The next morning, about seven o'clock, I called at the Archer home. Laura had revived "Uncle Henry." She said, "I had an awful time getting his bowels to move but I made it after awhile. He has already taken some soft food and I've given him a good bath."

After Henry was up and around, Laura explained to me that he had loaned her some of his pension money on several occasions and, in return, she was to care for him if he ever needed nursing care. She said, "I made him a solemn promise that I would come at any time if he needed me. He had only to get a message to me and you, Mr. Ellis, delivered his message."

Perhaps a Miracle

I had been Administrator of the Presque Isle General Hospital for only a short time when, as I was about to enter my office at 6:30 one morning, a nurse summoned me to the emergency room.

A young girl, about nine years of age, had just been brought in. At first glance, it appeared the child has passed away. She was white as chalk. There was not the least bit of color in her young face. I inquired, "If this child is living, why isn't something being done?" I was told, "She is one of Dr. Donahue's patents and he is on his way over."

I viewed the admission sheet. The girl's name was Bettina Gardner, daughter of Alice and Herbert Gardner.

The Doctor arrived and instructed the nurses to prepare a blood transfusion. I had not seen a case like this one so I began asking questions. Dr. Donahue said, "This child is a bleeder." Later, after the blood transfusion had been completed, the Doctor came to my office and explained about bleeders.

In a day or so, the girl was up and around as spry as any youngster. After she'd gone home the Doctor told me, "She's been in here before and she'll be back from time to time for as long as she lives."

A few weeks later, Bettina was back for another blood transfusion. At this time I asked the Doctor, "How long can anyone be expected to live like this?" He said, "It will be a miracle if I can keep this child living until her tenth birthday. The only thing known to medical science that can be done, I'm doing."

The days and months passed and the child continued to live. Her tenth birthday came and went. One day, when she was admitted for treatment, I said to the Doctor, "You have been doing a fine job. What is your opinion now as to how long she might live?"With tears running down his cheeks, Dr. Donahue said, "Phin, I've been fooled so far. Perhaps she may live to be thirteen or fourteen years old."

Time passed and Bettina lived on. One day when she was brought to the hospital, I had a feeling the Doctor felt this would be her last admission. The Doctor and the nurses completed the regular procedure and Bettina was put to bed in the children's ward. A day or so later, the Doctor requested the mother come to the hospital right away.

The mother arrived, quite upset about being called. She stopped by my office and inquired, "Do you think my daughter is really worse this time?" I answered, "I don't know what to say, Alice. I haven't been told just how ill Bettina is." Alice stated, "Phin, I'm almost afraid to go in and see her. Won't you come with me?" We went together to the girl's bedside.

I placed a chair by the bed for Alice and she placed her hands on Bettina's. I noticed she was praying. While she prayed, something seemed to say to me, "Tell the mother her prayers will be answered. Her daughter is going to get well."

At this point, I was a bit shaky. I placed my hands on Alice's and delivered the message, saying, "Alice, something seems to tell me your prayers will be answered. Bettina is going to get well."

The surprised mother looked up at me and smiled. In all her previous visits to see her daughter in the hospital, I had never seen her smile.

Bettina was soon well enough to go home and her trips to the hospital became less frequent. She eventually outgrew her problem. Bettina is married and now lives in New Hampshire where she teaches school.

Dr. Donahue was my doctor. Sometimes when I went to his office for my check ups, he would mention the strange case of Bettina Gardner. He would say, "I'm still wondering what brought about the change."

I never told him of the message I had received for the child's mother.

Fred Gates

My memories of Fred Gates, a fine gentleman, go back to my high school days. Not long after beginning my sophomore year, I became acquainted with the people at Union House, a hotel located near Dr. Hagerthy's home.

The hotel was operated by two proprietors, Mr. Junkins and Charles Sleeper. Mr. Gates was married to Charles Sleeper's daughter. Although Mr. Gates did not live at the hotel, he often assisted with the chores.

Nearly a quarter of a century later, when we had open roads, Mr. Gates was employed as a wingman on the state snow plow, which passed my home in Castle Hill. It was often necessary for the plow to be out nights during bad storms.

Many times, I would be up doing the barn chores when the plow passed by. I learned they only went down a mile or two below my home before turning and heading back toward Ashland. Another state plow from Presque Isle plowed the remainder of the State Road.

One cold blustery morning, it occurred to me that the men on the plow had been out most of the night and perhaps they would like to have a hot cup of coffee. They had passed my house and I knew they would be back in about half an hour. I hustled around feeding the stock in the barn then hurried to the house and put on a pot of coffee.

When the plow returned, I was standing beside the road waving for them to stop. At first, they thought there'd been a telephone call for them. I told them I thought it would be nice for them to take a break, come in and have a cup of hot coffee.

Mr. Gates and the driver of the plow were so pleased with the coffee and the doughnuts I served with it, that it seemed they could not thank me enough. This was just the beginning. Many other "coffee breaks" followed.

About the middle of August, 1956, I crossed paths with Fred Gates again when he was admitted to the Presque Isle General Hospital. I was administrator of the hospital at the time. Although he was now an old man, little did I realize his life's journey was about to end.

I noticed on his admission form that he would be eighty years old on August 18th. I asked Mildred if she would make a birthday cake for one of the men who used to appreciate the coffee and doughnuts served to them on some of those cold stormy mornings, years ago. Mildred thought this would be a kind thing to do and agreed to make the cake. She frosted it, wrote happy birthday on it and decorated it with candles.

On the morning of August 18, I took the cake to the hospital and placed it on my desk. Some of the nurses spied it and asked, "What's up?" I told them of my plans to present the cake to Mr. Gates. I said, "I became acquainted with this gentleman many years ago. When it is convenient, I would like to have several of you nurses come along with me. You can sing Happy Birthday." Never in my life had I seen anyone so surprised or so pleased. He shared the cake with the nurses and thanked us over and over.

Later that morning, some of the nurses came to my office and allowed that this was one of the nicest things they had ever seen done for a patient. One of them said, "Mr. Ellis, Mr. Gates told us about your high school days and how you worked so hard to get through school. He seems to have forgotten about his illness and wants to talk about the good things in life." During the next several days, I always found the time to stop by and say good morning to Mr. Gates.

On the night of September 5th, I was very restless all through the night. I thought I heard someone calling my name. Several times, I got up and went to the door to see if someone was there. I got up very early and had completed the chores when I got a premonition that I was wanted at the hospital. I kept this to myself for fear Mildred would say, "Don't take your work so seriously."

As soon as I'd eaten my breakfast, I hurried to Presque Isle. I entered my office and found a memo lying on the desk. It read, "Mr. Gates has been calling for you all night."

It was not six-thirty, the night crew was getting ready to leave and the day shift was coming to work. There were so many things to check on that I didn't go to see Mr. Gates right away. About eight o'clock, a nurse came running in saying, "Please come and see Mr. Gates. He wants you."

I went to his room and sat by his bedside. He said, "Phin, I want to tell you something. It is something I have wanted to tell you for quite a few days. I've been thinking about the little birthday party you had for me. Really, it was wonderful and the best thing that has been done for me. It has made my stay here more pleasant." He reached for my hand and continued on saying, "Thank you again, Phin. What you have done for me perhaps you can do for other patients while you work here at the hospital. I'm glad to see you this morning and I hope you have a good day. I'm sort of tired this morning. I didn't rest much last night. Help me fix this pillow under my head and I'll have a good rest while you go do your work."

About noon, a nurse came and said, "Mr. Gates has gone into a coma." This condition lasted a few days and Mr. Gates died on September 9th without regaining consciousness.

Mr. Gates' appreciation of the cake impressed me so much that I decided to carry out his suggestion and do this for other patients.

From that fall of 1956 until I left the employ of the hospital on December 31, 1962, every patient, except those too ill to be disturbed, who had a birthday while they were a patient in the hospital, received a cake. The nurses always sang Happy Birthday to them when it was presented.

Many of the cakes were brought from home but sometimes I would purchase one at the grocery store and have the kitchen frost and decorate it for me. We averaged more than one birthday a week.

Mr. Gates suggestion was carried out and I have always felt that each recipient appreciated the gesture just as much as Mr. Gates did.

Chapter 24

The Lynching of Jim Cullen

Jim Cullen came from a very lawless family living in Florenceville, New Brunswick. The boys of this family were harassed so much by the Canadian police that some of them shacked up on the American side of the border, back of Mars Hill Mountain, in a place known as Rogues Roost.

Beginning about the middle of the nineteenth century and continuing for many years after, considerable pine lumber was cut on land bordering the Aroostook River. Good axe men were hired to square up the timber. In the spring of each year, the squared timber, referred to as ten-timber, was driven down the Aroostook River to the Saint John River then on to the town of Saint John where it was sold, loaded on boats, and shipped to different parts of the world.

Many Canadians were hired each year to assist with the cutting of the logs. Ox teams were taken up to the camps in the fall to haul the pine timber, after it was squared, to the river banks. At least two of the Cullen boys were among those who would go up to the woods each year, stay until the cutting was finished and then assist with the driving of the lumber down to Saint John.

There was a trail, we will refer to it as the "short cut", to reach the town of Dalton (later renamed Ashland). The "short cut" came around Mars Hill Mountain to Mars Hill, continued north along the Aroostook Road, to a place some five miles south of Presque Isle that has always been known as Spragueville. Here the trail turned westerly, toward Chapman, then on to Ball's Mill (what is now Mapleton), Castle Hill, and by the Haystack Mountain Road to Dalton.

Only about three miles of the Haystack Road had been settled. From Haystack Mountain, up through the woods to Worcester Ridge, a distance of about four miles, the road had not been improved for summer use and was used very little in winter. At Worcester Ridge, the road to what is now Ashland had been improved. Many farms had been cleared and homes built along the way.

It was on one of the trips up to the lumber camps that Jim Cullen became acquainted with the woman that has been known down through the years as Mrs. Twist. (The Roe and Colby Atlas of 1877 shows the name Twist as belonging to one of the families living in Castle Hill on the Haystack Road.) Mrs. Twist was a young woman in her early twenties. She was very much overweight, weighing over 300 pounds, and was about five feet four inches tall. She was of a very jolly nature and was always giggling. When she giggled, she jiggled all over. This was entertaining for many young men who knew her. In this spring of 1873, Cullen and Mrs. Twist were living in a square house, one story in height and constructed of hewn timbers. (This house was remodeled into a two story house in 1895 and is still standing today.)

Jim Cullen was about 27 years old at the time of the lynching. He was over six feet tall and weighed 240 to 250 pounds. His hair and beard were fiery red and he had a receding forehead. From casual observation, one could compare the shape of his skull with that of an animal.

Cullen was of a troublesome nature and feared by all who knew him. He had the reputation of being a thief. His strength was unlimited, whenever he had an opportunity to demonstrate it.

Quite often merchants would miss merchandise from their stores after Cullen had come to make a purchase. Some people complained of losing clothes from their clothes lines and vegetables and canned goods from their cellars, yet nothing was done about it because everyone feared the man. It was a known fact that Cullen had been locked up in the Houlton jail a couple of times but always managed to escape by grasping the bars of the window and shaking the wall until it gave way and collapsed.

In April of 1873, Mr. J. T. Hoffses, living on what is now known as Lot No. 142 in Castle Hill, had timber hewn in the Haystack woods area and hauled to his farm. Work was in progress to frame and build a barn. The timber had been delivered to the location where the barn was to be built and most of it had to be moved again. Three or more men would take up one of those timbers and carry it to a place designated by the carpenter on the job to be tongued, mortised, and made ready to become part of the framework of the barn.

Jim Cullen came by at this time and offered to assist with the work. Mr. Hoffses said, "Sure, young man, your assistance will be appreciated." Cullen helped move a few timbers then allowed that he could do better moving them alone. The other men stepped back and Cullen demonstrated his strength by moving timber alone. From that time on, no one dared to make any statements that might cause this man to become angry.

The property on which Cullen was living is listed in the Roe and Colby Atlas of 1877 as belonging to Samuel Williamson. William Hubbard purchased the property from Samuel Williamson and came from Palmyra, Maine with his widowed mother to make his home in Castle Hill and begin farming. When he arrived, the house was occupied by Cullen and Mrs. Twist. Several attempts were made to get them out of the building but Cullen would not budge.

Mr. Hubbard boarded at J. T. Hoffses; perhaps his mother was boarded there also, and waited for the time he could move into the home he had purchased. He had called on Cullen several times to see what he was planning to do. Summer would soon be here and Mr. Hubbard planned to begin farming this spring. Mr. Hubbard was aware that Cullen showed some degree of jealousy about his calling but little did he realize what Cullen could do to him should they get into a scrap until his strength had been shown at the barn raising.

The last call that Mr. Hubbard made on Cullen and Mrs. Twist, he threatened them to either move out of the house he had purchased or he would take action through the law to have them moved.

At the village known as Ball's Mill (now Mapleton), there was a general storekeeper by the name of David Dudley who was very well respected by all who knew him. Mr. Dudley was a shrewd fellow and always seemed to know what to buy and when to buy merchandise or goods that would please his customers.

This spring of 1873, Mr. Dudley noticed Cullen's footwear was getting rather worn and he would soon be in need of a new pair of shoes. Cullen wore a size fourteen shoe, so Mr. Dudley ordered a pair and hung them in the front of the store so that Cullen could see them whenever he called to make a purchase.

On Monday morning, April 28th, 1873, Mr. Dudley came to open his store at the usual hour. After opening the door, he noticed the shoes were missing. Mr. Hubbard had arrived at the store about the same time as Mr. Dudley and they wondered how in "hell" those shoes could have ever been taken down without being noticed by someone. Mr. Hubbard went outside and looked around the building and, to his surprise, saw some very large footprints in the new snow that had fallen over the weekend. Mr. Dudley was called out to make an inspection of the tracks and, at this time, they found that a storm window had been removed from a back window and entrance gained to the store by raising the inside window. The tracks were so large that both Mr. Hubbard and Dave Dudley agreed that they could not have been made by any other than Jim Cullen.

Mr. Dudley was so angry that he probably would have taken a shot at Cullen had he appeared at that time. Mr. Dudley stated, "This is the last STRAW! I've put up with a lot from Jim Cullen, but no more!"

Mr. Hubbard confided in Mr. Dudley that he was getting disgusted with trying to get Cullen to move from his property. He stated that he was on his way to Presque Isle to arrange with a sheriff to remove Cullen from the house. Mr. Dudley said, "Bill, include me in on the deal. We've just got to have something done with no more fooling around. Cullen has gone the limit around here with his thievery. Today is the day…no more fooling with that CRITTER!"

It was seven miles to Presque Isle. The roads were still covered with snow and ice so William Hubbard walked and went to the hotel to inquire as to where he might find a sheriff. Much excitement was aroused when the word sheriff was mentioned. Mr. Hubbard told his story about Cullen making a theft at Dudley's Store as well as telling him that Cullen was a squatter in the house he had purchased.

Word soon got around town and a large crowd gathered at the hotel. Everyone present had heard a great deal about Cullen and of his reputation.

Mr. Kalloch was an elderly gentleman but agreed to go himself, apprehend Cullen, and bring him in for trial. Mr. Kalloch was cautioned not to go alone to arrest Cullen. He was told "You must take some husky fellow along with you."

Mr. Kalloch was already aware of the strength of the Cullen boys and stated, "One of this man's brothers came to Ashland last fall on his way up to the woods to work for the winter. The young fellow, to show off at the hotel, went to the veranda and turned several handsprings, one of them a double handspring and he allowed that he had walked nearly sixty miles that day. Believe me no one spoke, even in a whisper, of having a wrestling match that night."

Mr. Kalloch was preparing to go to Ball's Mill with the warrant for Cullen's arrest when Granville Hayden, who had a store directly across the street from the hotel, learned something of what was taking place. He came over and was informed of what Mr. Kalloch was preparing to do. Mr. Hayden told Mr. Kalloch, "You are too old a man to do this job."

Mr. Hayden was a deputy sheriff and had a way with arresting people. He always brought in his man without much trouble and was well respected by all who knew him. In a wrestling match, Mr. Hayden always floored his opponent. He allowed he would go in Mr. Kalloch's place. The crowd approved very heartily to this suggestion.

Mr. Hubbard was deputized to assist Granville Hayden with the arrest. The arrangement was to meet at Dudley's Store, as early as possible, the next morning, Tuesday, April 29th.

Mr. Hubbard returned to Castle Hill that day and went to meet Mr. Hayden, as planned, the next day at Dudley's Store. Mr. Hayden came with a horse and pung and, as the roads were soft and punchy, it was nearly noon when he arrived. Hubbard was there waiting. Mr. Hayden ate dinner at an eating place and a plan was drawn up as to the location of the home from which they planned to arrest Cullen and ideas were rehearsed as to what to do in case Jim Cullen got rough.

A farmer was in town with his double team and sled and offered to take Hayden and Hubbard to the house in Castle Hill where Cullen was living. It was approximately three-fourths of a mile from Ball's Mill.

Upon arriving at the house, Mr. Hayden went to the door and was greeted by Mrs. Twist. He asked for Cullen and stated that he had some business to do with him. Mrs. Twist said, "I'm sorry but Jim is not home. He went over to Florenceville yesterday to visit his mother before going up on the 'drive.' He plans to be away for three or four days."

Mr. Hayden and Hubbard, who was close by his side, went back out to the road where the farmer was waiting with the team. The three men held sort of a conference and it was decided that Mrs. Twist had lied and that they should return to the house, rush right in, and find out for sure whether Cullen was hiding there. Just as Hayden and Hubbard were about to return to the house, the farmer with the team called their attention to large footprints leading down across the field to the Chapman Road. The Chapman Road, at that time, was on the town line between Castle Hill and Ball's Mill. Inspection was made of the footprints in the snow as well as in the soil where the snow had melted off.

It was decided that perhaps Cullen had gone out to Swanback's camp as he sometimes had in the past. Due to the hard walking, it was doubted that Cullen would go very far. Mr. Hayden stated, "Now that we have the warrant for Cullen's arrest, an honest effort must be made to arrest him." It was decided to follow the tracks, so the farmer with the team returned to Ball's Mill and Hayden and Hubbard went on their way. The tracks eventually led to Swanback's camp, nearly seven miles away.

About three miles out, at a little settlement, they lost sight of the large footprints because teams had been out on the road. They asked several men along the way if they had seen Jim Cullen pass recently. No one had seen him but when they were passing Eben Garland's, the tracks were noticed again.

Hayden and Hubbard went into Garland's to inquire, as they had of others, if they had seen Jim Cullen. Mary Judkins, who lived nearby, came to the door. She had good news for these men. She answered, "Yes, Mr. Cullen stopped here yesterday and borrowed a pair of snowshoes. He said it was hard walking, that he was on his way over to Florenceville to see his folks and the snowshoes would be helpful in making the trip. He said he would be coming back in a few days and would return the snowshoes."

Once back in the road, Hayden and Hubbard stood for several minutes pointing. Sometimes back toward the direction from whence they came and sometimes toward Swanback's clearing. It must have been decided to continue on with the warrant for they went towards Swanback's. Although the snow had settled nearly to the bare ground in many places it was still very hard and tiresome walking. It was late in the afternoon when they reached Swanback's camp and they were getting very tired, especially Mr. Hayden, for he had not been walking much except for around his store.

Cullen was found here at the camp. Minot Bird was also there. Minot's home was on the same road as that of Cullen and he had been spending a few days helping Swanback shave shingles and had many bundles stacked up out a ways from the camp. These would be sold at Presque Isle just as soon as the snow was gone and the roads dried up.

After taking a good look at Cullen, Hayden decided he would not return that night but wait until morning to arrest Cullen and take him in after it became daylight. Swanback was called out in the camp yard by Hayden and informed as to why he and Bill Hubbard were there. Swanback allowed he had plenty of provisions on hand and it would be better not to return that night. While supper was being prepared, Mr. Hayden called Cullen out in the yard, away from the camp, and showed him the warrant. It was always felt by Swanback and Minot Bird, during the years that followed, that Hayden had given Cullen a chance to move on towards Canada. After supper, they all rested and told stories for awhile.

The camp was made of logs, perhaps all spruce logs, notched at the ends so as to make the corners of the camp good and solid. The cracks between the logs were chinked with moss. There were two small windows. The heating system was just an open fireplace walled up around the sides with rocks. The roof was of the "hip roof" style and covered with cedar splints. These splints, as they were called, were about three to three and a half feet in length and made of the choicest cedar (the same kind that was used in making shingles) which split out evenly all the way.

After a time, most everyone was getting very drowsy and Mr. Hayden suggested they all settle down for the night and get some rest. He wanted to get a good early start in the morning. A good supply of wood was brought in for the night. The kerosene lantern was filled and hung up. Mr. Hubbard had his suspicions that something might happen if all slept at the same time. Swanback and Hubbard went out to the camp yard. After talking things over, it was decided not to all sleep at once. Hayden was called out and told of the plan. He allowed that would be the proper thing to do and that he and Hubbard would take turns remaining awake.

After a couple of hours, Hubbard branded up the fire and woke Hayden to take a turn at being awake. Hayden stretched and began his turn at being watchman. Soon Hubbard was "dead to the world" for he was just about ready to drop from fatigue. Perhaps it was around midnight that Cullen got up, stoked the fire, looked all around, picked up his coat and cap and quietly left the camp, being careful not to make any noise. The snow had frozen some and Cullen's footsteps could be heard as he crunched along out the road towards his home. Bird and Swanback were very restless and hopped out of bed and whispered to Mr. Hayden, who was already on the alert. They opened the door of the camp very quietly and Cullen's footsteps could still be heard in the distance. Finally they faded away completely.

Hubbard was sleeping very soundly. The other three, Hayden, Swanback and Minot Bird, sat around the fire for quite a long time. All agreed that Cullen had decided it was best for "his hide" to clear out and had gone towards his home. Hayden mentioned, "Too bad that man hadn't gone towards Canada, then we would be rid of him."

After awhile, everything was quiet. Hayden had fallen into a sound sleep. Although Swanback and Minot had crawled back into their bunks, they were too nervous to sleep thinking of what might happen when Cullen was arrested at the place he was living in the morning. As they lay there, a noise like footsteps could be heard; as they listened, the noise in the crunching snow became louder. More than an hour had passed but it was now certain that Cullen was very quietly stealing his way back. Cullen stood outside the camp for several minutes then very quietly opened the door and entered.

He stood very quietly inside for a brief time then walked over to the fireplace and branded up the fire. Hayden and Hubbard were breathing loudly as they slept. It was certain that Cullen believed all were sleeping soundly. He reached and grasped an axe that was sticking in the wall and, with heavy strokes, split the heads of first Hayden, then Hubbard. With the bloody axe, he quickly stepped over to the bunks and prepared to strike when Swanback and Bird rose to their knees and pleaded for Cullen not to harm them, saying "We haven't done anything. We won't ever tell if you will just spare our lives." While they were pleading for their lives, the little dog became very much alive and began growling. His hair was standing straight up on his back and he was prepared to pounce on Cullen. Minot Bird, always through life, expressed the feeling that Swanback's dog, though small, perhaps had saved their lives.

Cullen stood quietly before the bunk beds for a minute or more as Swanback and Bird pleaded for their lives. Finally he lowered the axe and said, "All right, but climb out and help me get a lot of wood." Each was trembling like a leaf but they scrambled out to the camp floor and were preparing to put on their rubbers when Cullen snatched them away saying, "No, you don't put on any rubbers. Get on out there and bring me in a lot of wood." The camp door was opened. Cullen dragged the bodies of Hayden and Hubbard over and heaved them on the fire. Swanback and Bird began bringing in wood. Cullen kept shouting, "Now no tricks boys, if you know what is good for you keep busy, remember, no punches," and he continued on while piling wood on the fire.

Cullen became so busy with his fire that the "boys," as he referred to them, kept edging further away from the camp yard each time they went out to bring in an armful of wood. They always believed that Cullen intended to kill them too when he finished burning the bodies of Hayden and Hubbard. On one trip out for wood, Swanback whispered to Bird, "Come on. Let's go." In their stocking feet and without caps or jackets the "boys" took a chance on escaping.

The snow had hardened into a crust during the night and would hold them fairly well. Perhaps if Cullen started to follow, he would find it more difficult walking and would lose time in trying to catch them. The "boys" made good time and glanced back from time to time to make sure Cullen was not close behind. It was getting daylight by the time they reached the settlement, some three miles from the camp, and it would not be long before sunrise.

Andrew Judkins had tapped a number of maple trees that spring and, when the "boys" came running by, Mr. and Mrs. Judkins and their son, Ernest, were out on the crust gathering the sap. As the "boys" raced by, Swanback kept repeating "He kill one...he kill two...he kill one...he kill two." Without stopping to make an explanation, they ran on toward Ball's Mill.

Mr. Judkins, his wife and son went to the road side and observed the "boys" running for dear life without coats, caps or rubbers on their feet. Holes had worn in their stockings and blood from their feet could be seen in places on the crusty snow.

Swanback and Bird raced on, reached Ball's Mill, and spread the alarm. They were taken to Dudley's home and their bloodied feet were washed and bandaged. After they calmed down a bit and stopped trembling, a good warm breakfast was prepared for them.

By mid-forenoon, news of the tragedy had spread far and wide. A posse had formed at Ball's Mill and another at Spragueville for it was feared Cullen might escape by way of the "shortcut" and return to Canada. The farmer had brought back word, to Dudley's store the day before, of Mrs. Twist's remark, "Jim has gone to Canada to see his folks."

Cyrus Hayden, brother of Granville, was so confused when he heard of the tragedy that he hardly knew what to do or which way to turn. His first move was to have a box, used to put caskets in taken to Ball's Mill.

A Mr. Dorsey of Fort Fairfield, who had some fine teams of horses and did a considerable amount of toting, was in Presque Isle that morning with a high wagon and one of his teams. This was the first wagon seen out this spring. There was still snow on the roads, due to a late spring, and sleds had been used up to this time. Mr. Dorsey allowed that perhaps it would be easier and safer to make the trip to Ball's Mill by wagon and that he was available to go. (Note: the name Mr. Dorsey was mentioned many times by my grandmother as being the man who had the team but I have not seen this name in any of the stories written.) James Phair was hired to go with Mr. Dorsey and Fred Barker volunteered. Cyrus Hayden went by horse and sleigh and took Dr. Parker along with him.

Cyrus and the Doctor arrived at Ball's Mill nearly an hour ahead of the wagon. Their first stop was at Dudley's Store where a large group of men had gathered. Next, they went to Dudley's home to see Minot Bird and John Swanback to get firsthand information of the tragedy. It was at this time that Cyrus became aware the bodies had been burned and the box for his brother would not be needed.

Cyrus's horse was stabled and he and the Doctor were provided with a lunch at a near-by boarding house. The excitement continued to increase. Constable Hughes was trying his level best to quiet the group when some men came from the Chapman settlement spreading the news that Cullen had come from out of the woods and had gone up across the field to the place he called home.

About one o'clock, a posse was "armed to the teeth" and ready to go with Constable Hughes to help bring back Jim Cullen. Reports are that there were between twenty and thirty men in the posse that marched up the road. Several brought along their guns. When they arrived at the driveway, a careful search was made to make sure that Cullen had entered the house. New tracks were observed that could only have been made by a heavy person wearing a very large shoe.

Constable Hughes pushed the door open and called for Jim to come out "as we have some business to talk over with you." Jim did not reply but Mrs. Twist came to the door and inquired, "What in 'hell' is this all about, why such a mob as this?" She stated, "Jim is not here. He left Monday to go to Canada to visit his people before going up on the drive. I told the two men who were here yesterday just what I'm telling you now."

There was a few seconds pause then Constable Hughes said, "Why do you lie like this? Here are his tracks leading right up to the door." Mrs. Twist asked, "Has Jim done something awful that brings you men here?" Constable Hughes answered, "Yes, woman, he has killed Gran Hayden and Bill Hubbard." At that moment, he beckoned to those with him to enter. The door was pushed wide open and Mrs. Twist was told "get out of our way, we have come for Jim Cullen and we are coming in."

As many men as could crowded into the room. There was a small boy, perhaps two or three years old, walking around. Mrs. Twist was asked to take the boy over in the corner so he would not get hurt. A hasty search was made behind a curtain and under a bed but no Jim Cullen was found. Inquiry was again made of the woman to "Just tell us the truth of the whereabouts of Jim." Mrs. Twist stated, "I've told you all I know."

As a crowd milled about the room, one man tripped his foot on an iron ring that was fastened to the floor. "Look here, Mr. Hughes," he said, "What might this be." Constable Hughes took hold of the ring and pulled. Up came a trap door in the floor and a ladder was noticed leading to the cellar below.

"Are you down there, Jim?" Constable Hughes inquired. There was no reply. "Jim," Constable Hughes said, "We have some business to talk over with you. Now come on up." There was still no answer. Mrs. Twist kept repeating, "I tell you Jim is not here. Now clear out!" Some of the fellows with guns were getting disgusted and one said, "Come on boys, let's stop fooling and fill that cellar full of lead."

Several gun barrels were pointed down through the opening in the floor. Constable Hughes stated, "Go easy men, let's give Jim a chance. Come on, Jim, before these men get desperate and begin shooting. Come on up like a man and we will use you good." Still there was no answer.

By this time, Mrs. Twist was weakening and as she was repeating "I tell you Jim is not here" she was, at the same time, pointing to the cellar. Someone in the group spoke up and said, "Let's give Jim a dose of his own medicine. Here is some kerosene in a can and here is plenty of kindling wood. We will just burn the place down and that will save a lot of trouble. Bill Hubbard is dead and will not be needing the house now. So here goes, let's burn the damn place right here and now."

Mrs. Twist was handed a coat and a blanket and told, "Here, take these. Take the boy and scram for we are all done foolin' with Jim Cullen." In a very short period of time, Cullen was coming up the ladder saying, "Don't do that. I'll come up if you will use me good." Constable Hughes agreed to this and said, "That is just what we have been trying to tell you. Come on up."

Cullen scrambled up onto the floor and, as Constable Hughes was about to apply the handcuffs, Cullen began to get rough. Perhaps he would have thrown the whole group out if Albert Griffin hadn't screeched at the top of his voice "JIM" and at the same instant pulled the hammer back on the old "Muzzle Loader" and jammed the gun against Cullen's red whiskers. Suddenly Cullen wilted...all his strength left him...his hands and arms became limp and Constable Hughes applied the handcuffs without further trouble.

Cullen was given his cap and a jacket was fastened around his shoulders. Then, surrounded by the posse on all sides, he was marched down to Dave Dudley's store. A wooden box was placed near a post in the store. Cullen was asked to sit on it and a rope was passed through his arms and tied behind the post. Cullen was asked many questions about what he had done. He told the whole story and stated that he was sorry the two "boys" weren't piled up with the other bodies. Cyrus Hayden made several attempts to pounce on Cullen but was prevented from doing so by Constable Hughes.

Cullen did not give any particular reason for doing what he had done. Down through the years, it has always been reasoned out that after Cullen left the camp during the night he decided that if he came back, got rid of the four men and destroyed the warrant which Mr. Hayden had for his arrest that no one would ever "be the wiser" for he was supposed to be over in Canada visiting his folks. This may or may not have been the reason, yet it was only reasonable for people to arrive at this conclusion after Cullen's capture.

Perhaps it would be well to mention, at this point, that Sheriff Hayden was 37 years old and William Hubbard about 25 years of age. Minot Bird's records show that he was born in Brocton, Mass, on June 2, 1849, so was 23 years old at the time. Swanback was born in Germany in 1834 (this date has been verified from his army records) and was 39 years old.

After the capture and Cyrus Hayden had talked with Cullen, he decided to go to Swanback's opening and see for himself how things looked at the camp where the bodies had been burned. He inquired of the crowd hanging around as to what would be the best and quickest way for him to make the trip. The majority suggested that horseback would be the most sensible way to go. His brother's horse, which had been stabled here since the day before, was made ready and a fellow, who had a horse tied nearby, volunteered to go along. It was around three o'clock in the afternoon and the distance to be covered, out and back, was 14 miles, yet Cyrus insisted on making the trip.

As they rode out on the Chapman Road, Cyrus wished he had brought along a container in which to bring back some evidence of what might be found. As they came by my grandparent's home, my grandfather, Steve Wilcox, was splitting wood in sight of the road. Cyrus turned in with his horse and told my grandfather the purpose for his being out there and inquired if there might be a box or container that he could use. My grandmother made a search but nothing could be found, however she said, "I have a box of salt that is almost empty. I will put the salt in a dish and you may have the box if it will suffice." Mr. Hayden allowed that it would be okay if the slide cover was still with the box. It was, so the salt was put into another container and Cyrus took the empty salt box and the two men hurried on their way.

The going was too bad to jog the horses but the snow had settled enough so that good time was made just walking them. Cyrus and his companion arrived and found the camp had burned flat to the ground. They found a stake, out near the pile of shingles, and stirred the ashes in the rock fireplace. A bunch of keys, some buttons, buckles of leggings and pieces of bone were found. The salt box was filled with some of the remains and taken back to Ball's Mill.

They arrived back at the Mill around seven o'clock. The cover of the salt box was pulled back and the contents set before Cullen. Someone said, "These are the remains of Hayden and Hubbard." Cullen looked into the box and remarked, "They are looking well." The contents of the salt box did not bother him in the least. He said, "I'm not sorry a bit for what has happened. I just wish the ashes of those two men (Swanback and Bird) were mixed up with these." Cyrus was so upset and tired and became so angry with Cullen that he almost had to be tied to keep from pouncing on Cullen.

During the afternoon, Cullen had become quite fatigued from sitting in the same position, handcuffed and tied to the post. Sometime during his life, he had learned to whistle a few tunes. Perhaps he had learned the tunes from listening to Mrs. Twist. It has been said she was jolly all of the time and was always humming a song or hymn. Several times during his captivity, Cullen was heard whistling "Abide with Me." A church goer called at the store during the afternoon, heard Cullen whistling the hymn and suggested that "This man be untied and allowed to move around." A bystander said, "Yep that would be a hell-of-a-thing to do after what he has done since midnight last night." The bystander then cut off a good sized chew from a plug of tobacco and stuffed it in Cullen's mouth.

Cullen was to be taken to the Presque Isle jail for the night. Constable Hughes had selected two husky men to act as guards and organized a group to accompany them. He ordered the crowd to leave and "not cause any trouble." It was decided not to leave for Presque Isle until after dark. "So as," Constable Hughes stated, "not to have any trouble." Darkness came and Mr. Dorsey's team was brought to the store. Mr. Dorsey, James Phair, Dr. Parker and Fred Barker were on the wagon ready to go. Constable Hughes and the guards untied Cullen and rushed him out to the wagon. Hay had been brought for him to sit on and he was covered over with a blanket. The casket box, which had not been needed, was used as a seat by some of the men.

Cyrus Hayden drove his horse and sleigh and hired a fellow to drive his brother Granville's. It has always been assumed that these two drove close behind the wagon.

Constable Hughes was off to a good start with his prisoner but soon got a surprise that he never forgot. A posse, that has been estimated to be from 100 to 200 men, had gathered on the other side of the large hill just out of Ball's Mill. Just about dark, they had begun to gather. Some had come walking, many came on horseback and others had come with double hitches on sleds or with a single horse and sleigh. Many tied their horses to a barnyard fence, on the left hand side of the road, belonging to a Mr. Higgins. Mr. Higgins heard the noises in his barnyard and went out to see what all the excitement was about. Several men, with hoods over their heads or scarves over their faces, met him. "What is going on out here?" inquired Mr. Higgins. "Never mind," said the leader of the group. "We are going to a necktie party. No harm is going to come to you and there will not be any damage to your property. Now, Mr. Higgins, you march yourself right back into the house and just forget, now and forever, that you ever saw or heard anyone around here. Now remember, secrecy is the word. Please remain inside and just forget you talked with anyone tonight."

Mr. Higgins was puzzled and a bit shaky about seeing such a mob, but he obeyed and returned to the house. The posse marched out to the road and toward the brow of the hill. They idled back and forth in the chilly spring air on this evening of April 30, 1873.

When the wagon carrying Cullen was heard coming over the brow of the hill, the posse, en masse, marched to meet it. The team was halted and the horses held by their bridles. The hooded men completely surrounded the wagon.

Constable Hughes shouted, "What is this all about? What is going on here?" Someone inquired, "Where are you going with this team this time of night?" Constable Hughes answered, "That is none of your business. Now clear out and let the team pass." "Have you got a passenger on there by the name of Jim Cullen?" someone shouted. "That is none of your business," answered Constable Hughes.

At this time, several searched the wagon and discovered Cullen, who was under the blanket. Then the action began, hastily and in a rough way. Constable Hughes was pulled down from the wagon and several men gaffeled on to him. He was marched around behind the wagon and given instruction to go right home. He was told, "Don't even look back. Now get going while the going is good. Your services won't be needed anymore tonight. Now get going! Hear what we say! Get going!"

During the time Constable Hughes was being started back to his home, Cullen was pulled from the wagon and a rope looped around his neck. He was yanked along, grunting and groaning, about 150 feet into the woods. The rope was thrown over a limb on a maple tree and his body pulled up until his feet were at least two or three feet above the ground. Several of the men in the posse formed a circle around Cullen and stomped around to keep warm. The horses were still being held by their bridles and the large group completely blocked the road.

After a time, Dr. Parker was helped down from the wagon and asked to "Come and make an examination to see if Cullen is dead." Dr. Parker felt for the pulse then he unbuttoned Cullen's clothes at the waist and passed his hand up under the shirts toward the area of the heart. After a pause, he stated, "I think the man is dead but to be positively sure, let the body hang for a few minutes longer." After a short while, which seemed like hours to the nervous group, Dr. Parker gave the word, "Okay now."

The body was brought to the side of the road near the wagon and the hooded visitors dispersed. None had been recognized either by their voices or looks.

Now the question was "What shall be done with the body tonight?" It was decided to place Cullen's body in the box and take it along to Presque Isle. Mr. Barker, who owned a store on Bridge Street (now State Street) in Presque Isle, allowed that the box with the body in it could be placed in an empty room of the store for the night.

It was well past midnight when the team arrived at the store. The town was as quiet as "a Quaker meeting house." No one was on the street. It was suspected that many men in the posse were good friends of the Hayden's; if so, all had gone to their homes. Cyrus Hayden and the fellow driving his brother's horse had driven on ahead after leaving Higgins' driveway and they too had vanished for the night.

The box with Cullen's body was taken inside. A couple of empty barrels were put in the center of the room and some boards placed on them. Cullen's body was taken from the box and placed on the boards.

The next day was May 1st. Word had spread throughout the County. People came from far and wide to view the body of Jim Cullen who was known as a thief and was feared by all. His body "lay in state" nearly all day.

The Sunrise, a paper printed in Presque Isle, in their April 30th edition printed only what had been learned of the tragedy up to press time at four o'clock. Other information was included in the next week's May 7th, issue. (Photostatic copies of both editions are on file at the Presque Isle Library.)

Daniel Foster, coroner for this area, whose home was in Fort Fairfield, was notified that a job was waiting for him here at Presque Isle. Mr. Foster came during the morning of May 1st, and viewed the body of Cullen.

He was told that Constable Hughes, who had custody of Cullen, had been taken from the wagon and sent home and a group of hooded men took over. After the hanging, the body was brought to the roadside and placed near the wagon. The crowd quickly dispersed and no one was recognized.

Shortly after noon, on May 1st, Mr. Foster chose a jury of six men. They were Nathan Perry, James Phair, Francis A. Soule, B.B. Glidden, Fred Barker and H.R. Forbes. Later in the day, they met in the room where Cullen's body lay and a hearing was held. The only story of the lynching that could be obtained was from those who were on the wagon that night. No evidence could be found and no one had been recognized. After an hour or so, the hearing was called to a close by Mr. Foster.

Now came the problem of what should be done with the body. No one wanted to take part in saying what should be done with it. Finally, after it was decided not to have a shroud made, Cyrus gave permission for the box to be used.

With some twenty people in the room, Darius McGuire, a resident of Presque Isle, was called in. Mr. Foster asked him to listen to the verdict of the jury. "It has been found that the body lying in this box is that of Jim Cullen. It has been decided that he is dead." Mr. Foster then said, "Now, I'm asking you to swear to the facts that I have just stated, place the cover on this box and nail it down good and solid with these nails." (A hammer and nails were provided.)

Mr. McGuire stated, "Gentlemen of the jury, I have viewed this corpse and swear it is the body of Jim Cullen. I further swear that Jim Cullen is dead and that his body is contained in this box." He then placed the cover on the box and nailed it down.

The question now was how and where to take the box for burial. No one in the group felt that Cullen was entitled to any sort of a funeral. It finally was decided to get a high wagon and take the body out to the town dump, which was out on the road leading back to Ball's Mill. All of the men present volunteered to accompany the wagon. When they arrived at the dump, the question of where to dig the grave came up. There was still a considerable amount of snow in the woods and still frost in the ground, except close by the dump where waste was burned daily. A place was chosen east of the dump and on the same side of the road some thirty or thirty-five feet from the highway.

Shovels and pickaxes had been brought along. Those present took turns digging the grave and the box was lowered into the ground without ceremony of any kind. After the earth was placed back on the area, some of the men present remarked, "It is good to know that the killer had been captured and buried. Now all those who knew him can rest nights and not live in fear of their lives."

The group returned to Mr. Barker's store. Mr. Foster announced that the inquest was closed and he thanked those who had assisted that day. (I never heard that anyone in the group received any pay for their services, except the coroner, who may have been paid by the County.)

Late in October of 1873, Professor L.C. Bateman from Bates College came to Presque Isle lecturing on phrenology. He brought along several human skulls to be used in his lectures. During his stay in Presque Isle, Professor Bateman, who had heard much about Cullen through the papers, inquired as to how he might acquire his skull.

People, to whom he inquired, informed him that it was definitely against the law to molest a grave and it was suggested that the idea be forgotten. Professor Bateman persisted so much about making a deal with someone to dig up the skull that he was told, one evening at the hotel, to close his "yap" or go see a lawyer. He decided to do the latter and called on a young man, by the name of Smith, who was a law student. Mr. Smith listened to Professor Batman for awhile and then said, "Professor Bateman, it is against the law to molest a grave…so you had better forget the idea."

Professor Bateman paused for awhile, apparently very much disappointed. He finally said, "I'll give $25 to anyone who will go with me to open the grave and get the skull." Twenty-five dollars was a lot of money in those days. Mr. Smith was a young student, with very little money, who was trying to become a lawyer. When money was mentioned, he suddenly became interested and said, "Well now, let's see, perhaps some way might be devised to help you. Let me think it over." Professor Bateman continued making plans. Smith was listening and thinking at the same time of how much the money would mean to him. Finally he said, "I know where the grave is located and after dark tonight, I'll go and help you."

When evening came and darkness set in, the two men met at the bridge on Bridge Street and started walking toward the town dump. Professor Bateman brought along a pail, a hammer, a pick-axe, a shovel, a jimmy bar, and a kerosene lantern. He also brought along a bottle of gin. Except for the pail and lantern, they concealed the things under their coats.

It took only fifteen to twenty minutes to reach the grave. Due to the time of the year and the lateness of the evening, they hoped they would not be seen. Mr. Smith stated, "In case a team does come along, we will step back in the bushes."

There was not much dirt over the box in which Cullen's body lay and it was removed in a very few minutes. The jimmy bar and hammer was brought into use and part of the cover removed. At his first look at the decomposed body of Cullen, Smith said, "Oh, Professor Bateman, I just can't go on with the deal." At this point, the Professor took the bottle of gin from his overcoat, took a swig himself and invited Mr. Smith to do the same. Mr. Smith had a good sized drink and the two talked for some time.

Soon, Professor Bateman said, "Here young man, have another sip and we will go back to work." Smith obeyed and the two began separating the grisly decomposed head from the body. When the task was only partly done, Mr. Smith allowed that he needed the money but not badly enough to go on. He was helped to his feet and requested to "take another swig." He obeyed. By this time he was feeling the effects of the gin and said, "Come on Professor, I've decided I will obtain the skull for you and perhaps I will skin the whole body if you want me to."

The head was brought out of the box in a minute or two. Mr. Smith nailed the cover back on and replaced the dirt. A lot of leaves, which had fallen from the trees, were spread on the area so it would not be noticed that the grave had been dug up.

Professor Bateman took the head back to the dump where a fire was still burning. The two men found a couple of old pails and went to a nearby brook for some water. The head was in the pail that was brought along. It was covered over with water and boiled over the open fire. They cautiously listened all of the time for a team that might pass even at this late hour. Mr. Smith was familiar with the habits of the farmers and told Professor Bateman, "If a team is out tonight on this road, chances are they will have bells on for most people have bells on their horses this time of year."

After boiling the skull three of four times, Professor Bateman allowed the task had been completed and stated, "It is time to return to town and get some rest." Mr. Smith was paid the $25 as promised. He was offered another swig of gin but he refused it. Professor Bateman carefully concealed the red hair and whiskers and the pail was left behind. He took another sip of the gin threw the bottle on the fire, wrapped the skull in a cloth which he had brought, placed it under his heavy coat and the two men marched back to town.

The next morning, Professor Bateman packed his luggage and material used in his lectures, which now included the sterilized skull of Jim Cullen, and became a passenger on the stage going to Bangor.

To tie in the facts of my story, we must at this time, mention a reporter's story written of a lecture given by Professor L.C. Bateman at Easton, Maine in 1887. Many people had gathered to hear the lecture. Among the crowd was a Fred Smith. Professor Bateman's lecture was very interesting. As he lectured, he demonstrated with several skulls he had brought. During one part of the lecture, a few listeners noticed his statements, concerning one particular skull, coincided with the life of Jim Cullen, whom a few had known many years ago.

After the meeting when all but a few had left for their homes, Mr. Fred Smith asked Professor Bateman if it would be ethical to ask a few questions. Professor Bateman gave consent to the request. Mr.

Smith placed the skull with the receding forehead where all could see it and said, "Your lecture relative to this skull, tallies exactly with what we have heard down through the years about Jim Cullen. This man Jim Cullen was a Canadian and had lived around Castle Hill for some years. I have heard so much about the man I just had to stay and compare notes with you."

Professor Bateman began to repeat his version of the life of a person with such a skull when he suddenly paused and said, "Gentlemen, it is getting late. There are only a few of us here and I will confide that this is the skull of Jim Cullen. Many years have passed and probably there is not any suspicion that anyone ever molested the grave. During the fall of 1873, late in October, I lectured in Presque Isle. I got acquainted with a young man who was hard up for money, a fellow who did not fear God, man, or the devil. I confided in him that I'd like to visit Cullen's grave and offered him $25 to come and help me exhume the body and obtain the skull."

The Professor explained how they went about the task and, with the support of a bottle of gin, the job was accomplished. The Professor did not mention the name of the young man and he was not questioned about it.

As they were about to say good night to each other, Fred Smith had to speak his little piece about some of the many stories he had heard. Among his remarks, Fred said that his brother, who had become a prominent lawyer in Presque Isle, told many times of attending the coroner's inquest and of going out with the group to the town dump to assist with the digging of the grave. He also mentioned that his brother, George, had a piece of the limb from the tree upon which Cullin was hanged. He said, "My brother George never knew the name of a single person who took part in the lynching and it is doubtful if any name will ever be told of those who were in that hanging party of April 30, 1873."

Little did Professor Bateman or Fred Smith dream that a secret was being unfolded that evening concerning who had helped open the grave. Professor Bateman remembered the name Smith as belonging to the young law student; however, he referred to the fellow who had assisted him as a rough guy who did not fear God, man, or the devil. This was so the small group he had confided in would not suspect anyone they might know.

Chapter 25

Acquiring Information of the Jim Cullen Lynching

From as far back as I can remember, information and stories have been told and repeated by many people many times.

My father, Jasper O. Ellis, was about four years of age when the lynching took place and many times, down through the years, I have heard him compare notes of memory with others who also had heard much about the tragedy.

My grandparents, Steven and Eucebia Wilcox, lived on the Chapman Road at that time. My mother, Lucy, was later born there in the home that is known today as the Tingley place. My grandmother told me the story many times when I was a boy.

Dr. Hagerthy first pointed out the stump of the tree to me, on which Cullen was hanged, as we were driving to Presque Isle in the spring of 1913. That same day, he stopped near Jim Cullen's grave and let me discover for myself the depression in the ground. He related to me the stories he had heard pertaining to the lynching since coming to Ashland nine years before.

While employed at Mapleton from 1920 to 1923, many people told me about the tragedy and of Cullen, as they knew him, and of Mrs. Twist. Many of those living at that time remembered the little boy growing to manhood. He was always referred to as Dummy Cullen or Dummy Twist. Like Jim Cullen, he had red hair and a red beard. Many years of his life were spent at the Town Farm in Presque Isle.

Lewis Griffin, who was living in Castle Hill within sight of the house where Cullen was captured, came to the grist mill several times while I was employed there and told me about the affair. Mr. Griffin seemed proud to remember that it was his father who poked the muzzle loader in Cullen's face, causing him to give up. Never once, at that time, did I take notes. It did not dawn on me that this information would help sometime in telling or lecturing about the tragedy.

Mr. Swanback returned to where his camp had stood, built another nearby and continued to shave shingles, for which there was a good demand in those years. He later married Mrs. Akeley, a widow. Mr. Will Akeley, her son, used to bring grist of wheat to the mill. He was a prominent farmer in Chapman and probably knew much about the affair; if only I had been making notes at that time.

Minot Bird married Edith Ellis of Ashland on June 24, 1882. Edith was a cousin of my father. From this source, perhaps a good book could have been written. Minot Bird, in 1873, was living at his father's home in Castle Hill. He had a brother named Will Bird. I became very well acquainted with Will during the time I was carrying mail by the Haystack Road (1917 and 1918).

Many people told me their versions of the tragedy and it did not occur to me that this information would be needed some day to present a true account of the story until Ernest Judkins told me all about it. In the spring of 1952, Mr. Ernest Judkins, a Mapleton resident, was the last living person who remembered Jim Cullen. I am indebted to Mr. Judkins for the actual description of Cullen.

The latter part of April, 1952, while working at the Town Office in Mapleton as Town Manager for two towns, Castle Hill and Mapleton, I received a call saying that I was wanted at the home of Ernest Judkins. "What's up?" I inquired. The caller answered, "Ernest has passed away or is dying and Mrs. Judkins wants you to come right over."

I just about wilted for Mr. Judkins was the last person who remembered Jim Cullen. It had been five years since I had become Town Manager for Mapleton and Castle Hill. During those years, Mr. Judkins had always wanted to tell me the Cullen story. I told him many times, "I'll take some time some day and make a good write-up of the tragedy as you tell it to me." But I always put it off.

On my way over to the Judkins' home, I was feeling guilty for not getting firsthand information from a person who had known all of the fellows who had taken part in the capture of Cullen and knew the names of those who were hanging around Dave Dudley's store that afternoon of April 30, 1873, and of those who watched Cullen being loaded on the high wagon to be taken to Presque Isle.

In a very short time after receiving the phone call, I arrived at the Judkins' home. Mrs. Judkins met me at the door and I inquired, "Is

Ernest very sick?" "Well," she answered, "I really think he has passed away." I got a chair and sat by the bedside and made some observations. His pulse, if any, was too weak to be detected. His body felt stone cold. After awhile, I could get a faint pulse beat now and then. I asked Mrs. Judkins to bring me a small mirror. She brought it and I held it near the man's nose. A little vapor appeared on the mirror and I showed this to Mrs. Judkins. I stated, "He is not dead. Let me call a doctor." She replied, "No, I haven't any money to pay a doctor." Well, then," I said, "Let me have a doctor come at the town's expense." She firmly answered "NO" that they would never accept charity. "Well then, Mrs. Judkins," I said, "I have my checkbook down at the town office. Let me call the doctor at my expense." Mrs. Judkins said, "I don't want you to do that. Ern has reached the end of his journey. You can do just as well as anyone now. Just stay with me for a little while."

The faith Mrs. Judkins had in me sort of bolstered me up and I remembered what Dr. Hagerthy used to say, "Phinagin, always remember where there is life, there is hope…never give up."

As I pondered just what to do, a voice from nowhere spoke to me and seemed to say, "Get busy…there is still life…you may win!" Again I used the mirror and still got a little vapor but the pulse was very weak and hardly noticeable. I asked Mr. Judkins for a little brandy. "Bless your soul, we haven't such a thing in the house. What would you do with brandy?" I replied, "I have a hunch that with a stimulant perhaps 'Jud' will pull through."

As I massaged his arms, a thought came to me; this man had become very excited the many times he had mentioned the Cullen story. I said, "I will talk to him about the Cullen tragedy, perhaps he can hear even if he can't talk. Perhaps this will serve as a means of waking him."

Mrs. Judkins brought in some wood for the stove and I asked her for something made of wool. "Now what have you thought of?" she asked. "Oh," I replied as I took off my coat and rolled up my sleeves, "You feel that I can do just as good as a doctor, now, with the faith you have in me, I'll just go to work. Ernest needs a stimulant." Some woolen blankets were brought. I kept warming them by the stove and applied the warm blankets all around his body. I kept massaging his arms and legs, thinking perhaps it would enhance the circulation.

All of the time that I was massaging and applying warm blankets, I kept asking the man questions regarding the Cullen tragedy, hoping that he could hear and perhaps this would serve as a stimulant.

After a few minutes, it was noticed that his body was becoming warmer. Soon perspiration was observed and, before a half hour was up, his eyelids began to twitch. I continued to ask questions while applying warm blankets. He began to appear normal and looked to be only asleep. I felt his pulse and it was "getting back to normal." I continued talking and said, "Well Jud, I'm sorry that I never listened to you and wrote a story as told by the last person living who actually knew most of the people involved. Now that you are feeling better, I'll come up here soon and take notes." What a surprise it was to notice that this man was trying to raise his head and he spoke right out loud saying, "Why don't I tell you the story right now while you are here."

Mrs. Judkins heard his voice and came on the run, asking, "Was that Ern that spoke?" I replied, "Yes, he is coming along just fine. All he needed was a good stimulant." I fixed the pillow so that he would be more comfortable and asked, "Could you drink some hot tea?" Ernest answered, "Yes."

"Jud," I said, "I've got to get back to the office and see how things are going. In about half an hour I'll be back. I'll bring a notebook and take notes while you tell me the whole story." Again Jud spoke, "That's good, Phin, I'll be ready to tell the story. You'll hear it right from the last person living who actually saw the people involved." His voice was good, his pulse was about normal and he was perspiring well. Boy, what a thrill it was to see what had taken place in such a short time.

Very soon and before eating my dinner, I returned. I swung Jud around so that he could sit on the side of the bed and, during the next three quarters of an hour, took many notes concerning the tragedy. Best of all, this man was up and walking around the room with only his union suit on before he finished telling the story.

As I was taking my leave, he and I made plans to visit Swanback opening. He wanted to show me the old landmarks along the way as well as where the bodies had been burned. Mrs. Judkins was sobbing with joy because Mr. Judkins had revived. I told these people that I had decided to write up a lecture and pass the true story along to others during the rest of my lifetime. Mrs. Judkins said, "Thank you for coming; perhaps sometime we may be able to repay you." I said, "Mrs. Judkins, please forget about that. By getting the facts of this story, I feel very well paid."

Twice during the summer of 1952, Mr. Judkins and I drove, with my car, to Swanback opening. The location of the old fireplace, which had been in the camp, was easily located. The circle of stones was still visible although grass and small bushes were growing in the area. I took a small axe, which I had in the car, and cut a stake which I drove in the center of what was the fireplace.

People told me time and time again about a large pine tree that was standing about 100 feet from the camp and was supposed to be still there. Dr. Doble had purchased the land for lumber but had forbidden anyone from cutting the tree. The stump was still there but someone had cut and taken the pine tree away.

I made a second trip out to Swanback opening that summer to learn more of the whole area which had been known for many years as the "Bloody Half Acre."

For the next two years, I kept making notes and tried to write a story that would bring out the whole truth of the tragedy.

Late in the summer of 1954, it came my turn to have a program for the Washburn Rotary Club, of which I had been a member for more than six years. I thought, perhaps this would be a good time to tell the story of the "Lynching of Jim Cullen." This was the night to make the "debut." I had no idea of the time it would require. I mentioned to the members, "I'm not a public speaker; however, I think I have a program that will be of great interest to you all."

For the next forty minutes the room was very quiet. There was not even a squeak from a chair. The table girl had vanished or was sitting over in a far corner of the room listening. After I had concluded, it appeared that the story had been accepted very well for each and every member came forward to compliment me for a program well given.

There were several visitors from other clubs present that evening. Requests were already being made, "You will just have to come and be my program at our Rotary Club." In the years since the "debut" in 1954, I have told the story many times in various clubs and have been asked to relate the story to various schools in the area.

During the years I have lectured about the Jim Cullen story, the conveyance that went to Ball's Mill on April 30, 1873, carrying the casket box, was referred to as a sled or a long heavy pung, such as was used around the livery stable in that era. As many as three seats could be placed on the sled at one time but it was mostly used with only one seat leaving plenty of room for hauling goods. Several times, writers have referred to the vehicle used as a hay wagon. This never sounded right to me. During this winter of 1974-75, I vowed to resolve this question. I read and reread stories at the libraries and in the old scrap books that belonged to my mother.

One day, I stumbled on an article pertaining to high wagons that were used back before the turn of the century. The article also told of the "birth" of the gigger wagon. Many of us remember the gigger wagons that were used in this century. Here was the answer to this puzzling question. Some writer, or reporter, had misspelled the word high and written hay. This answer made sense. The high wagon would have been the vehicle used, on that tragic day, to carry the large casket box to Ball's Mill.

Recently, at the Ashland library, I saw Dr. Burtt, a veterinarian. I have known Dr. Burtt for many years. Although I do not know his age, it is my guess that this man is around three score years and ten. I told him of my hours of research trying to verify just what type of vehicle was used on that trip to Ball's Mill. I remembered that my grandfather Ellis had a high wagon with wooden axles and wooden hubs. I asked, "Would you say, Dr. Burtt, that I am correct in calling the vehicle a high wagon instead of a hay wagon as mentioned by some reporters." He answered, "Yes Phin, I'm positive that you are correct and the trip to Ball's Mill carrying the large box would have been made with the high wagon. At that time, it would have been the most sensible way to carry it."

Dr. Burtt went on to tell me of his early life some sixty miles north or west of the Maine border. He described how those wooden wagons were made and said they were used extensively even after the turn of the century.

One time, about 1955 or 56, after lecturing at one of the clubs in Presque Isle, someone phoned my home and asked if I would like to use the handcuffs that were used on Cullen the day of his capture. "Sure," I replied, "Who is calling?" The caller answered, "I can't tell you that, but go to the police station in Presque Isle the next time you are in town and pick them up. You may use the handcuffs for as long as you tell the story, and then please return them to the police station." I went and received the handcuffs and was requested to "not ask questions."

The handcuffs were made of iron and were very heavy. A key had to be used to lock them on a prisoner. It would require a threat with a gun, as in the Cullen case, or a rough fellow would have to be knocked out before this type of handcuff could be used. Perhaps it was the only type available one hundred years ago.

In 1972 the handcuffs were called for and I returned them to the police station. They were picked up and placed in the Presque Isle Museum.

I also have a piece of the limb from the maple tree on which Cullen was hanged. This was loaned to me to be used in my lectures.

Ivan Sawyer of Castle Hill has in his possession the old muzzle loader that was used to subdue Cullen. Albert Griffin, who used it, was Ivan's grandfather.

I believe that I am the last person living who has made an honest effort to obtain the truth of this tragedy that took place in April of 1873.

I am indebted to the Presque Isle Library, to my mother's old scrap book, to Ernest Judkins, Sr., and to all the others who, in years gone by, told me what they remembered of Jim Cullen and Mrs. Twist.

With the information that I have acquired from these sources, I honestly believe that no truer account will ever be written.

Chapter 26

Weather Observations & Forecasts

Even when I was very young, my mother and father taught me to observe weather signs. Down through the years, from as far back as I can remember, I don't believe a day went by that there wasn't some reference made to the weather. My father often mentioned the following weather observations. Frost on the trees in the morning was a sign of rain or a thaw. After a snow storm, if the snow stayed on the trees, expect more snow. If it fell off, better weather ahead. Before a rain, the leaves on many kinds of trees and bushes appear to turn completely over. (To get their backs washed, I was told.) Pine needles will stand up before a storm (especially before a rain). When fog hovered over a hill in the morning, he would say, "This will be a poor hay day, perhaps we will have showers." If, after being milked, the cows went to high ground it would be a "poor hay day" for sure. If the cows stayed on flat or lower ground, that was a sign that it was "safe to cut hay today."

Before a storm, deer come out to feed in the fields. In fair weather, deer are seldom seen feeding in the fields. If a horse garps (yawns), look out for a thaw. Hogs scratching their backs on fence posts are a sign of wind. Before a thaw, water in a brook will rise.

In winter, wet places on logging or dirt roads is a sign of a storm or a thaw. A circle around the moon is a good sign of a storm and the number of stars that can be counted designates the number of days before the storm. If many stars can be seen in an evening, foul weather is in store. In fair weather, not so many stars are visible.

Before a thaw, skunk cedar will give off a scent resembling that of a skunk. When the balm of Gilead trees give off a very strong odor that can be detected some distance away, spring has arrived. Black specks (called snow fleas) on new snow, is a sign of a thaw.

If your corns ache, a storm is coming. Watch for a storm from the South when you see heavy bank of clouds in the North. A heavy bank of clouds in the West, at night, is a sign to watch out for a "down-easter" which could be a very bad storm, especially in winter.

If the sun sets clear on Friday night, there will be a storm before Monday night. Bad weather on Saturday means there will be a "sweet" Monday morning. Rain before seven, clear before eleven.

A whirlwind turning away from the direction of the sun is a sign of a dry spell. A whirlwind turning in the same direction as the sun means better weather in store.

In winter, if the horse's hair looks rough it is going to be cold. If the hair is smooth and flat, the weather will be fine. When pumping water from the well, if you observe small round bubbles rolling around on the water in the pail, look out for a storm. When steam-like vapor comes off the fields in the spring, it is time to plant. It is time to sow grain when the swallows arrive. Hornets nest built high above the ground signifies deep snow. When the hornet nests are built low you can expect a mild winter. (By watching this year after year, I find it is fairly correct.)

It is a sign of a thaw when spiders crawl out. It is a sign of a good day when there is heavy dew on the grass in the morning. If there is no dew, it is apt to rain or shower before the day is over.

My mother used to say there would be a change in the weather when creosote burned in the stovepipe. When the cat was seen scratching its back on the doorways or elsewhere, the wind was expected to blow. When the buttermilk riled in the jar, a storm was brewing.

Mornings when the fog could be seen going down the river, we expected to have a fair day but when it was drifting up river, look out for rain or showers.

When the air was "hollow," expect a storm. By hollow I mean when sounds could be heard for a long distance. At times we could hear the Sheridan Mill whistle quite plainly and the mill was seven miles away. The same with the bell on the Catholic Church that was four miles away located on the Frenchville Road.

Red sky at night, farmer's delight. If the sky was red at night, we looked for good weather the next day. A red sky in the morning, take warning and expect rain or showers. If thunder was heard in the morning, we expected to have a long storm or a very cold spell.

Quite often the kettles would burn dry when the meals were being cooked. This was a sign of rain or a storm. If the smoke from the stove pipe settled down toward the ground, expect rain or snow. If it went straight up in the air, fair weather was forthcoming.

Birds sitting on the telephone wires indicated showers or rain. When the birds were flying high, foul weather was in store. When the woodpeckers were pecking on the trees in the lowlands, rain was expected. When their thumping could be heard from the ridge or high ground, cold weather was coming.

When it would start to rain, the hens out in the yard would run for cover. If they stayed under cover, we would expect only a brief shower but if they came right back out and stayed out in the rain, it was expected to be a rainy day.

When hauling loads, if the horses began sweating it was a sign of a thaw.

A morning can be very cloudy and seem like a very poor day to do any kind of outdoor work, but watch the sky in the North. If the clouds break away, go after whatever work you have to do. Chances are ninety-nine out of a hundred that it will be a good day.

Mackerel skies indicate rain or snow. Mare's tails (wavy clouds strung out like horse's tails) are a sign of a storm.

When we could hear sounds coming against the wind, it was a sign a bad storm was brewing. Many times, when the old covered bridge was at Washburn (eight miles away, as the crow flies) we could hear the sounds made by teams crossing, even against the wind. Whenever these sounds could be heard, we would say, "Foul weather is in store."

I was always interested in watching the northern lights. If they were streaming rapidly up and down, colder weather was in store. If they were more bank-like, warmer weather would be forth coming.

Today people listen to their radios and televisions for weather forecasts and pay little attention to these weather signs. Perhaps people of the younger generations have never before heard of them. I hope all those who read my book find them interesting.

Made in the USA
Monee, IL
24 February 2021

61263362R00148